KU-536-932

LIBRARY

Contents

Illustrations

Figures

Tables

Foreword

Literacy teaching and literacy research have been dominated by reading teaching, reading research, reading surveys and reading results. The contribution of spelling and writing has to a large extent been ignored or relegated to a minor role. Knight and Smith (2000: 85) said that although spelling had been extensively researched there appeared to be gaps between the current research and its application in classrooms. Although there is certainly a gap between what the research tells us and what is done in classrooms, the research on spelling is dwarfed by that on reading.

Remediation theory, research and practice likewise have been almost entirely geared to reading. It is for this reason that this book looks at literacy from the viewpoint of spelling and handwriting to try to show that their contribution to literacy has a far greater impact than they are given credit for.

To be literate is to be able to read and write with the same facility and understanding as that by which we speak. There will be an acquisition, a development and a fluent stage and the processes, the methods of teaching, the research and operation may need to be different for each.

These represent just a few issues which are raised as soon as we begin to investigate literacy and writing. Writing itself involves three main areas – spelling, handwriting and composition.

Note: as this is a book about English writing the usual convention of changing s to z in words for an international audience has not been adopted: for example, organisation and recognise are used, as this affects the spelling teaching which is discussed.

Part 1

Introduction

Introduction

The first three chapters in this book examine the nature of spelling, handwriting and dyslexia and their relationship to becoming literate and to each other. The key theme which links them is how can an understanding of each of them help us design and develop interventions which will work better and faster so that children become literate more easily and earlier. In the meantime we have to recognise that some will take more time and effort and we need to cater for this.

Teachers are daily confronted with the problem of deciding if, for those with slowly developing or poor literacy skills, they should:

* teach to strengths or weaknesses?
* make compensatory or remedial provision or both?
* take account of learning styles?
* offer individual or small group provision?

Each response has had a period when it has been in fashion, and cost has had a significant influence. Training and trainers have to deal with these issues and too often advice has occurred in a piecemeal fashion such as how to develop worksheets for the less literate, how to cater for different learning styles, if indeed they exist (Coffield 2005), and whether 'mind mapping', visual training or neurolinguistic programming will make a difference.

Looking at the needs of underachievers across the ability range we find that their major areas of difficulty lie in an inability to cope with all the written work that schools require them to do. Whatever the reasons for their difficulties there are enough of such pupils for us to thoroughly review the general teaching and learning needs of children. This has led me in a number of researches and publications to propose that education in schools is over didactic and teacher dominated, a methodology which has been promoted by successive governments and their agencies. It involves much teacher talk and pupil writing but these forms of teaching and learning need to be questioned for efficacy with school pupils.

Although the ultimate aim of education may well be to develop the potential of each individual to the full, simply telling children information and practising responses is not the only way to do this. My view of a 'good' education is one which enables children to think efficiently and to communicate those thoughts succinctly in whatever subject area is under consideration and whatever the age the pupil.

To promote such learning objectives modest changes in the curriculum are needed. By this I mean that we should reframe the provision in mainstream education by developing in every curriculum subject: a cognitive curriculum; a talking curriculum; a positive supportive behaviour policy; and a developmental writing and recording policy. These would not involve a change in curriculum content but small changes in the ways in which we teach it and the ways in which we enable children to learn.

The cognitive curriculum

This consists of:

- developmental positive cognitive intervention (PCI, see below)
- cognitively challenging questioning – open and problem posing
- deliberate teaching of thinking skills and protocols
- reflective teaching and learning
- creativity training
- cognitive process teaching methods e.g. cognitive study and research skills, investigative learning and real problem solving, experiential learning, games and simulations, language experience approaches, collaborative learning.

What was clear from using these methods was that intrinsic motivation was developed and children's time on–task extended in their enjoyment long after the lessons ended. Disaffected children remained at school and more able students recorded such things as 'This is much better than the usual boring stuff we get'. They all began to spend extended periods of time on, instead of off–task. The quality of their work frequently exceeded all expectations, as did that of the most modest of learners and there were sometimes the most surprisingly interesting and creative responses from unsuspected sources. The collaborative nature of many of the tasks meant that mixed ability groups could easily access the work and all could be included in the same tasks with no diminution of the achievements of any.

The talking curriculum

This is intimately related to the cognitive curriculum. It consists of the following techniques:

- TPS think – pair – share
- circle time
- small group work
- group problem solving
- collaborative learning
- reciprocal teaching
- peer tutoring
- thinkback (Lockhead 2001)
- role play, games and drama
- debates and 'book clubs' (Godinho and Clements 2002)
- presentations and 'teach-ins'

- poster presentations
- exhibitions and demonstrations
- organised meetings.

Underachievers in particular need to talk things through before they are set to writing them down. In fact all young learners need such opportunities for often we do not know what we think until we try to explain it to someone else. Where such children come from disadvantaged cultural and linguistic environments the talking approaches are essential. This not only helps vocabulary learning and comprehension but also develops organisational skills in composition. To support the organisational abilities, direct teaching of 'scaffolds' can be especially helpful and is the logical extension of the developmental writing curriculum.

When the talking approach to the cognitive curriculum was used with pupils, their feedback showed that enjoyment and legitimised social interaction were not often connected in their minds with school learning. This meant that at each stage they had to be shown in explicit ways that this was real school work, how much they had learned and how their work was improving. This was done by giving detailed comments on their work and their learning processes, both verbally and in writing, couched in constructive terms.

A positive approach to behaviour management in classrooms

Positive behaviour management and classroom control were extensively researched in the observation and feedback to teachers in over 1250 lessons. During this research four interrelated strategies for improving teaching and reducing behaviour problems were evolved, as described below.

C.B.G: 'Catch them being good'

The C.B.G. strategy requires that the teacher positively reinforces any pupil's correct social and on-task responses with nods, smiles, and by paraphrasing correct responses and statements and supporting their on-task academic responses with such phrases as, 'Yes, good' and 'Well done'. Incorrect responses should not be negated but the pupil should be encouraged to have another try, or watch a model, and the teacher prompts with, 'Yes, nearly', 'Yes, and what else ...', and 'Good so far, can anyone help [him or her] out?' and so on.

3 Ms: management, monitoring and maintenance

The 3Ms represent a series of tactics which effective teachers use to gain and maintain pupils' attention whatever teaching method or style they subsequently use. When teachers with classroom management disciplining problems were taught to use these strategies in observation and feedback sessions they became effective teachers.

PCI: positive cognitive intervention

During the steady move round the room the teacher should look at the work with the pupil and offer *developmental PCI* advice in which a positive statement about progress thus far is made and then ideas and suggestions for extension are offered. Alternatively, through constructive questioning the pupils are helped to see how to make the work better or achieve the goals they have set themselves. When the work has been completed again there should be further written or spoken *constructive and positive comments* and further ideas suggested.

Tactical lesson planning (TLP)

Lesson plans need to be structured into timed phases for pupil learning not teacher talk; e.g. title/lesson objective or focus; introduction (teacher talk, Q/A); phase 1 (pupils reading); phase 2 (pupils doing practical work); phase 3 (pupils speaking – sharing experiences); phase 4 (pupils writing and recording work and ideas); concluding activity (Q/A reporting back to the class). Getting the TLP right improves the pace of the lesson and increases pupil time on-task.

A developmental writing and recording policy

Writing and recording are not the same. Recording may take place in writing or in a range of other forms such as cartoons, maps, diagrams, pictures, videos and audio tapes. Each of these options should be available at some point in the curriculum as well as considering if recording is needed at all. For example, why should every subject require pupils to write their own textbooks? Are there better methods of learning and consolidation?

The rest of this book will offer an analysis of writing and writing difficulties, because these seem to be a neglected area of study, and so that a developmental writing policy may be developed. The evidence and the methods associated with the above may be found in the following books by the author: *Reversing Lower Attainment* (2003); *Able Underachievers* (2000a); and *Helping Teachers Develop through Classroom Observation* (2002).

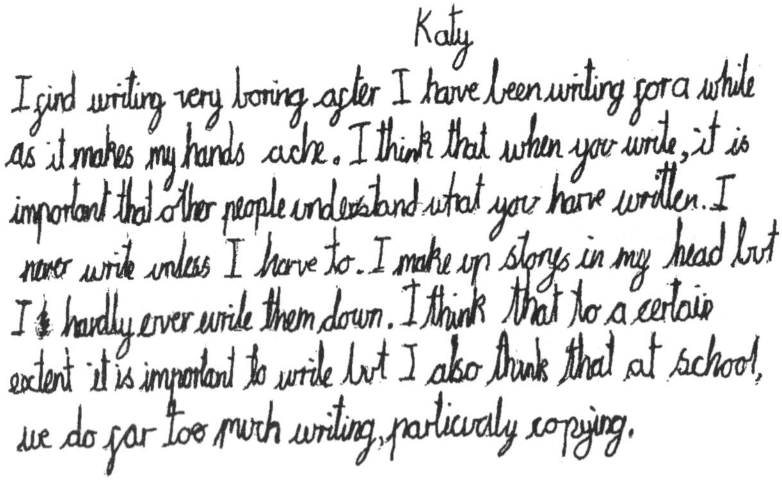

Katy

I find writing very boring after I have been writing for a while as it makes my hands ache. I think that when you write, it is important that other people understand what you have written. I never write unless I have to. I make up storys in my head but I hardly ever write them down. I think that to a certain extent it is important to write but I also think that at school, we do far too much writing, particularly copying.

Figure 0.1 Views on writing of Katy, aged seven

Chapter 1

Spelling
Learning and teaching

Introduction

At the simplest level, spelling is the association of alphabetic symbols called *graphemes* with speech sounds called *phonemes*, the smallest identifiable sounds in speech. In English we use 44 distinct phonemes out of a possible 70 or so including clicks which have been identified in human speech worldwide. The association of speech sounds with the alphabet symbols is called 'sound–symbol correspondence' or systematic 'phonics'. Phonics permits simple regular spellings such as d-o-g for 'dog', and b-e-d for 'bed' and so on. It is thought that when the alphabet was first invented several centuries BC, most words could be transcribed thus, but over time this simple correspondence between sound and symbol called *one-to-one correspondence* has, in many languages, gradually slipped. In this respect Turkish and Italian are more regular than Greek which is more regular than English. In earlier centuries English was more 'regular' but this correspondence slipped for a variety of reasons, some of which will have been the 'freezing' of the spelling convention at the time of the introduction of the printing press and then again following the publication of Johnson's dictionary of the English language in the eighteenth century, plus the nature of English itself.

In addition, pronunciation and dialects of the English speaking peoples have changed and developed over time. For example the words 'class', 'path' and 'bath' are now pronounced with a longer 'a' sound as in 'clarss', 'parth' and 'barth' in the southern counties of England whilst in the North the older, original form with the short vowel sound is preserved. This also makes it easier for beginning spellers in the North to spell the word correctly without the intrusive 'r'.

Before the Puritans were forced to leave the country to settle in America we must have pronounced words such as 'shone' with the long vowel sound. Now we only hear this form in certain North American dialects and here in England we say 'shon'. They also tend to preserve the old form of 'dove' for 'dived' just as you may occasionally still hear 'dove', 'snew' for snowed, and 'tret' for treated in East Anglia.

It has become necessary for all members of a modern society to become able to communicate in writing by committing spelling patterns to paper or screen. This is a more difficult task than *recognising* all the letters when they are present in context in a book. Spelling requires the *recall* of spellings from the memory in exactly the correct order or the *construction* of such spellings if they are not already stored in the word memory store or lexicon.

A controversy exists between most teachers and researchers who contend that spelling is a natural extension of reading and others such as Chomsky (1971) and Clay (1975, 1989), who argue that writing is a more concrete task, and developmentally occurs first. Nevertheless, agreement does exist that spelling is a more difficult task than reading (Frith 1980; Mastropieri and Scruggs 1995). 'It requires production of an exact sequence of letters, offers no contextual clues, and requires greater numbers of grapheme-to-phoneme decisions' (Fulk and Stormont-Spurgin 1995: 488).

Prior to the introduction of the printing press and even for some while afterwards spelling by scribes and clerks was much more variable than it is now and such variations were accepted. Today only correct spelling is acceptable and poor spelling is regarded, often quite wrongly, as indicative of poor intellectual ability or carelessness and such applicants for jobs are often screened out. Word processor spell checkers can now be used to conceal most poor spelling but as soon as we send emails or handwrite notes and exam essays it is revealed. Employers now often insist on job applications being handwritten to discover spelling difficulties and other personal characteristics.

English spelling also reflects its complex history, making it more difficult than many other languages to spell. Our modern alphabet has only 26 letters to accommodate the 44 English phonemes. Thus double vowels (r-oa-d, b-ea-d), diphthongs (r-ou-nd; c-ow) and six consonant digraphs (ch-, sh-, ph-, wh- and th- (voiced and unvoiced)) supplement them to preserve sound–symbol correspondence with graphemes.

In English, morphemes are also as significant as phonemes and the language itself can be said to be morphological in structure. *Morphemes* such as cat, -ing, I, a, -ed are the smallest elements of meaningful speech sound and can be single letters which when in isolation or added to a word are meaningful or change the meaning. There is thus a conflict between phonemic representation – writing the spoken language directly as it sounds now – and morphemics – representing the meaning and often the historical origins of the language, showing where the words have come from and how they sounded then. It is the convention in English to preserve the history over the current sound, thus *sheep herder* is spelt as *shepherd* rather than *sheperd* or *shepperd*. In the evolution of this spelling we may have pronounced *sheep* as *shep*, or we may have transcribed *sheep* as *shep* as some poor or beginning spellers might today.

English spelling is rich in history of this kind and so methods of teaching which offer an understanding of both the origins of the language through morphemics as well as its phonemic structure are important; however, they are rare.

The origins of the alphabet writing system

Writing systems first appeared about the same time some 5000 years ago in several different locations: Egypt, Mesopotamia, Hyrapus in Pakistan, and China. These writing systems evolved throughout history ranging from *hieroglyphs* – sacred characters used in ancient Egyptian picture writing and picture writing in general, to *logographs* – the use of single signs or symbols in Chinese representing words, to *syllabaries* – a set of characters representing syllables, to *rebus* – an enigmatic representation of a word or part of a word by pictures. It is maintained however that the *alphabet* system was only ever invented once (Delpire and Monory 1962; Gelb 1963).

Phoenician traders were believed to have invented the first alphabet in about the seventh century BC for their commercial needs as a maritime trading nation. The Greeks are thought to have experimented with its use and added vowel symbols to adapt it to their Indo-European language, and by the fourth century BC a common Hellenic alphabet and language were constructed. The Romans appeared to have acquired this alphabet from the Greeks (Delpire and Monory 1962) and disseminated it through their conquests to the Roman Empire. The medieval Christians then added the definitive distinction between 'i' and 'j' and 'u' and 'v'.

What is of interest and significance is that the alphabet was only invented once, presumably by some stroke of genius. A second important feature in its development was that it was invented in the context of a Semitic language. This Semitic language was consonantal and the Phoenicians developed 22 signs based upon common things such as whips and horses' heads (Jarman 1979) to fit the sounds of their language. If the alphabet was to be invented today in English it would have to consist of a set of symbols which would represent the 44 sounds that make up all the words in this language. This of course was done in 1961 and published as a new alphabet, the *initial teaching alphabet* (i.t.a.) by Pitman (1961) and later phonics schemes have adopted the principle (Lloyd 1993) but not the alphabet.

Different languages use different numbers of phonemes. The Japanese use several different writing systems but their language uses only 22 phonemes and thus they have problems learning the extra sounds of English and especially confuse 'l' and 'r'.

Although graphemes originally had a pictorial reference or meaning, now they as well as the phonemes are *abstract perceptual units* and this can create difficulties for some learners.The significance of the alphabet and consonantal language will be shown in later chapters to be an important principle for spelling development and dyslexia.

Methods of teaching spelling and links with handwriting

Alphabetic systems and the ABC method

In earlier centuries the traditional way to learn to read and spell was by an alphabetic method in which children had to master the 'criss-cross row' or 'Hornbook'. This was a sheet of paper mounted on a board covered with a thin layer of horn. There was a cross in the top left-hand corner and the alphabet was written in Roman letters, or 'black letter', the medieval Gothic form, and italic. The alphabet was learned by the child pointing to each letter in turn and then *naming* it. Sounds were not introduced at this stage. Learning the alphabet was followed by learning the sounds of vowels and then punctuation marks. The sounds of the vowels helped to master the 'syllabarium' which followed. The syllables were taught by first naming the letters thus: ay, bee, ab-ee, bee-eb (Chalmers 1976).

abcdefghijklm

nopqrstuvwxyz

ABCDEFG

Figure 1.1a An example of black letter or Gothic

More from the syllabarium:
   ab eb ib ob ub
   ba be bi bo bu
   ca ce ci co cu (and of course 'fah fee fi fo fum')

In rote order the pupils spelled the syllabarium through forwards and backwards, down, up and across until each meaningless syllable was fully memorised. A teacher could leave a monitor to hear groups and classes of 50 or more chanting the hours away. Learning to read was incidental to this process. Most teaching then consisted of rote memorising vast quantities of poetry, prose and the scriptures: a stultifying experience for any pupil and particularly so for the able or creative learner. Failure to memorise could and frequently did bring about severe punishments. School was more a torture to be endured and a luxury many could not afford. Aversion to this 'spelling grind' was widespread.

The last item in the Hornbook was the Lord's Prayer, which was spelled out word by word and read aloud. After this the pupils were 'ready' to spell out the words in the Bible. As can be envisaged, reading for meaning played little part in this system although whole word recognition may have developed incidentally in the process. According to Diack (1965) this method had remained largely unchanged since medieval times.

The persistence of the alphabetic method had apparently occurred because the spelling method was particularly suited to 'black letter' and because of the late introduction of Roman type for vernacular use (Chalmers 1976). 'Black letter' was to be found in cheap books well into the first half of the eighteenth century. Black letter is difficult to read and dots on 'i's were added to help overcome part of this problem.

Although compilers of spelling books in the early eighteenth century used the Hornbook as the basis for their books and began with the alphabet and lists of syllables to be spelled out, there was an increasing awareness of the importance of the sounds of the letters. Newer books combined simple phonic, alphabetic and syllabic methods. The books were intended for use by the parents and private tutors, for

minimum

Figure 1.1b A problem with black letter

most reading teaching then took place in the home and in the Sunday Schools run by the Society for the Promotion of Christian Knowledge (SPCK).

From 1770 Hornbooks which had often been used as bats were superseded by 'battledores'. These were small three-leaved cards costing about a penny which could be folded into an oblong with a flap left over to form a handle. Battledores contained alphabets, numerals, easy reading lessons and wood cuts.

At the beginning of the nineteenth century, Mrs Trimmer's book *Teacher's Assistant* was published and ran to 22 editions. This still used the spelling method and rote learning but the Anglican catechism was used as the 'reading book'. The method was synthetic for spelling, blending words from sounds, involving extensive drill in the alphabet, and analytic, breaking down words into syllables and letters to aid word recognition for reading. The catechism was learned section by section using this method. Writing was only introduced when children could read competently. This is quite different from today when reading and writing are introduced at the same time whether or not the children have the necessary fine motor coordination skills or any spelling competency. Occupying children's time plays a significant role in both approaches!

Phonics teaching methods

The ABC spelling method of teaching began to change during the late nineteenth century and a phonics and rule-based method began to replace it. However, even into the early twentieth century alphabetic methods were still found lingering in many country schools, and extensive periods of the school day were spent in rote memorising activities (Barnard 1961). A major feature of this form of education was to associate with it the teaching of copperplate handwriting, and late nineteenth-century copy books were numerous (Jarman 1979).

Copperplate handwriting was derived from the script used by those etching into copper blocks. It was essential that the flow of the writing was continuous and so a very precise and elaborate hand was produced. Variations of copperplate were taught in nineteenth-century schools and persisted well into Edwardian times.

What was written in the copy books became a prime source of early reading material. The fundamentals of the phonic approach were that the *sounds* of the letters singly and in combination became the overriding targets for children's learning. Alphabet learning now took second place. Even when phonics became well developed in the twentieth century it was still linked to extensive rote learning and copy writing. By this stage the pupils were learning a modified form of joined writing, called 'civil service hand' which had fewer loops and curls and was thought to be easier for beginners. In a survey of handwriting Piggott found 42 per cent of teachers were still using the style up to 1958.

Figure 1.2 An example of copperplate writing

The sounds of the lower case letters ('small letters') were introduced in alphabetical order. When the sounds of the letters had been learnt they were used in a simple way to decipher text. A popular item was: 'The' c-a-t 'cat' s-a-t 'sat' o-n 'on', th-e 'the' m-a-t 'mat'. Some common words were not always broken down into single phonic units but were presented as whole words. Putting the sounds together to blend words, known as phonic synthesis, was somewhat restrictive for there are a limited number of words which can be treated in this way. It gave rise to the development of rather bizarre story lines such as: 'The pig with a wig did a jig in the bog.'

By this phonics method it could take about six months to teach the rudiments of spelling and reading sufficient to tackle more interesting text and by then some

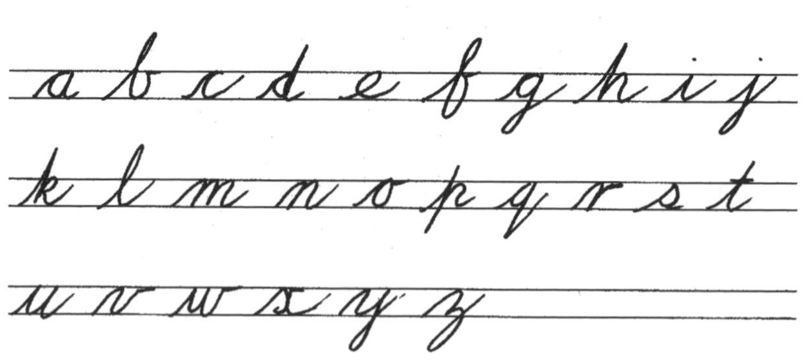

Figure 1.3 Civil service hand

children's motivation might have waned. Able children with quick memories would not need the rote methods and could easily become bored. The very slowest to learn stayed in the class with the beginners repeating their lessons until they had sufficient skills to be moved up into 'standard two'.

Purely phonics methods of this nature ignore the fact that the eye and brain are much quicker at processing than the ear and brain. The eye simultaneously processes data, whereas the ear must deal with them sequentially. Thus whilst we are 'spelling by ear' we should perhaps be 'reading by eye' using the phonic knowledge not only to guess words from context and initial sounds, but also by building up whole word memories as well as part word knowledge from the visual patterns they form. The two types of information should be linked so that the one process supports the other. Teaching phonics for reading needs to be *analytic for word decoding* in context whereas teaching phonics for spelling needs to be *synthetic for encoding* or building words in the absence of context.

A very popular phonics-based scheme with stories and fables, teaching notes and letter and blend cards which could be assembled to construct words was introduced in 1929 by Fassett, called *The Beacon Readers*. It was published by Ginn who are still active in the literacy programmes field. This graded scheme could be found in schools throughout the country well into the 1950s.

In North America, phonics methods were actually introduced from the UK in the 1920s to try to counteract what were considered to be the deleterious effects of their 'look and say' methods. Teaching schemes such as *The Writing Road to Reading*, the Spalding and Spalding (1967) method, taught a set of 70 phonograms as the basics before reading books were introduced.

Phonics teaching, or *code emphasis* methods, predominated in UK schools throughout the first half of the twentieth century. They had been expanded in this period to teach both reading and spelling in combination. The method was supported at least in the first few decades by the teaching of a cursive form of handwriting using copy books. However, all this was set to change.

'Look and say' methods

From the middle of the twentieth century a revolution in literacy teaching began in the UK as the method called 'look and say' was introduced from the USA. It needed a graded scheme of reading books and this was provided by the 'Janet and John' series in which children learned a basic sight vocabulary of 50 words by memorising words on 'flash' cards and saying them aloud. After ten such sightings and sayings it was expected that most would be able to commit a whole word to memory and then be able to read it when they met it in the story line. This *meaning emphasis* method quickly became widespread and replaced the phonics method in England and Wales and was in use well into the 1990s (Goodacre 1971; Hinson and Smith 1993). With it the entire focus had moved from reading and spelling to reading reinforced by copy writing and as Peters (1967, 1985) concluded, spelling was 'caught' rather than taught in this process.

It was argued that in the meaning emphasis method more interesting text could be provided which would enhance the motivation of children to read. Children took tins of flashcards home to learn their words for reading. Teachers now had to devote considerable time in the reception and infant school years to hearing individual children read. Whilst the teacher heard one child reading the rest of the class needed to be occupied and so they were engaged in copy writing and tracing their news and then drawing a picture of it, followed by activities of their own choosing such as painting, and sand and water play. These other activities could be supervised by teaching assistants and nursery nurses. Even hearing reading was shared out among parent helpers so that reading time could be increased. Often the teachers themselves had little training in ways of developing literacy through hearing reading. So what with drawing pictures of news and tracing lines to pictures of what the words represented in workbooks and on worksheets, a considerable amount of literacy learning time was wasted.

Studies by Southgate-Booth (1986) showed that on average teachers were giving about 15 seconds each to hearing children read per day and more time to managing the behaviour of the rest of the class during the process. The teachers were working exceptionally hard and she advised that they should be doing less but teaching more. This would be by organising individual, group and class teaching sessions for reading and that all children should have to learn the basic sight vocabulary of 200 words to support this. Teachers, she asserted, should learn to delegate many of the simpler tasks to classroom helpers. This strategy formed the basis of what was contained in the NLS literacy hour format (DfEE 1998).

By this stage phonics teaching was almost eradicated in some schools' reception classes and it became usual to introduce initial letter sounds only *after* a basic vocabulary of 50 sight words had been learned, or as a remedial programme at seven or eight years when particular children had failed to learn to read other than a few common words. Even so the phonics consisted of single letter sounds and a few rules, such as 'magic e' and 'i before e except after c' thus there was very little direct teaching to support early spelling development. The main method of its development was in copy writing and tracing over letters and words. As early as 1967, Chall's survey of teaching methods had shown that to delay the introduction of sound values in this way slowed down the acquisition of reading (and spelling) skills in a considerable number of vulnerable learners.

During the 'look and say' period it became common practice to introduce the letters in groups which it was believed had similar writing patterns: a c o e s or c a o d g, and l t f. However, what looked the same was not the same nor equally easy to make in handwriting. Children were not taught the alphabet under this scheme and lost the sense of alphabetical order; it then needed to be separately taught. Visual processes and visualisation strategies were emphasised for learning spellings and reinforced during copy writing. Compilation of pupil word dictionaries was widely used to support writing.

Whole language approaches and 'real books'

These methods are variants of the meaning emphasis approach and were encouraged by the work of Smith (1973, 1978, 1988). Learning to read was described by him as a 'psycholinguistic guessing game' in which the learner guessed words in context using picture, semantic and syntactic cues in 'top down' processing, thus it was and still is most important to develop speaking and listening skills, language competence and performance to support reading.

Peters and Smith (1986) reported that pupils entering secondary school unable to read were just as aware of their spelling as their reading difficulties. However, whilst there had been consistent pressure upon them to read and they were given support for their reading, the same kind of pressure had never been placed upon their spelling. They might well have had several years of remedial 'phonics', simple reading books and activity workbooks to help them but the teacher had always been there to give them the word and to correct their spelling mistakes; even so they had not learned to spell correctly. It is also clear that the so-called 'remedial phonics' of the period had not been effective.

The 'real books' movement followed from the whole language approaches and children were enabled to choose for themselves the books they wanted to read from the story book chest and sat down with the teacher or helper to read. It did of course mean they often chose books for the interesting picture on the cover and quickly found the text was too advanced for them. As a result many teachers colour coded the levels of difficulty so we were back to a 'Rainbow Reading System' of a kind. The notion behind 'real books' goes back to Witty and Kopel (1936) who found that the best training for reading was reading itself and beginners needed an *apprenticeship* in reading. The effectiveness of an apprenticeship approach was demonstrated by Waterland (1986) in her classroom.

What these methods failed to do was help those with average or poor visual memories acquire correct spellings. The instructions pupils complained of were 'mind your spelling', 'learn this word', 'write this word out five times', and 'use a dictionary', but 'nobody tells us how Miss'. They did not know how to correct their misspellings and most teachers did not seem to teach them. Pupils do not make spelling mistakes deliberately or out of laziness and would use a dictionary if they knew more or less how to spell the word in the first place. What was observed was *learned helplessness*.

Although it had been popularly believed that schools were giving insufficient attention to basic skills (reading, spelling and numeracy) during the 1970s and early 1980s, the National Foundation for Educational Research (NFER) report by Barker-Lunn (1984) found to the contrary. Teachers were found to have spent a high proportion of their time engaged in such pursuits and many gave regular spelling tests. Spelling tests had been a weekly and often daily feature of the old phonics system. However, as Southgate-Booth (1986) found, the time and attention was not always given to the most effective methods for literacy teaching.

The main methods of teaching spelling identified by Tansley and Pankhurst (1981) in their survey are outlined below.

- Pupils engaged in extensive copy *writing*, especially in reception class.
- After this, when the pupils had learned a basic spelling vocabulary, some teachers taught *common letter strings*.
- The *look-cover-write-check* system for correcting errors was becoming popular.
- Some teachers asked pupils to guess the spellings, particularly *the initial sound* and would provide the correct spelling after this.

- Some teachers taught some *basic phonics* and *simple blending* to form words, for example c-a-t.
- Many of the classes of children kept *personal word dictionaries* of the most common words that they either could spell or used a lot in open-ended story writing.

The major underlying method observed was rote learning and it did not begin to change until the introduction of the National Literacy Strategy in 1998.

The National Curriculum and spelling (NCC 1989)

The National Curriculum in English was designed to improve literacy standards and the teaching of literacy skills within the context of the study of English. Levels of attainment were set out by 'expert' groups.

Levels of spelling attainment in the National Curriculum (NC)

The following lists set out for each level what the children should be able to do at that level.

Level 1:

- begin to show an understanding of the difference between drawing and writing and between numbers and letters;
- write some letter shapes in response to sounds and letter names;
- use single letters or pairs of letters to represent whole words or parts of words.

Level 2 (Target set for the seven-year-old age group – Key Stage 1 (DfE 1995)):

- produce recognisable (though not necessarily always correct) spelling of a range of common words;
- know that spelling has patterns, and begin to apply that knowledge in order to attempt the spelling of a wider range of words;
- spell correctly words in regular use in their own writing which observe common patterns.

Level 3:

- spell correctly less common words which are important in the learning context in which they occur (e.g. technical vocabulary in science);
- show a growing awareness of word families and their relationships;
- check their own writing for accurate spelling;
- recognise and use correctly regular patterns for vowel sounds and common letter strings of increasing complexity.

Level 4 (Target set for the 11-year-old age group – Key Stage 2 (DfE 1995)):

- spell correctly words which display the other main patterns in English spelling including the main prefixes and suffixes.

Level 5:

- spell correctly words of some complexity, including words with inflectional suffixes (e.g. -ed, -ing), consonant doubling, etc.; and words where the spelling
  highlights semantic relationships (e.g. sign, signature).

Note: at each level of attainment the use of technological aids by pupils who
depend on them to produce their written work is acceptable DES (1989).

These specifications include a code which teachers recognised and implemented. The key word indicants are 'recognise letter shapes', 'letter patterns',
'common letter strings', and 'word families'. These show that the NLS writers have
espoused the visual theory of spelling acquisition and rote training in letter patterns and strings. These are all more appropriate to teaching reading than spelling.
The level 5 criteria needed to be dispersed around level 3 and replaced by 'spell a
wider technical and specialist vocabulary' and 'reduction in the number of errors
in homonyms, apostrophe use and punctuation errors'. Thus we can see that little
had changed in teaching orthodoxy since the research of Tansley and Pankhurst.

Spelling, teaching and the National Literacy Strategy (NLS)

In 1996 a National Commission on Education into standards in literacy and numeracy 1948–1995 found that one in five school leavers lacked the literacy and
numeracy skills demanded by the modern workplace. Reading standards had
changed little over the period but the needs of society had increased. An NFER
Briefing Paper (1992: 23) reported that 1 per cent of school leavers were illiterate, 15
per cent struggled with reading and writing and 20 per cent had limited numeracy
skills. These standards were not regarded as high enough nor good enough in comparison with international standards (TIMSS 1997) and led to the introduction of the
NLS (DfEE 1998).

After one year of the NLS, 71 per cent of pupils had achieved level 4 or above in
reading in 1998 but only 53 per cent achieved it in writing. From 2000 to 2004 it had
plateaued at around 80 per cent when the target set was 85 per cent and writing
performance rose from 60 to 63 per cent. By 2005 although 83 per cent of students
at 11 years had reached level 4 in reading, still only 63 per cent had met this criterion in writing. Tymms (2004), however, challenged the evidence that literacy had
improved as much as the Government had claimed. In his analysis of the results,
from a low of 48 per cent in 1995, only 60 per cent had achieved level 4 in English
by 2004.

The differences between the results of girls and boys were also concerning. In
reading, 87 per cent of girls and 79 per cent of boys had reached level 4 but in writing, 71 per cent of girls and 57 per cent of boys had reached it in 2004 (Tidmas 2005).
At GCSE boys' achievements were found to be on average 10 per cent worse than
girls although at A levels they appear to catch up.

A House of Commons Inquiry was set up in 2005 to investigate the shortcomings
of the NLS and DfES commissioned a review of the situation by Jim Rose. Although
the NLS introduced phonics teaching earlier than before, it allowed teachers to follow the patterns of the past, teaching the names and sounds in alphabetical order,

then initial sounds and endings, visual patterns and letter strings to aid word recognition. It was found that in some classes children learned the sounds of all the letters within a few months, while others took three years.

The evidence presented now pointed to the inadequate teaching of phonics, in particular a lack of *synthetic phonics* and not teaching it early enough. It was thus advocated that teaching for literacy should be 'synthetic phonics fast, first and alone' and there should be a greater emphasis in the early years on speaking and listening. An onset and rime and a 'top down' language approach at first might only confuse pupils.

In 2006, following the Rose Review, the NLS was withdrawn and a consultation paper circulated with the results to be implemented in September 2006. The literacy hour will remain but its rigid format will not. Instead teachers are going to be allowed to develop their own programmes but must give more time to synthetic phonics and teach this from the outset. Literacy consultants will be trained and the training will be 'cascaded'.

Since the introduction of meaning emphasis methods, reading teaching has tended to predominate, whilst spelling and handwriting have been used in a supportive role. The same dominance can be seen in literacy research and in the dyslexia field. We read of 'dyslexia, or reading difficulties' in *Excellence for All Children* (DfEE 1997: 15) when the majority of dyslexics have both a reading and a spelling problem (Vellutino 1979; Frith 1980).

Is there a spelling problem in schools today?

At Year 7 when pupils enter secondary school, according to the NLS they should be competent spellers for everyday purposes, and fluent writers. In 2000 HMI had published a discussion paper *The Teaching of Writing in Primary Schools: Could Do Better*. This paper gave the main findings from the observation of 300 Literacy Hour lessons and concluded that not enough time was spent on 'it'; 25 per cent of lessons were unsatisfactory; and the balance between the teaching of reading and writing was not yet achieved.

HMI concerns were however more about compositional techniques than spelling and penmanship. However, the two best early predictors of compositional ability have been found to be the rapidity of writing the alphabet (Berninger 2004), and the rapidity of coding orthographic material – spelling to dictation (Berninger *et al.* 1997; Graham *et al.*, 2000).

In controlled studies Scannel and Marshall (1966) and Briggs (1980) found that poorly spelled work was downgraded by teachers whatever the contents. These seemingly low level skills of spelling and handwriting appear to play an important role in the achievement of standards because they are fundamental to the development of compositional abilities. The reason might be because once we can write and spell with relative ease and fluency, and achieve automaticity, the processing power of the brain is free to contemplate higher order things.

What seems not to be taken into account in the national surveys and the NLS is that because of its difficulty, the development of spelling can be expected to lag behind reading by six months in normal circumstances during the school years (Myklebust 1973). A target of 80 per cent to reach level 4 in spelling at age 11 might thus be more appropriate than one of 85 per cent. In 1994 the NC targets for spelling and handwriting had been merged, making the separate contributions of spelling, handwriting and composition even more difficult to unravel.

Cohort analyses of spelling after two, four and seven years of the NLS (Montgomery 2006)

In this research pupils were set a 20-minute essay-writing task on a topic of their own choice (after Allcock 2001). They were given a two-minute planning session. The task modelled those they might be expected to do in extended writing tasks in examinations, whereas writing the alphabet, dictations, and three-, five-, ten- and fifteen-minute essays do not model such tasks and have been a criticism of many earlier studies.

After each five-minute period the student leaves a line space and continues. Overall it is found that they write rapidly in the first ten minutes, slow up in the third segment (thinking time) and speed up again in the final five minutes.

It is important to note that some pupils will have adopted the strategy of trying to write within their known correct spelling repertoire and so the error counts are likely to be a conservative estimate of the true spelling situation. Proofreading was not part of the exercise because of lesson time constraints and control issues. The results are shown in Table 1.1.

The 'dyslexic' group were defined by having made 20 or more errors per script. The majority of dyslexics will have a spelling difficulty which is as severe as the reading problem if not more so. It is the spelling problem which is difficult to resolve even when reading has attained normal levels (Vellutino 1979; Frith 1980; Snowling 2000).

According to Allcock's (2001) research the mean speed of Year 7 groups (N=2701) is 13.9 words per minute. Pupils in School C are writing more slowly than the average, but their spelling ability is better than the earlier cohorts. We could suggest that having three extra NLS years to learn the sight vocabulary of 200 words has had some effect.

Table 1.1 Comparison of scores for writing speed and spelling in three Year 7 cohorts

School A: After two years of the NLS (2000)				
	N	Words per minute	Mean spelling errors	'Dyslexic'
Set 1	28	15.66	7.11	2
Set 2, 3, 4	63	12.04	8.65	6
Set 5	15	10.88	12.73	2
Means	N=106	13.97	8.82	(10%)
School B: After four years of the NLS (mixed ability sets) (2002)				
Means	N=160	13.64	12.18	(18.5%)
School C: After seven years of the NLS (mixed ability sets) (2005)				
Means	N=251	12.44	10.79	(16.4%)

The writing speed was faster and the spelling ability higher in the most able set in School A. We could ask if they are in Set A as a result of this. Lyth (2004) has evidence to suggest this may be so.

In School C after seven years of the NLS:

- 16.4 per cent of the cohort showed 'dyslexic' type spelling difficulties;
- the ratio of 'dyslexic' boys to girls was 1.6 to 1;
- 32 per cent of the cohort failed the HMI spelling criterion making five or more errors per 100 words;
- the ratio of boys to girls failing the HMI criterion was 1.5 to 1;
- 28 per cent of 'dyslexics' also had slow or problematic handwriting.

The number of errors of boys and girls has gone down after seven years of the NLS. Alternatively teachers have improved their teaching of the NLS, or in one catchment area are more skilled than in the other.

Tansley and Pankhurst (1981) found that 10 per cent of the population in their survey had literacy difficulties. The British Dyslexia Association (BDA 2004) also put the figures for dyslexics at 10 per cent with 4 per cent having severe literacy problems. In addition to this it looks as if a further 20 per cent of cohort C have literacy difficulties related to spelling which will hamper their achievement. Silverman (2004) has also identified writing difficulties as a significant contribution to underachievement (UAch).

Although these results are not absolute in that questions can be raised about the methodology, there do appear to be a significant number of pupils in the cohorts whose spelling must be of concern. There are also significantly more boys with problems than girls, in the ratio of 1.6 to one. This is not far from the ratio of two to one found by Rutter *et al.* (2004) in four large epidemiological studies.

Poor written work and avoidance of it wherever possible may be the only indication of a learning difficulty in the presence of seemingly higher potential. But the conclusion most often drawn is that these students are lazy, unmotivated and do not take care with school work, not that they have a problem for which they need help and so we can see a cycle of rejection, underachievement and failure with consequent loss of self-esteem. This is the classic profile seen in underachievement (Whitmore 1980; Butler-Por 1987; Silverman 1989; Wallace 2000), and in truants (Southwell 2006).

Underachieving pupils may simply withdraw and try to go unnoticed or may become so frustrated and bored they engage in problem behaviour such as disruption or clowning and become set upon a career in deviance. Does this in part account for the rise in social, emotional and behavioural difficulties (SEBD)?

Table 1.2 Spelling results of boys and girls in cohorts B and C

	School B: Four years NLS More than five errors per 100 words	School C: Seven years NLS More than five errors per 100 words
Girls	N=96 (30%)	N=129 (25%)
Boys	N=64 (50%)	N=122 (38%)
Totals	N=160 (40%)	N=251 (32%)

Developmental stages in spelling

What is of interest when studying spelling as it is 'caught' during reading is what successful readers are doing when they learn, either specifically taught or not. Clay (1979) found that the behaviour of high progress readers involved anticipating or predicting what can occur in meaning and language structure, searching for cues, self-correcting and forming intuitive rules that took them beyond what they already knew. She found that the reading was organised at the phrase and sentence level and attention focused on meaning, with the reader checking meaning cues with other cues related to syntax, concepts of print such as punctuation and direction, the visual impact of the print and the sound-to-letter associations. Attention was directed to meaning and finding a fit within this integrated cue-searching behaviour so that the reader was immediately aware when a mistake had been made and would search again for a better fit. This self-correction inevitably led to a greater independence in reading. The readers were behaving as problem solvers and used a wide range of cognitive strategies and skills which enabled them to gain more knowledge and skill. We can see here that Smith's (1973) psycholinguistic guessing game was very much in progress.

Clay found that the low progress readers organised their reading at the letter and word level and used a narrower range of cues. They tended to rely on remembering words by sight and their attention to letters was usually restricted to the first letter. The resulting 'fractured utterances' caused the reader to lose track of what the message of the text was about. When a mistake was made, the reader was thus unaware of it and so self-correction did not occur and the pupil remained dependent on the teacher to give help to continue the reading.

Rather than teach poor readers to engage in 'top down' processing they need perhaps to be equipped with the basic skills to proceed to this level of operation. In other words 'bottom up' and 'top down' processing may reflect two developmental levels of reading that students pass through either slowly or more quickly to reach fluency. Francis' (1982) research tends to support this. She found that good beginning readers taught by 'look and say' nevertheless inferred the alphabetic principle and used this information in their word attack skills. The slow readers had difficulties doing this. Later, those who developed reading difficulties showed a tendency to overuse the phonic strategy and tried to sound out all the words they did not know. Since most of the words could not be decoded by this strategy they quickly faltered and needed help from the teacher.

This does not mean as some teachers inferred that the children should not learn further phonics but that the phonics they did know should be supplemented by teaching them synthetic phonics for spelling and analytic phonics for reading. These children were stuck at a lower level of development in 'bottom up' processing where their knowledge for reading and spelling was not secure and could not be readily used as tools in development.

What successful spellers learn to do

If children relied wholly on the limited system of rote training for spelling described, it would be difficult to see how many of them could become accomplished spellers, for their main exposure would be through reading and copying. This would place too great a burden on the visual memory.

There is a pressure for accuracy observed in many classrooms rather than an encouragement of exploration but through the work of Chomsky (1971), Clay (1979, 1989) and Read (1986) in particular, insight has been gained into what successful spellers are doing. They found that a child's first literate response is *to write* and not read. This natural tendency they advocated should be encouraged starting with marks on paper. In a method called 'emergent writing', 'developmental writing' or 'creative spelling' children are encouraged to muster any spelling skills they can and to write their messages and stories. The teacher then teaches the spelling skills and strategies that will prove most useful in making the spellings more like standard orthography. The teacher ignores most of the misspellings but supplies limited but helpful information such as knowledge of sounds not yet learnt and rules if problems persist. Parents of course do need this method carefully explained to them for they like to see correctly spelled work in the books. According to Read (1986) the children's 'creative spellings' may look bizarre at first but if the teacher persists with an analysis it can be seen that the spellings are based upon reasonable principles such as spellings representing sounds, and similar sounds perhaps having similar spellings. The children may often be found to have a surprising amount of spelling knowledge when they enter school, which they have picked up from books, television, and advertising in the street and in shops.

In addition to absorbing spelling information from the environment and from the teacher in the classroom it has become clear that the eye and brain are doing a considerable amount of additional processing work on their own. Children taught entirely by a 'look and say' method developed knowledge of letter sounds without

Figure 1.4 The emergent spelling of three five-year-olds

Emma – five years two months: 'once upon a time there was a christmas fairy'

wuns a pon tyme tcer as a crisms fariy

Yacob – five years two months: 'I went to bed Yacob'

I weto peto yocp

Kelly – five years one month: 'She is in bed. She is sick. She has chickenpox'

She si in BaD. She si sip. She haS Chpspo

ever being directly taught. The children in the phonics systems of earlier times learned to read and spell a much wider range of words than were in the schemes and could read and spell words which could not be sounded out phonically. There are thus as many routes to learning to spell as to read. An emphasis upon 'look and say' alone can hamper and slow down the learning but not actually cut it off (Chall 1967; Adams 1990).

An interactive approach using a judicious mixture of the best of the teaching approaches in the correct sequence in both reading and spelling is obviously to be recommended, for this will facilitate the learning of the able and support that of the pupils with difficulties, teaching them the strategies which they have not inferred from contact with print. It could then be envisaged that almost all school children would meet the National Curriculum attainment targets for spelling at the appropriate level for their age and ability, or indeed earlier for there is no guarantee that the NC staging and levels are correct.

Theories of spelling development

Pupils do not suddenly move from a state of no spelling knowledge to one of complete spelling accuracy and success. There are a number of theories and models which have been proposed that trace spelling progress and link it to a model or models of spelling development.

The theorising usually first arises within the context of a particular education system and teaching context. Thus findings from spellers in a 'look and say' regime might not be quite the same as from those in 'whole language' and phonics schemes and this has led inadvertently to different aspects or emphases in the developmental models.

Simon and Simon (1973) proposed an information processing model of spelling in which, once the spellings of skilled writers were phonetically accurate, a number of alternative phonemic spellings were generated and the correct one was selected by comparison with partial information in visual memory. Marsh *et al.* (1980) however found that very proficient spellers made heavy use of visual information and even mediocre spellers were able to go to a visual information store and spell new words and non-words by analogy with already known words. This led them to propose a series of developmental stages which the normal speller moved through.

They suggested that initially, a *sequential encoding* strategy is used in which a word is processed in a left-to-right serial order when spelling unknown words. Later, a *hierarchical coding* strategy based upon conditional rules is evolved. Examples would be where c is softened before e, i and y and the silent e at the end of a syllable indicates that the preceding vowel is long or 'says its name' as in 'late' and 'rote' etc. The researchers suggested that this strategy developed more slowly and over a longer period of time but reached a ceiling by about fifth grade whereas this was not so for reading. The final stage of spelling was identified as the use of *analogy,* that is, spelling unknown words by comparing their sound with wholes and parts of already known words and selecting the most likely combination. They also found that there appeared to be a developmental shift towards the use of analogy strategies in both reading and spelling between second and fifth grade.

More recently Goswami (1993) showed that beginning readers and spellers also use analogy strategies, or these are available to them if they are encouraged to use them. This has led her to reject the notion of a stage theory and to promote the teaching of the use of initial sounds and analogy strategies to beginning readers. This approach using *onsets* and *rimes* is based on the work of Bryant and Bradley (1985). Onsets are initial sounds and rimes are endings of syllables such as 'ig' in pig, fig and wig. Teaching this strategy to older dyslexics has been called a *phonological approach to teaching* (PAT) (Wilson 1994).

In summary these theories identify *information processing strategies* which are available or could be made available to beginning and proficient spellers. A somewhat different view has been developed by Frith (1980). She identified different stages at which spellers arrived as they accumulated spelling information and skill. These could be indicative of the invariant mental structures which it was believed by Gibson and Levin (1975) were built from contact with print. In essence this theory reflects the *products* of learning as well as the processes.

Frith's model was first a three-stage model as described below.

Logographic stage

This is the first stage in which an instant recognition of familiar words is seen. A range of graphic features may act as cues in this process. Letter order is generally ignored and phonological aspects are secondary considerations – the pupils pronounce the words after they have recognised them. They usually refuse to respond if they do not recognise the word.

Alphabetic stage

Letter order and phonological factors now play a crucial role. Pupils begin to use a systematic approach, decoding grapheme by grapheme. At this stage the pupils may use these strategies to pronounce new and nonsense words although they may not do this correctly.

Orthographic stage

Here the instant analysis of words into orthographic units is seen without phonological conversion. Strategies are systematic and non-visual and operate on larger units than phonological ones. These could coincide with morphemic meaningful units or could just be letter strings. This will vary depending on the strategy emphasised in teaching if taught at all.

In 1985 Frith redeveloped this basic framework as a six-step model. She proposed that normal reading and spelling proceed out of step, with each of the three stages divided into two in which either reading or spelling may be the pacemaker. In logographic reading step 1a the skill is presented in a very basic form; at level 1b logographically it is ready to be adopted for writing. At stage 2a in reading, the strategy may continue to be logographic and only at the next step 2b becomes alphabetic, whereas writing at 2a becomes alphabetic at a simple level, continues into 2b and on into 3a before developing into the orthographic mode. Her rationale for the six-step model was that the alphabet is tailor-made for spelling rather than reading and that in acquired disorders, phonological reading is always accompanied by phonological spelling but not vice versa. In general, progress in literacy skills in normal subjects she regards as 'an alternating shift of balance between reading and spelling. Reading is the pacemaker for the logographic strategy, writing for the alphabetic strategy, and reading again for the orthographic one' (1985: 313).

From the six-step model, Frith (1985) identified the classical developmental dyslexic's problem as a failure to proceed to the alphabetic stage, quoting Makita (1968) and the relative absence of developmental dyslexia in Japan where the Kanji script involves logographic and syllabic but not alphabetic skills. Makita's (1968) survey of 9195 school children had shown that the incidence of reading disabilities of any type was about 0.98 per cent.

This figure of about 1 per cent is close to that found by Clark (1970) and Chall (1967) in phonic teaching regimes and to those who after Clay's Reading Recovery programme were referred on for specialist help. It is close also to the 1.5 per cent discovered by HMI (SED 1978) in their Scottish schools survey. It compares favourably with the 4 per cent identified by Rutter et al. (1970) in their Isle of Wight survey which was taken to be a representative sample of the position likely to be found in England and Wales excluding major inner city areas where overall the results were found to be more than 9 per cent (Rutter et al. (1979). More recently the British Dyslexia Association has estimated the current incidence of dyslexia to be 10 per cent with 4 per cent of these in the severe range (BDA 2004).

Makita's results have now been challenged by Amano (1992) who has found that the lockstep progression through the Japanese curriculum, requiring extensive memorising at all levels with children spending many hours in the evenings and at weekends in private 'crammer' classes, is causing larger numbers of failures and truancy than had previously been revealed. In order to achieve basic literacy, 2000 characters have to be learned by very young children and many of them are failing to do this and keep up with the pace expected of them. In addition they are also expected later to transfer to Kana which is a more alphabetically based script. However, failure to learn because of poor teaching does not make pupils dyslexic.

From the model shown in Table 1.3 it becomes clear how one can meet a beginner who reads logographically but spells alphabetically and can write correctly some simple regular words which he or she cannot read, as Bradley (1980) found. At a

Table 1.3 Frith's (1985) six-step model of stages in reading and writing acquisition

Step	Reading	Spelling
1a	Logographic	(Symbolic)
1b	Logographic	Logographic
2a	Logographic	Alphabetic
2b	Alphabetic	Alphabetic
3a	Orthographic	Alphabetic
3b	Orthographic	Orthographic

later stage, it is possible to find competent orthographic reading whilst spelling remains alphabetic (Frith 1980). Frith (1985) argued that achievement of orthographic competence in reading is not in itself sufficient for attainment of this level in spelling and did indeed identify a group of subjects who were average and even good readers who were disabled spellers. As will be seen later, this is not an uncommon problem.

Frith (1985) compared the three-stage model with methods of teaching reading. The logographic strategy was compared with the 'look and say' method and dominated the first stage of reading acquisition during which a sizeable sight vocabulary was normally developed. The alphabetic strategy was compared with 'phonics' and she noted that '[i]t is generally agreed that a "phonics" stage in reading is of great importance and cannot simply be skipped' (p. 309). The orthographic stage she compared with the morphemic approach in 'structural reading' of Stern and Gould (1965) and to the later stages of the Gillingham–Stillman (1956) programme. However, we have to question what the model might show if Frith had been investigating dyslexia in a 'phonics first' schooling system as Read (1986) was doing in the USA.

Gentry (1981) closely analysed the writing of 'normal' (non-dyslexic) children and proposed five stages in the process of spelling development. These can be compared with the levels of spelling development in the National Curriculum and Frith's stages.

Gentry's (1981) levels of spelling development

- Precommunicative – scribble writing in which children may tell a story as they scribble and draw.
- Prephonetic – the creative or invented spelling stage where a single letter may represent a word or a group of letters e.g. H or h for 'high'.
- Phonetic – letter-by-letter transcriptions of sounds e.g. 'hi'.
- Transitional – the spellings look more like standard spelling influenced by origin and rules e.g. 'hye'.
- Correct – standard spelling e.g. 'high'.

Having decided the level of development, the assessment on the same form can be used again at the end of the intervention period to see if there has been progress

Table 1.4 Developmental spelling error analysis based on Gentry's levels

Level	0	1	2	3	4
Word	Precommunicative	Semiphonetic	Phonetic	Transitional	Correct
1	Random letters	mtr	mostr	monstur	monster
2	Random	u	unitid	younighted	united
3	Random	jrs	jras	dres	dress
4	Random	bt	bodm	bottum	bottom

(Source: Fiderer 1998)

Table 1.5 Comparison of theories and levels of spelling development and the National Curriculum

Frith (1980)	Gentry (1981)	National Curriculum
Logographic	Precommunicative	Level 1
	Prephonetic	Level 2
Alphabetic	Phonetic	
Orthographic	Transitional	Level 3
	Correct	Level 4/5

across the stages. A score overall for improvement can be calculated. Looking at spelling from a developmental point of view can prove useful for teacher and learner; however, when some spellers get stuck and show multiple levels the analysis cannot help. It is more useful if the developmental progression analysis is seen as a backcloth to the actual intervention.

As can be seen from Table 1.5, the nature and levels of spelling development are not definitive but offer guidelines from which to assess a pupil's general level when the method of introductory teaching is taken into account. For example, the impact of a phonics-only approach will be different from a 'look and say' one with more alphabetic knowledge to be seen in the writing at an early stage.

Who has spelling problems?

The UK Government has encouraged up to 5 per cent of marks to be deducted for poor spelling and set targets for writing which were the same as for reading, showing that spelling and spelling progress were not understood. In rapid writing, especially in tests and under duress, we all can make spelling mistakes and 'slips of the pen'. Mistakes frequently occur as homophones (e.g. there for their) and endings may be missed (e.g. the for they), but if we have time to proofread they can usually be corrected.

Dyslexic students not only have reading difficulties; they also have spelling problems. Even after reading improves they may carry their spelling disability into adulthood. Students who can read adequately but make multiple spelling errors also appear to have 'dyslexic type' difficulties. Their difficulties are often ignored in schools because they can read well enough.

In addition to dyslexics there appear to be a large number of students who have difficulties in learning to spell accurately. These are often students whose handwriting is illegible, sometimes because their thoughts run faster than their handwriting skills can capture them but more frequently they have a mild handwriting coordination difficulty. This slows down their writing and so they get less practice in spelling. This is illustrated in the case of Maria, shown in Figure 1.5.

Maria is bilingual in German and English and speaks both languages fluently. She is highly verbal and a fluent reader. She taught herself to read at the age of four, before entry into school. Highly able children writing like Maria will be overlooked in busy classrooms and will be considered low-average in ability, seemingly of the standard of the writing.

Annette – aged five years eleven months, showing 11 of 20 lines written from memory in ten minutes in fully joined script, with no spelling problems, only an occasional misspelling.

'Wild animals often live in woodland, the fox, the squirrel, the woodmouse and the shrew, the largest of these animals is the fox, the fox is carniverous which means he eats meat. The shrew is the smallest of the animals mentioned, and he is about two inches long at the most. The pigmy shrew is about one and a half centimetres. The squirrel is often a pest because he will dig up the roots of varios plants. Squirrels eats nuts and sometimes pine cones. Occasionally rabbits are seen in the wood, they are grey brown and have very large ears—- I once found a dead adder'

Maria – aged five years ten months, writing from memory in ten minutes in print script. She has a spelling problem, and wrote 3 lines.

'I wnt to the Titic Esbtn
I swo srm thes fom the Titic
and srm thes war reil'

Translation: I went to the Titanic Exhibition. I saw some things from the Titanic and some of these were real.

Figure 1.5 Examples of the spelling of two highly able students

Other poor spellers with disabilities may include:

- Children with hearing difficulties. Their sentence structure may reflect that of British sign language. They may miss endings and high frequency sounds in words.
- Those with language impairments. They will also show the impact of this in spelling and composition when they are unable to pronounce words correctly, use complex ideas and words and follow normal grammatical rules.
- Second language learners, who may import their mother tongue features into English spelling and composition and take time to catch up.
- Slower learners, who will show a slower profile of development in literacy skills more typical of younger children and with a simpler vocabulary and sentence structure.

In addition, poor teaching, slowness to learn and missed schooling all play a part. The spelling development of some learners is slowed down by the teaching regime. This can be seen in the writing of Luke at age four years six months and then again at six years in Year 1 (see Figure 1.6). At six he has signs of a mild handwriting coordination problem as well.

Friday March 13th
My diary ye
Yesterday It was
Book Day I made
sum caks and a
Flower we mad a
cafe we rot som
sygns and sum menys
we playd in the
cafe I l-was a bider

Figure 1.6 Examples of the writing of Luke at four years and six years

New directions in the teaching of spelling?

Having so many poor spellers and so many vulnerable to spelling difficulties, it is surprising that something as difficult as learning to spell has not been given more detailed consideration from teachers and researchers rather than being just bundled into reading.

Spelling teaching in schools seems so elemental for such a complex topic in dealing mainly with phonological representation. If the language is morphological and guided by morphemics, where is there a consideration of this aspect in the NLS and secondary classrooms throughout the country? Nowhere except in isolated pockets.

Current spelling teaching where it exists serves many children poorly and they fail to achieve reasonable levels of competence suitable for employment. The answer is not to change or regularise our spelling system for it would be at great cost to the grand history of the language and the communication of concepts and ideas for which the language is so suited. The minor attempts made in this direction in the USA led to confusion rather than simplification e.g. *colour* was regularised to *color* rather than *colur* when perhaps it should really have been *culla* or even *kulla*.

In Chapter 6, suggestions for some new directions in teaching spelling will be explored to show how miscues analyses of spelling errors can help target appropriate interventions of a phonological and morphological nature. They can be used with ordinary and dyslexic spellers to develop problem solving and motivational approaches to spelling and obtain transfer to general writing.

Summary and conclusions

This chapter gives an outline of the nature of spelling and how it has been taught over the centuries to the present. Links are made between past and present techniques and their relative effectiveness is discussed, for it is not uncommon for old methods to be recycled or transformed to become the 'new'.

Methods of teaching spelling such as the alphabetic method, phonics and being 'caught', during reading and reinforced in copy writing are discussed and lead to the conclusion that some are necessary but not sufficient methods for developing good spelling. Currently spelling teaching seems somewhat haphazard.

Theories of spelling development are outlined and matched to National Curriculum levels. The points at which errors might occur are indicated for example in the failure of dyslexics to enter the alphabetic stage despite a large amount of 'remedial phonics' teaching, and then having broken through their difficulties at the later orthographic stage, only to fail again.

Spelling 'problems' are identified in separate groups: normal developmental spelling errors, spelling errors due to missed opportunities, spelling errors due to slowness in ability to learn standard orthography, those made by dyslexics, errors due to other learning difficulties in language and hearing, and spelling difficulties due to cultural factors. Error analyses will be explored in later chapters.

It is concluded from cohort analyses of spelling after two, four, and seven years of the NLS that although it has had some positive effects on improving reading standards it has not been sufficient in improving spelling. The reasons for this are suggested to be a reading focused training package not geared sufficiently to teaching spelling and handwriting, and because these skills were wrongly assumed to follow from improving reading. Achieving automaticity in spelling and handwriting have been found to be intimately related to and predictive of good compositional abilities in the later stages of schooling and this needs more focus in the NLS.

Chapter 2

Handwriting
Learning and teaching

Introduction

Associated with spelling there has been an equally long history of handwriting teaching going back beyond the Middle Ages. From ancient times the most important skill of all was *calligraphy* first seen in the illuminated manuscripts of the Church written in Latin by monks. Now all members of our society learn to write in English in school and calligraphy is regarded as an art form. The main purpose of handwriting in schools is for *communication* but some schools and teachers do confuse communication and calligraphy.

In general terms, handwriting is a recent acquisition for the human race especially in alphabetic scripts and it requires an additional set of skills on top of being able to spell. Despite the widespread use of word processors and electronic mail a considerable amount of handwriting still takes place in the form of note taking, list making, examination writing and general communication purposes. In schools it is still an essential skill although Project 21 (QCA 2005) is reviewing this. However, for the foreseeable future children will have to be taught to develop it from making marks on paper to producing a clear, legible script, correctly spelled and presenting a coherent narrative. Classroom observation shows that up to 80 per cent of time is still taken up with writing. At university most students still make handwritten notes in lectures and take examinations which require extended handwriting periods.

Handwriting is almost entirely a *motor skill* but one which is conceptually driven, for it is possible to write one's name and address with the eyes shut and people who cannot see can learn to use it as a communication system.

In 1989 targets for achievement were set for handwriting (see below) in the first specified National Curriculum for England and Wales. In 1994 the targets for spelling and handwriting were merged. By 1998, after nine years of the National Curriculum, Her Majesty's Chief Inspector in his annual report (HMCI 1998) stated that the weakest element of literacy teaching and learning was writing and it 'must now be seen as a priority for schools, literacy consultants and local authorities' (24). Despite this the greatest emphasis in the National Literacy Strategy (DfEE 1998), published in the same year, was reading. In fact very little was said about writing and penmanship; schools could decide on their own policy.

In the paper *The Teaching of Writing in Primary Schools: Could Do Better* (HMI 2001) the main findings from observation of 300 Literacy Hour lessons were as follows:

- Insufficient time spent on teaching writing within the Literacy Hour.
- Where writing was taught a quarter of the lessons were unsatisfactory.
- Time spent writing outside the Literacy Hour was seen as practising writing rather than being taught how to improve it.
- The balance between the teaching of reading and writing was not yet achieved.
- There was 'shared' writing in only a quarter of the lessons seen, but there was 'guided' writing in half of them.
- The transfer of skills taught in the Literacy Hour was not being achieved; teachers were missing the opportunities.

This must be of concern, for the two best early predictors of compositional ability have been found to be the rapidity of writing the alphabet (Berninger *et al.* 1997; Graham *et al.* 2000; Berninger 2004), and the rapidity of coding orthographic material – spelling to dictation (Graham *et al.* 1996). Handwriting would thus appear to be fundamental to the development of compositional abilities although HMI concerns were more about composition.

In May 2001, the NLS team published guidelines on *Developing Early Writing* (DfEE 2001a) directed to teachers in the Foundation Year and Key Stage 1. As previously, it allowed schools to choose their own preferred handwriting style, stipulating only that the style must enable joining in the later years and help children write in a legible, fluent and fast hand. It advised that 15 minutes per day should be spent on developing the skill outside the Literacy Hour and cursive should be introduced as soon as possible.

For more than five decades, infant schools have determined the style of handwriting which their pupils will learn and in England this has mainly been a print script thought to be easy for infants (Johnston 1913 cited in Jarman 1979: 2). Research however suggests that this style can be problematic for a significant number of learners and may actually cause problems for some with coordination difficulties (Wedell 1973; Early 1976; Montgomery 1997a).

Connelly and Hurst (2001) investigated whether transcription skills (spelling and handwriting) contributed to the quality of written composition in later primary and secondary children. They used TOWL-3 (Test of Written Language-3) and Berninger *et al.*'s (1991) speed test (writing letters of the alphabet for 60 seconds) and found that their sample of 65 had not developed sufficient speed in handwriting or enough spelling knowledge and thus their higher order writing processes were constrained. There was also considerable variability in the sample.

In a later study, Connolly *et al.* (2005b) found:

> the writing skills of dyslexic students at university are poorer than age matched peers and were highly tied to spelling and handwriting fluency levels ... the thinking and arguing skills of the students were no less than of age matched peers.
>
> (p. 42)

By 2005 it became clear that the NLS had still not been entirely successful. For although 83 per cent of pupils at 11 years had now reached level 4 in reading, only 63 per cent had met this criterion in writing. However, Tymms' (2004) analysis of the results showed that from a low of 48 per cent in 1995, only 60 per cent had achieved level 4 in English by 2004. Within this, writing would have improved very little over five decades.

The ultimate goal of the NLS is to enable the students to read and write fluently so that they can become literate members of the society and in the interim pass GCSEs and other public examinations at a good standard. These examinations mainly require the writing of extended text, or composition of various types, for periods of up to 20 minutes or longer, although secondary teachers report that currently there is little time to give to practising extended writing. Even though the House of Commons Inquiry (2005) and the Rose Review (2005) examined the problems of the NLS they failed to address handwriting teaching. Improving handwriting speed and fluency are very important targets for both primary and secondary teachers if we wish to improve compositional skills.

Handwriting

When we learn to write, posture, grip and movement are all involved and the sequence is put together by the motor cortex in the cerebral hemispheres concerned with voluntary movements. If a letter is taught as a whole fluid movement in the air, on a whiteboard, in sand and so on and then written on paper from memory this emphasises the motor memory aspects and gradually the size can be adjusted to fit on the page and the line.

Much copying and tracing is used in early writing but this practice needs to be questioned. These strategies can extend the time taken to establish motor memories and when children are left to their own devices it can lead them to draw the letters rather than to lay down correct motor writing programmes as in Figure 2.1.

Harry is benefiting from the finger strengthening aspect of copying but not developing the correct motor programme for his name which is the real target.

In order to develop the fine motor control required to produce handwriting there are many stages that have to be reached and developmental phases that

Figure 2.1 Illustration of copy writing by beginning writer Harry (aged 4.5 years)

have to be achieved in using one's hands and fingers precisely in a skilled activity. Good fine motor skill stems from solid sensory and motor foundations and it is important to have muscle and joint stability, especially in the neck, trunk and upper extremities. Not least is a consideration of the whole body's posture and the appropriateness of the furniture, especially in the acquisition stages (Sassoon 1989).

Accurate tactile discrimination and hand and finger strength aid in the control of pens and pencils. In addition the ability to motor plan, the coordination of the two sides of the body and the development of hand and eye dominance are also involved in establishing pre-writing skills. However, visual control tends to be overemphasised instead of cognitive control.

Handwriting is a motor activity which needs to be taught; it is not a natural skill that will develop like walking. The motor memory controls the direction and shape of each letter, and therefore a continuous joined handwriting style, established as early as possible, can help to gain automaticity.

> the skill of handwriting is not only one of the fundamental building blocks of literacy, it also provides children with access to other parts of the curriculum.[...] An automatic style releases the brain to concentrate on other ideas i.e. spelling, grammar, syntax, style and content.
>
> (Stainthorp *et al.* 2001: 1)

Handwriting is regarded by Alston (1993) as an underpinning skill, essential if children are to succeed in writing and spelling. Thus any student who has not been able to develop a fast and legible script is at a disadvantage and likely to underachieve in school.

According to Ellis (1995: 70) two or three stages of planning intervene between the grapheme level and the movements of the arm, wrist and hand that produce handwriting. The first step involves selecting the particular letter shapes that are to be used. Is it to be A or a? The different forms that the same grapheme can take are sometimes referred to, following linguistic terminology, as *allographs*. After the allograph has been selected, the writer must then generate the sequence of movements that will result in the letters being written correctly. That movement sequence is sometimes referred to as the 'graphic motor pattern'. It will specify the force and direction of the strokes needed to create the required size as well as the shape of letters. All that is required to complete the writing process is for the graphic motor pattern to be implemented as a sequence of instructions by the necessary group of muscles.

Learning to write however is not the same sort of process as using fluent writing and needing to select allographs. In schools we are first of all dealing with learning to write and the laying down of allographs and Marr (cited in Calder 1970) has shown that this is dependent on different neurological processes.

Learning to write in the brain

Two areas of the brain are involved in the motor control of handwriting. The first is the voluntary motor cortex in the cerebral hemispheres which lies just in front of the Sylvian fissure in the frontal lobes. The left hemisphere is usually responsible for controlling the right hand and vice versa. Twelve per cent of the population are left handed (Henderson *et al.* 1982) but only about half of them will have the control in the right hemisphere, thus being 'true' left handers.

When we are learning to handwrite, the voluntary motor cortex is responsible for learning the skill and putting all the parts of it together so that over time it gradually becomes a fluid and economical form. The representation of motor control in all parts of the body is seen as an 'inverted homunculus' in the brain. There is a huge area devoted to the thumb and fingers for manipulation of objects, and to the lips and tongue in speech. This represents their importance and the amount of control needed to be exerted over them.

Developing motor skills can be a lengthy process in which muscles have to be strengthened and for this spaced practice is the most effective. Guided practice with the feedback from a mentor, the teacher, is important in the acquisition stage as with a 'sports approach' or coach. This enables the correct penhold, the tripod grip, to be established and the most efficient form of motor movement to be executed. Because cognitive control is involved it is essential that this is exerted from the outset. To do this the child is shown the model, the teacher makes the shape in the air, on the board and so on and then wipes it off. The child should then try to reproduce the movement in the air and then on a board and eventually on paper. All these movements can be supported by singing and painting and drawing activities to strengthen the muscles and fingers.

What we see in classrooms is not always as described above. Children are shown the model and then left to copy or trace over letters. Their pencil grip is not adjusted to the tripod grip and the problems of bendy joints and grasp are not noted and compensated. Thus habits develop which are later difficult to change.

Fluency, automaticity and the role of the cerebellum

All the while that we are learning a new motor skill another area of the brain is shadowing this process and this is the cerebellum (the hind brain). The surface of the cerebellum consists almost entirely of a vast array of 30 million nerve fibres running in parallel with each other (Eccles 1973) fed by a series of cell complexes rather like a wiring diagram in series. It is laid out differently from the rest of the brain, especially the cerebral hemispheres, for its unique purpose.

In essence the cerebellum is a recording machine which memorises all the complex muscular actions involved in a particular skilled movement. It 'shadows' the skill acquisition and development of the motor cortex in the 'roof of the brain' in the cerebral hemispheres. It soon begins to take over control of the operation and this leaves the main brain free to think about new things. Repeated firing of the parallel circuits in a particular format creates connections between them that fire the whole motor programme. Thus one day when I was putting up ceiling tiles and had a small segment to glue, I spread the glue with the knife and started to put the tile in my mouth. The feeding programme had been elicited and because I was talking whilst I worked my attention was distracted and the wrong programme was activated. When driving we often feel that a large black gap exists in a regular journey where the brain was switched off but if an emergency stop was called for we would still make it. These examples illustrate situations where the cerebellum with minimal perceptual and cognitive cues runs its programmes. It means that once we have learnt to play the piano, swim, ride a bicycle or write, we do not forget how to do them, and even after 20 years it can take a very little exercise to get us back on form.

If the work of the cerebellum is damaged or disrupted in any way then we see persons unable to perform skilled movements easily. They may stagger when walking and be unable to get a cup to the lips without spilling it and so on. In developmental coordination difficulties (DCD) there may be a number of barriers to learning in such a system which inhibit the smooth and easy development of motor skills. These might be difficulties in the cerebral learning areas, problems in the pathways between the cerebral hemispheres and the cerebellum and problems in the cerebellum itself. Difficulties in using tools for eating and in bead threading may be early indicators of a DCD problem which will also affect handwriting. DCD may affect all aspects of movement including gross motor skills or they may just affect fine motor skills when the problem is less likely to be detected before entry to school.

It will be shown that we must consider the ways in which we teach handwriting much more carefully because of these dual processes, for many of our methods are creating additional barriers to learning. In addition there are implications for remedial and corrective approaches to spelling and handwriting.

Teaching handwriting in schools

Handwriting for communication needs a *'fast running hand'*. Herein lies the problem. Ten per cent or more of pupils have mild handwriting coordination difficulties (Gubbay 1976; Laszlo *et al.* 1988; Alston and Taylor 1993). They have difficulty in learning to form letters correctly and in producing a neat style on a page at a reasonable speed. Teachers are very concerned that pupils do develop and use neat writing and some can pressurise pupils unmercifully to do so. But it is rare that speed features in the teaching process (Stainthorp *et al.* 2001).

There may be such a concern for neatness that it is at the expense of content and studies have shown that neat writers, more often girls, tend to be awarded higher marks in many classrooms. Untidily written scripts were downgraded although the content was exactly the same (Soloff 1973; Briggs 1980). The pressure focuses upon the production of a neat print script which is easily readable for the teacher. It is modelled upon the simple style currently found in infant texts. This *print script* became so popular that throughout England and Wales it replaced the earlier joined 'civil service hand' or *cursive.*

Handwriting style – print?

Because children's stories and reading schemes were in print script it encouraged teachers to teach it in reception and then introduce joining as soon as a neat print had been achieved. A consensus developed that this was at about eight years of age and it became the role of many junior schools to teach joining. However, there was no evidence to support the view that print was easier as children had managed perfectly well before when learning cursive. In fact in the majority of countries throughout the world cursive is taught from the outset and French education focuses more on teaching handwriting in the first two years than on reading and spelling (Thomas 1998).

Reception class teachers in the UK even adopted the practice of simplifying the print form further so that it became the development of a series of ball- and stick-like forms. This practice was challenged by handwriting experts such as Marion Richardson who included ligatures to help with later joining.

Even after the introduction of the NLS, print is still the main form introduced in reception classes but to ease joining, ligatures are added to the letters. Alternatively they are introduced in Years 1 and 2 when joining is promoted. Thus the age at which joining is taught varies but has become lower. Unfortunately this means that children are being taught to develop one set of programmes then must change to another. This is easy for some but hard for many. Marion Richardson's view was 'start as you mean to go on'.

Figure 2.2a Early print script: 'ball and stick' form

Figure. 2.2b Later print script: single line form (letters formed using a continous line but no ligatures)

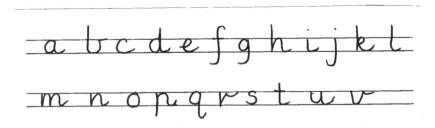

Figure 2.2c Marion Richardson style

Pupils and students who use a print script often prefer to do so because they feel that it looks neater. Occasionally parents have been encountered in my school-based programmes who refuse to permit their children to learn cursive.

Print, even with ligatures, is ergonomically problematic for many children, especially those with mild or more serious motor coordination difficulties. Such children *must learn* a joined hand (Wedell 1973). Once the cerebellum has learnt the print form, *learning cursive means learning a new set of motor programmes.* The former is not a step on the way to the latter and ligatures are not the answer for pupils with difficulties.

Teaching methods that require the copying of letters, whole words and sentences in infant unjoined print should be challenged. Teaching handwriting needs to begin with movement training and penhold exercises and develop into writing letters and simple words from 'inside the head', i.e. from memory. Copying from the board (far point copying) involves holding the spelling in short-term memory for a time and writing from this temporary memory store and thus extra errors can creep in. Even near point copying (writing below teacher's model) can give rise to similar errors. Tracing does not involve the word memory store; it only involves strengthening exercise in the motor movements which can be more fluently taught in other ways.

The NLS insisted that children must gradually learn the 200 basic 'sight' words found in their readers and of course this too encouraged the copy writing approach without phonics or morphemics. Teachers used the 'look, say and write' approach or the 'look – cover – write – check' method but significant numbers do not learn well by this method and remain poor spellers as evidenced in Chapter 1.

Handwriting is essentially a highly complex motor skill and needs to be linked with spelling which is a complex set of cognitive and recall skills. Either we have to recall complete spellings stored in the lexicon (word memory store) or we have to construct them as we go along from 'particles' of other information also stored in the lexicon, or from elements generated from the speech organs. Learning to write the particles such as base words (form, bed) and affixes (-ing, -ed, -s and re-) as whole writing units helps them lodge in the lexicon for that appears to be how they are stored (Kuczaj 1979). Writing separate letters as in print methods does not facilitate spelling of particles and leads to omissions of letters and syllables (concatenation) even when ligatures are included.

Handwriting style – cursive?

Cursive or joined script can be used to link the particles in words especially if it is done from the outset as soon as two letters have been learned. Only in a few areas such as Kingston-upon-Thames, Hampshire, Avon and Kent was cursive writing to be found taught in reception in the late 1980s and early 1990s. Even then, not all the schools started with cursive as so many teachers' attitudes were fixed against it. New headteachers entering the areas and not part of the original training programmes often permitted the practice to lapse and print script returned to the reception classes (Portsmouth LEA 2001).

It is noticeable that the scripts of undergraduate students, the 'successes' of the school system, also demonstrate a range of handwriting problems and many of them fail to produce a fast running hand in their final examinations (Montgomery 1997a). Often writing was a poorly formed, rounded hand, based upon half print and half joined script. Unjoined, large and rounded script takes fractionally longer to form and thus in examinations these writers could write less and their arguments would be shorter and supporting statements more limited than those with a fluent script. Stainthorp (1990) found 20 per cent of her B.Ed. students were unable to produce a fluent cursive script and half of them could not join letters at all. They were to become the teachers of the NLS.

There is a range of cursive styles with and without lead-in strokes, with and without loops above and below, or on some letters rather than others, but what is needed for teaching is the choice of a basic serviceable style which learners can modify later to suit their needs. Lead-in stokes are to be recommended as then all initial and separate letters start on the line. Loops above the line are to be avoided as they tend to cause more confusions and tangle with loops below the line from above. They also make the writing look more cluttered but are not as important as loops below which facilitate joining.

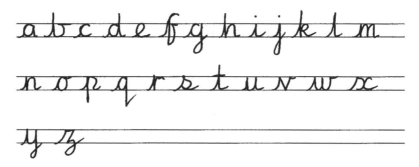

Figure 2.3a An example of 'Kingston' or Palmer cursive: a round, upright style

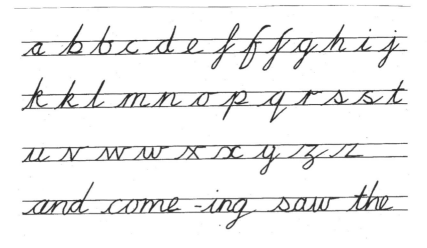

Figure 2.3b An example of the Learning Difficulties Research Project (LDRP) cursive: an ovoid, leaning style

In the remedial field it had been clear for a number of decades that the teaching of a remedial cursive was beneficial to the pupils. It was an important factor in over-coming incorrect motor habits and it had an appeal because it looked 'more grown up'. In working with the teachers at the Kingston Reading Centre it became appar-ent that many classroom teachers would not permit pupils to use the remedial hand in the work in the classroom which was a serious handicap to the pupils and slowed their progress. It was also distressing to the remedial teachers and so we jointly ran in-service training courses to try to change these perceptions. Students in training and those on in-service courses undertook research projects investigating ways of achieving policy change and the relative effectiveness of cursive over print learning in reception and with remedial pupils. As a result 16 schools in the LEA introduced cursive writing teaching in reception class (Morse 1991). Two years later at seven years the vast majority of pupils had achievements at level 3 in the National Curriculum writing area.

Handwriting style – italic?

Italic is frequently taught as a form of lettering in art classes and some people have absorbed this into their general handwriting style. It was originally designed in Renaissance Italy for speeding up writing and copying large amounts of text. It is a compressed slanting style based on an elliptical O with contrasting thick and thin strokes and simple serifs. It may well have speeded up the writing 400 years ago but today we have developed even faster forms. My concerns were first aroused when my undergraduate artist students used italic in their education exams and could write much less of what they knew in the three-hour papers.

The slanting O basis does have merit in that it is quicker and easier to make in a fluid form than an upright round O. The thick and thin strokes are an accomplish-ment which many with poor pen control and especially beginners would find beyond their powers. However, there are schools which after the infant stage have adopted italic as the school's formal handwriting style. It is important to warn against this. Calligraphy should be regarded as an art form and left for art lessons to be learnt later as it is difficult and time-consuming to form. Pupils with coordina-tion difficulties should not be required to learn it.

Figure 2.3c The italic style of writing: a calligraphic style

Handwriting – not teaching it at all?

At some periods in the twentieth century and even in some schools today it is not always thought necessary for children to be precisely taught how to write, and the consequences of teaching and not teaching have important negative outcomes shown later in this chapter. The whole writing area is unfortunately beset by some very rigid attitudes and beliefs not necessarily based on evidence and which hamper children's progress.

The National Curriculum (1989) on handwriting and presentation

The UK NC in English for handwriting and presentation specifies that the following areas should be taught:

At Key Stage 1

In order to develop a legible style, pupils should be taught:

Handwriting

1   how to hold a pencil/pen
2   to write from left to right and top to bottom of a page
3   to start and finish letters correctly
4   to form letters of regular size and shape
5   to put regular spaces between letters and words
6   how to form lower and uppercase letters
7   how to join letters

Presentation

8   the importance of clear and neat presentation in order to communicate their meaning effectively.

These are incorporated into *statements of attainment* as follows:

- At level 1 pupils should be able to begin to form letters with some control over the size, shape and orientation of letters or lines of writing.
- At level 2
  a) produce legible upper and lower case letters in one style and use them consistently (i.e. not randomly mixed within words)
  b) produce letters that are recognisably formed and properly orientated and that have clear ascenders and descenders where necessary (e.g. b and d, p and q).
- At level 3
  a) begin to produce clear and legible joined-up writing
  b) produce more fluent joined-up writing in independent work.

At Key Stage 2

Pupils should be taught to:

1   write legibly in both joined and printed styles with increasing fluency and speed;
2   use different forms of handwriting for different purposes (for example, print for labelling maps or diagrams, a clear, neat hand for finished presented work, a faster script for notes).

At Key Stage 3

Pupils should be taught to write with fluency and, when required, speed. In presenting final polished work, pupils should be taught to:

1   ensure that work is neat and clear;
2   write legibly, if their work is handwritten;
3   make full use of different presentational devices where appropriate.

Pupils may be exempted from this target if they need to use a non-sighted form of writing such as Braille or if they have such a degree of physical disability that the attainment target is unattainable (NCC 1989).

What can be observed is that the style is left to the discretion of teachers and joining only begins at level 3. This has reinforced the practice of teaching print first then changing to cursive later. By this time the print motor programmes have been stored and are difficult to change.

A negative attitude has also existed with respect to the use of lines for writing in reception class but Burnhill *et al.* (1975) found their use of lines helped the learner with placing and letter construction and made a significant and positive contribution to improving the overall appearance. There is a notion that lines are too difficult for infants to place their letters upon whereas early writing is more difficult to do well without them. Nor do lines hamper their creativity! In remedial teaching, lines (both double and treble) are recommended to help orientation, placing and structure of the letters.

Is there a problem with handwriting today?

There are a number of formal measures that can be used to diagnose handwriting problems but these are more research tools still in development than standardised and accepted tests. For example: TOLH – Test of Legible Handwriting; ETCH – Evaluation Tool of Children's Handwriting; CHES – Children's Handwriting Evaluation Scale; TOWL – Test of Written Language; DRHP – Diagnosis and Remediation of Handwriting Problems. None of these include writing tasks similar to those in schools and they all generally fail to relate the process to the product (Rosenblum *et al.* 2003).

Speed is most widely tested, for it easily lends itself to statistical analysis and can be quick and simple to administer; however, the measures used need to reflect the tasks of the school-age child more than many of them do if we are to improve handwriting and handwriting teaching. For example, some clinical diagnosis is also necessary as part of a more rounded approach to intervention or to deciding whether handwriting should be taught at all in the most severe cases. A range of teacher-based techniques can be used, such as:

- a diagnosis of motor coordination difficulties using a key indicants checklist (see below);
- an analysis of writing form and style as in Table 2.3 below;
- a test of handwriting speed;
- a check for penhold, paper position and posture.

Legibility is an issue which is more difficult to assess accurately as it is much a matter of personal opinion, eyesight, acuity and experience.

In the study described below, items 1 to 3 were tested using the written data. In ongoing research Bladon (2004) is examining the effects of irregular penhold on school achievement. Preliminary results suggest that grips other than the flexible or rigid tripod grips lead to a falling off of achievement in secondary schools as writing pressures increase.

The cohort pupils were given two minutes to plan their essay and then required to write for 20 minutes on any topic which interested them such as favourite people, games, pets and so on (after Allcock 2001). This test task is designed to match what might be expected of pupils in schools after Year 5 having achieved the writing standard. In addition, clinical assessment of form, style and handwriting coordination were undertaken to develop profiles of performance.

Handwriting speed

When handwriting speed was investigated by Roaf (1998) using a 10-minute test, she found that 25 per cent of secondary school students were unable to write faster than 15 words per minute and these were the pupils who were struggling in all

Table 2.1 The pattern of handwriting speed results in the three Year 7 cohorts

School A: After two years of the NLS			
	N	HW speed	Words per min
Set 1	28	317.30	15.66
Set 2, 3, 4	63	278.00	12.04
Set 5	15	217.60	10.88
Means	N=106	279.36	13.97
School B: After four years of the NLS (all sets mixed ability) from Tidmas's data			
Means	N=160	272.80	13.64
School C: After seven years of the NLS (all sets mixed ability)			
Means	N=251	248.80	12.44

Source: Montgomery 2006

lessons where a lot of writing was required. She also found a close link between self concept and handwriting presentation. The majority of the slow writers showed difficulties with motor coordination, spelling, and letter formation. She regarded a speed of 25 words per minute as a successful rate.

In Table 2.1 we see that the mean speeds are well below 25 words per minute, although comparable in schools A and B to Allcock's large sample in Table 2.2 below.

Allcock's (2001) survey found that with a speed of 25 per cent below the mean per minute pupils might benefit from an extension of their examination time by 25 per cent to be able to do themselves justice, even though at first some might say they had nothing more they wanted to write. Like sportsmen and women they need training for the event both in handwriting and writing scaffolds. Those who were 40 per cent slower she advised needed an amanuensis. Many pupils questioned after examinations feel they could have gained extra marks if they had been allowed some extra time to complete their themes.

Summary of results from cohort B

- No student could write at a speed of 25 words per minute
- 95 per cent could not write at a speed faster than 20 words per minute
- 26 per cent wrote significantly too slowly (25 per cent below average speed for the age group)
- 11 per cent wrote slower than 8.5 words per minute (40 per cent below the average speed)

Differences between boys and girls, cohort B

In GCSEs boys have been performing less well than girls by about 10 per cent, although at A level this difference tends to disappear. This is not a new phenomenon – boys appear to have been underachieving to this extent for over 300 years – it is just that SATs have recently enabled us to see the differences on a national scale. Many reasons have been put forward to account for this (Montgomery 2005) but it may in part arise from some more basic issues than currently supposed. For example, could maturational issues related to coordination be involved as well as the many motivational factors and 'boy codes' suggested in current literature? Of the 26 per cent writing so slowly 36.67 per cent were boys and 19 per cent were girls and there were clear indicants of DCD in each case.

Table 2.2 Average writing speeds in secondary schools in words per minute

Year (Chron. age)	Y7 (12)	Y8 (13)	Y9 (14)	Y10 (15)	Y11 (16)
Mean speed	13.9	14.6	15.7	16.3	16.9
Problem speed (25% slower)	10.4 (10)	10.9 (11)	11.8 (12)	12.2 (12)	12.7 (13)

N = 2701
Source: Allcock, 2001

Summary of results from cohort C

After seven years following the NLS similar issues arise with this cohort in comparison with other Year 7s.

- Overall the cohort is writing significantly more slowly (12.44 w.p.m.) than expected for their age and experience.
- Boys, not unexpectedly, are writing more slowly than girls by 19 per cent (11.14 to 13.69 w.p.m.).
- One girl is writing at 26 words per minute which is the speed Roaf suggested is needed to cope with the secondary school curriculum.
- 0.6 per cent (15 pupils) write at 20–25 words per minute which is probably the appropriate target speed for this age group and length of task to cope with the curriculum (three boys and 12 girls).
- 37.45 per cent (94 pupils) write at a speed of 13–20 words per minute putting them in the above average speed range (32 boys and 62 girls). The obverse is that 62.55 per cent are writing too slowly.
- 19.16 per cent (48 pupils) are writing at significantly slow speeds, 40 per cent below the mean, and can be expected to be failing in all lessons where writing is needed. Thirteen girls and 35 boys appear to have SEN in this area.
- Three boys appear severely disabled in the writing area. They write at six words or fewer per minute.

Speed in examinations in general has been investigated by Lyth (2004) in relation to the MidYIS additional test. Pupils take this test in Year 8 and go on to take Key Stage 3 exams in Year 9 and GCSEs in Year 11. His results are based upon approximately 15,000 pupils who took MidYIS in 1999 and GCSEs in 2003. The pupils are asked to copy repeatedly for two minutes the single same sentence 'I can write clearly and quickly all day long'. They are told their writing must be clear and legible and each sentence must fit exactly onto one line. The results were that the mean number of lines completed was 5.8 with a mean of 112 characters per minute. At 10 words per line this gives an average speed of 29 words per minute. This is a faster rate than that obtained by Allcock (2001) and Roaf (1998) but the tasks are radically different. It is easier to write rapidly for two minutes from copy or the same sentence than for 20 from memory and thinking.

Despite the limitations of the task other useful insights were obtained by Lyth. He found the speed varied from writing one line to 13 lines and showed a normal distribution function. Boys' writing speed (5.4 lines) was slower overall than that of girls (5.7 lines) and showed more variability. State school pupils' writing was slower than that of Independent school pupils (6.0 boys; 6.3 girls). He was able to conclude that generally, average ability rises with handwriting speed but this trend breaks down at the extremes. Those with the slowest speeds have ability higher than expected or predicted from the speed and at the upper end very high writing speed is associated with lower ability than expected.

It would appear that pupils need more help in developing fluency and speed in handwriting even after seven years of NLS training. Primary teachers however seldom encourage this, for Stainthorp et al. (2001) found that 84 per cent of primary teachers in their sample did not encourage children to write fast at all.

Keyboarding may not be the answer for it may well improve legibility but still contains strong motor components which can disadvantage the most severely disabled writers so that voice activation systems need to be considered for school work as well as examinations. There was little overlap in skills found (15 per cent) between ability in handwriting and word processing (Priest and May 2002).

Handwriting style in the cohorts

The data from the two cohorts in Table 2.3 follow the same pattern. They indicate that print script is still strongly established in primary schools despite some encouragement in the NLS for earlier and easier joining. It shows too that the majority of these pupils have not met the literacy target and achieved a fluent joined hand by 11 years.

It seemed to Tidmas that the boys in her cohort tended to see joined writing as more adult. Girls seemed to favour print because to them it looked neater. In my data these attitudes may well have had some slight effect but a stronger influence was possibly that of the teacher teaching them, for a clear policy on some aspects of joining was apparent and this was to discourage loops below the line. This prohibits a join. Some of the pupils with difficulties had clearly been exposed to a fully joined remedial programme.

Both samples B and C seemed to have equal numbers of print, mixed and joined scripts which were less legible and less neat and a few of each which were neither legible nor neat.

Speed and style were not at this age closely associated. It is argued elsewhere (Montgomery 1997a) that cursive can not only encourage fluency but also promotes writing legibly at a reasonable speed. In these pupils, changing from print to script which many appear to be in the process of doing may have slowed down their writing speed or at least not allowed it to speed up.

Table 2.3 Writing styles of the Year 7 cohorts

	Print	Mixed	Joined
Tidmas data (N = 160)			
2005 (Four yrs NLS)	24%	46%	30%
Montgomery data (N = 251)			
2006 (Seven yrs NLS)	30%	49%	21%

Table 2.4 The different stylistic achievements of boys and girls

	Tidmas data		Montgomery data	
	Boys	Girls	Boys	Girls
Print	18%	28%	31%	28%
Mixed	37%	52%	45%	54%
Joined	45%	20%	24%	18%

Handwriting form

Form difficulties often arise through inadequate teaching and learning or from no real teaching at all as well as from mild fine motor coordination difficulties in children with DCD.

The best way in which the form indicants can be used with Year 7s is to let the pupils analyse their own writing form using the error list and discuss the results with them. Then two basic interventions should be implemented:

*   Pupils practise writing small useful words between double lines so that all the bodies of the letters are the same size. Rules: start each word with a lead-in stroke on the line and complete the word in one writing movement.
*   Make all ascenders and descenders slope in the same direction whether forwards, backwards or straight.

Figure 2.12 later shows case work intervention results achieved in two weeks using this type of unisensory training on key words.

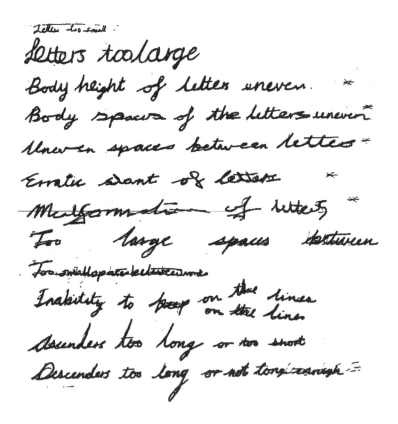

Figure 2.4 Form indicants in diagnosing writing difficulties (half size)
Source: Montgomery 1990

The essence is that the pupil has to be keen to want to change the writing and to understand why it can help. Key words are selected and practised for a few minutes each day in the new style over a period of a fortnight. When the pupil feels confident the style is then practised in some homework or class work and the results are studied pre and post to see the effects. In some rare cases the effect will not be transformative and then a serious coordination problem is implicated and other methods need to be considered.

Christensen and Jones (2000) found that one hour of INSED training for teachers from 14 schools could effect significant improvements in pupils' handwriting. Over eight weeks 900 pupils in control and experimental groups were given ten minutes' training per day. At the outset the groups were judged the same but after one year all the experimental group were better than the top 1 per cent of the controls.

Handwriting coordination difficulties in cohort C

A wide range of pupils will be likely to have mild handwriting difficulties. These may arise from developmental coordination difficulties (DCD) or from poor habits built up during inadequate or non teaching regimes. Earlier difficulties in pencil control and letter formation may clear up, also leaving a poorly integrated level of skill, so that extended writing causes aches and pains. These difficulties are not only indicated in problems in the formation of the letters but also in a series of other indicants as in the checklist below.

The figures in Table 2.5 indicate that nearly 30 per cent of the cohort appear to have some coordination difficulties in handwriting and of that group nearly a third (27 per cent) have severe problems. Over one-third of the cohort show form difficulties in their handwriting. In total after seven years of the NLS nearly two-thirds of the cohort appear to have some difficulties in producing legible and fluent handwriting and would benefit from some developmental, corrective or remedial help.

The following checklist shows the key indicants for diagnosing developmental coordination difficulties (DCD) in handwriting – developmental dysgraphia (Montgomery 2003).

- The letters do not stay on the line.
- The writing drags in from the margin towards the mid line.
- Wobble and shake observable on strokes in letters.
- Variation in 'colour' of words, lightness and dark as pressure varies or fatigue sets in.
- Spaces between letters are too wide.
- Spaces between words are too large and sometimes too small.
- Rivers of space run down between the words.

Table 2.5 Numbers of coordination and form difficulties in cohort C

	Coordination	Severe coord difficulties	Form	Total
N = 251	70 (27.9%)	19 (0.75%)	90 (35.4%)	63.75%

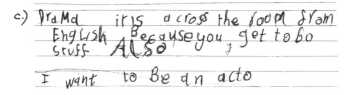

a) the day I whent to my Best friend part it was
out Safend peter pans we was haveing grat fun
We whent on fun rind like the water Logo
the terail ~~~~~~ swing and the say drop
38
139
~~~~~~ and a Lot more
When it got dark we when on relly
serey rind like the clorw We hard
grat fun meg take 7 friend Haner
CHalot Lorey Sam Josh CHalot and me

b.) My favourite part of accer is
the bodykits the re a main part
of a car. yow can get g body
kits to Fit any car youcan get
bodykits of many neope the
most common makes are veils's
demontlee eks and streetd emens.

c.) Prama iris across the loop dram
English Because you get to bo
stuff Also 7
I want to Be an acto

Figure 2.5 Extracts of legible writing showing coordination difficulties in the Year 7 cohort (half size)

- Difficulties making complex letters so they appear large or as capital forms T, W, S, K, F.
- Variations in size of other letters so they appear as large or capital forms e.g. n, m, u, h.

In addition:

- A non standard pencil grip (e.g. not a tripod grip, flexible or rigid) can hamper writing and achievement.
- Great pressure hampers fluency and makes holes or dents in the paper which can be felt on the reverse side.
- Contra lateral body and arm movements may be observed.
- Effort and grip causes whitening of the knuckles.
- Tongue may be stuck out.
- Fatigue rapidly sets in.
- Complains of aches and pains after only short periods of writing.

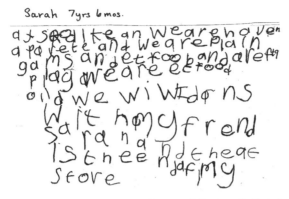

Figure 2.6 Extract exemplifying handwriting coordination difficulties (half size)

A score of four or five such indicants would warrant further investigation and intervention.

Poor handwriting and underachievement

Pupils with handwriting difficulties from whatever cause try to avoid, whenever they can, any written task and some even become disruptive when they are required to sit down to write. Teachers well know that, 'Now write it down' can bring forth a chorus of groans. But avoidance and difficulties with writing tasks can also have a serious effect on spelling and handwriting development through consistent lack of practice.

Although cross comparisons and trends cannot be predicted from these different samples, similar patterns appeared to exist within them when samples B and C were analysed in further detail. Handwriting appears to play a much more significant role in underachievement than has often been realised (Silverman 2004). Estimates of developmental coordination difficulties vary. Ten per cent or more of pupils have mild handwriting coordination difficulties (Gubbay 1976; Laszlo *et al.* 1988). Rubin and Henderson (1982) found that 12 per cent of pupils were considered by their teachers to have serious handwriting difficulties.

In a survey carried out with third year junior school pupils in Cheshire, Alston (1993) found that according to assessments made by five experienced remedial teachers just over 20 per cent of pupils were not writing well enough for the needs of the secondary school curriculum. In urban schools this figure rose to 40 per cent. She also found that 40 to 60 per cent of her secondary school pupils complained of pain and slowness and lack of fluency in writing.

Sassoon's (1989) research showed that in her study of 100 15-year-olds, 40 per cent of girls and 25 per cent of boys had actually said that writing was painful for them. The Assessment of Performance Unit (APU 1991) surveyed 2000 pupils at 11 and 15 years and found that 20 per cent of boys and 10 per cent of girls said they hated writing. Twice this number, 60 per cent, said they avoided writing whenever possible.

The profiles of typical able underachievers in school (Kellmer-Pringle 1970; Whitmore 1980; Butler-Por 1987; Silverman 1989; Wallace 2000; Montgomery 2000a) showed that handwriting, spelling and composition played a highly significant role in their difficulties. They were gifted, talented and illegible and exhibited the following traits:

- large gap between oral and written work
- failure to complete school work
- poor execution of work
- persistent dissatisfaction with achievements
- avoidance of trying new activities
- inability to function well in groups
- lacking in concentration
- poor attitudes to school
- dislike of drill and memorisation
- difficulties with peers
- low self image
- unrealistic goals set

Case examples

Karla could recite the alphabet at two years and took over story reading at four and a half. She would read to the 'little ones' in reception class but preferred to discuss and question rather than write. As the years progressed others caught up and passed her. In Year 2 her teacher was less sympathetic and demanded written work. Karla became progressively more chatty and was regularly punished for untidy, careless work. At home she grew anxious and irritable and at school evaded work whenever possible and was at times disruptive. Her SATs results put her just in the average range but her behaviour worsened until she was referred for her problem behaviour in Year 3, precipitated it was thought by her parent's separation and divorce. An IEP was drawn up for improving her behaviour. It worked temporarily and then Karla returned to her problem behaviours. By Year 6 she was due to be statemented and a career in disruption and exclusion from school was anticipated if she became more difficult to manage in her move to secondary school.

Postscript: Karla did indeed finish up excluded and in a PRU (Pupil Referral Unit). A teacher's research project found her there. She had a developmental coordination difficulty (mild dyspraxia) and dysgraphia, a handwriting coordination difficulty. The records showed that all the interventions over time had been directed to her behaviours not her learning disability.

Adam was overweight, the target of bullying and had poor relationships with peers. He was described by some teachers as an 'obnoxious and truly annoying boy'. In Year 3 he had been statemented for dyslexia and dyspraxia. He had a real talent for singing and puppet plays, owning a puppet theatre at home. His mother was a secondary headteacher.

He did not attend revision classes as it was thought he would only get Ws as he did so little work at school. However, in a one-to-one situation with an adult the extent of his ability was evident. He could explain his ideas clearly, hold a reasoned argument and had a good memory. He would talk knowledgeably on a range of subjects from dinosaurs and outer space to famous people and the existence or otherwise of God. At the end of the year he gained straight 5s using a laptop to write his English instead of a pen.

As can be seen, the underlying theme in underachievement is an inability to produce written work of a suitable quality to match the perceived potential. This also had secondary consequences such as inattention, avoidance, low motivation, low self esteem, negativism and behavioural problems. The illegibility might arise from a variety of causes such as a mild coordination difficulty, bendy joints, lack of teaching, inadequate teaching, and speed of thought which made the hand unable to record. Poor spelling was frequently associated with the slow and illegible handwriting and thus it was necessary to address both together.

Bravar (2005) found that 70 per cent of Italian children referred for underachievement had writing difficulties. Of these 47 per cent had poor handwriting and the writing of 23 per cent was illegible. Only 6 per cent had actually been referred for writing problems.

Teaching writing: why cursive?

In the early half of the twentieth century all our great grandparents learned a fully joined or cursive script from the outset with no more apparent difficulty than current print learners. Since then, experiments in teaching cursive from the outset have taken place in a number of LEAs and have proved highly successful in achieving writing targets earlier and for a larger number of children (Morse 1988; Low 1990). It is also found to be equally readable. However, custom and practice or 'teaching wisdom' is very hard to change and extremely rigid attitudes are frequently found against cursive (Montgomery 1998).

The research of Early (1976) advocated the exclusive use of cursive from the beginning. This was because it was found that the major advantage of cursive lay in the fact that each word or syllable consists of one continuous line where all the elements flow together. This means that the child experiences more readily the total form or shape of a given word as he or she monitors the kinaesthetic feedback from the writing movements. Handwriting therefore supports spelling and this contributes to literacy development.

Ott (1997) defined cursive as 'handwriting which is joined up and is a continuous flowing movement. The lower case begins on the line and the pen is not raised until the whole word is written' (99). Figure 2.3b on p.40 illustrates the LDRP cursive which is ovoid rather than upright to promote fluency and seeks to find the most efficient joining strategies.

A crucial factor of academic success at secondary level is a student's writing speed. It determines how easily and comprehensively he/she can take notes in class and can have a major influence on success in examinations. Ziviani and Watson-Will (1998) found that cursive script appears to facilitate writing speed. Differences may also be found between types of cursive, whether upright (Kingston-Palmer style) or ovoid LDRP sloping. In a study of the role of handwriting in examination success Barnett et al. (1998) found that boys who struggled to join up their letters scored half a grade lower than classmates of a similar potential in English, and girls scored a whole grade lower. Pupils who gained higher than expected grades in GCSE English language based on CAT score pre-dictions (Thorndike *et al.* 1986) had a better handwriting style and tended to write at a higher speed than underachievers.

The reasons for teaching cursive writing are particularly relevant to students with handwriting coordination difficulties (developmental dysgraphia). Remedial writing teaching and research (Gillingham and Stillman 1956; Hickey 1977; Cowdery *et al.* 1994; Montgomery 1997a) show that cursive:

- aids left-to-right movement through words across the page;
- stops reversals and inversions of letters;
- induces greater fluency in writing which enables greater speed to be developed without loss of legibility;
- enables more to be written in the time;
- can make a difference of a grade at GCSE, A level or in degree programmes through increased speed and fluency;
- can improve spelling accuracy, as the motor programmes for spelling words, particularly their bases and affixes, are stored together by the brain (Kuczaj 1979);
- results in orderly and automatic space between letters and between words;
- enables a more efficient, fluent and personal style to be developed;
- reduces the pain and difficulty experienced by pupils with handwriting coordi-nation difficulties;
- improves legibility of writing;
- reinforces multisensory learning linking spelling, writing and speaking.

In addition of course if taught from the outset:

- it eliminates the need to relearn a whole new set of motor programmes after the infant stage;
- there is a more efficient use of movement because of cursive's flow.

Children with coordination difficulties must learn to use a continuous writing movement. Dysgraphics such as these have difficulties, once they find where to make contact with the paper, in making the required shape and to the precise size and length. As soon as they lift the pen from the paper again in print script to make the next letter the directional, orientational and locational problems begin all over again. The effort involved becomes greater, the pen is seized more tightly, the knuckles go white and the whole body tenses and there is a further loss of fluency. To aid focus and concentration and stop contra-lateral movements the edge of the desk may be held and the tongue stuck out. It can take half an hour of formidable effort to produce a neat sentence.

When selecting a style or a scheme there are many around but they are not all of equal fitness for purpose. Cripps (1988) for example has produced a joined hand-writing training scheme, *A Hand for Spelling*, with a series of developmental workbooks. He has based his scheme on the research of Peters (1967, 1985) in adopt-ing a visual emphasis and a rote training approach to letter strings for spelling. His script, like that of the Nelson scheme and the NLS, is of incomplete joining.

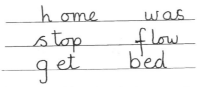

Figure 2.7 Example of incomplete joining which will slow down speed and fluency

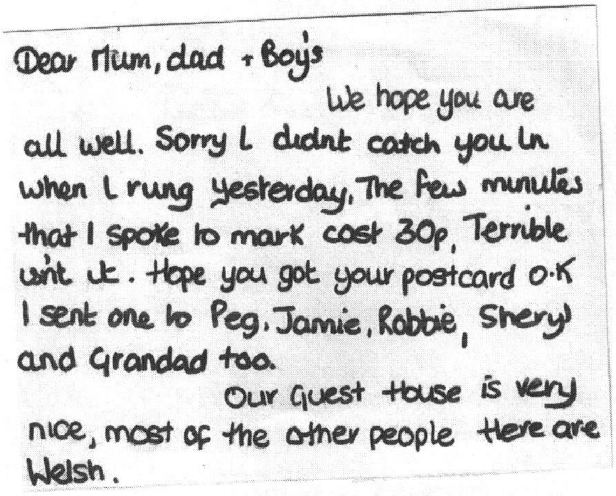

Dear Mum, dad + Boy's
                  We hope you are
all well. Sorry L didnt catch you Ln
when L rung yesterday, The few minutes
that I spoke to mark cost 30p, Terrible
isn't it. Hope you got your postcard o·K
I sent one to Peg, Jamie, Robbie, Sheryl
and Grandad too.
                  Our Guest House is very
nice, most of the other people Here are
Welsh.

Figure 2.8 Example of half joined script (half size)

Although the letters have small ligatures to encourage joining they are initially formed as print script from the top of the letters. For potentially good writers and spellers this is not going to pose too much of a problem but it does make difficulties for the pupil with spelling and coordination difficulties. Nevertheless, his evaluation studies (Cripps and Cox 1987) showed marked improvement in spelling and writing in the trained groups, showing that linking spelling and handwriting has positive benefits and that systematic training in handwriting will improve it.

Not using lead-in strokes is disadvantageous to children with learning difficulties. However, in converting later from print to cursive it has to be tolerated as children do find it easier not always to have a lead-in stroke for all their words. In the cohort scripts it was quite clear that many teachers were following a scheme which 'banned' loops below the line on letters such as g, y, f and a lead-up stroke from q. This also leads to a half joined form and disrupts the 'particle' approach to writing to support spelling.

Remedial handwriting teaching methods

Unisensory word training

This is the most common method of handwriting training. If as part of the developmental or remedial strategy the common words used in early writing and reading are worked on as whole units this can prove helpful to spelling as well. Each new

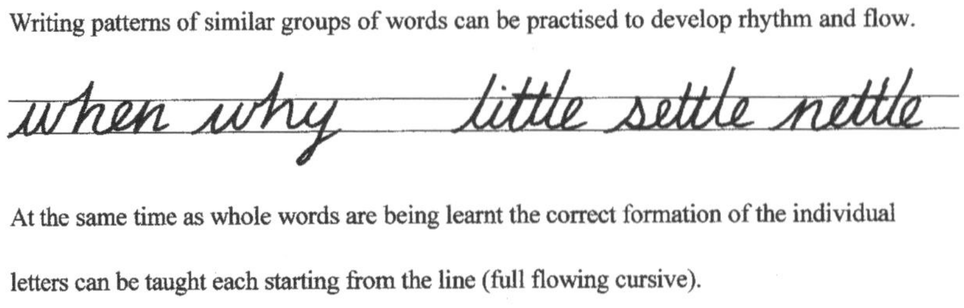

Writing patterns of similar groups of words can be practised to develop rhythm and flow.

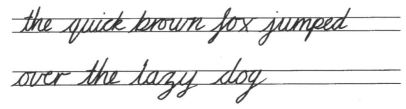

At the same time as whole words are being learnt the correct formation of the individual

letters can be taught each starting from the line (full flowing cursive).

Figure 2.9a Unisensory writing patterns

Figure. 2. 9b An all-letter check in cursive

single-syllabled word to be learned needs to be taught as a whole writing unit with a continuous line, then as far as possible a continuous line writing through the first and second syllables. So that the pupil always knows where to begin the word it should be taught as always starting *on the line,* and an *ovoid shape* to the body of the letter should be encouraged to enhance fluency. This form of unisensory training was found by Brown (1994) to improve writing and spelling. An example is given in Figure 2.9a.

Multisensory writing training

This involves teaching spelling with the handwriting not just as a motor pattern for words but as part of the synthetic phonic and morphemic linguistic process (Montgomery 1997a). This scheme begins with teaching letters in order of frequency of occurrence in children's scripts. Fry (1964) identified these as i, t, p, d, n, s, and a. It is not surprising that remedial schemes selected i, t, p, n, and s as the first letters to be taught (Gillingham *et al.* 1940; Gillingham and Stillman 1956) as some of the easiest to form and the least confusable, hence 'd' and 'a' were left till later. After 'i' is learnt and then 't' the two are used to build words – synthetic phonics: I, it, tit. This strategy is further developed in Chapter 5.

Cursive look – cover – write – check (LCWC) and look – say – cover – write – check

In a study with matched groups of 24 experimental and control subjects who were all remedial readers, spellers and writers, Vincent (1983) found that there was a highly significant improvement in the writing and spelling of the experimental group who were given cursive writing training in look – cover – write – check whilst controls were given print script training. Bueckhardt (1986) confirmed this in a similar study and equally importantly found that the class teachers' attitudes became more favourable to the pupils because of the neater writing. There are more effective versions of this type of method discussed in Chapters 4 and 5 as Simultaneous Oral Spelling (SOS).

Phonogram cursive writing training

Spalding and Spalding (1967) in *The Writing Road to Reading* described a system of teaching 70 phonograms through cursive writing training which, once learnt, would enable the pupil to read any of the early reading texts. They claimed success for their method in teaching both reading and writing. The phonograms begin with initial letter sounds, blends and digraphs and progress to -ing, -igh, and -tion, for example. They reported that it took about six months by their system to learn all the 70 phonograms with daily tuition but that both reading and writing involving the phonograms could be practised from the earliest stages.

Other aspects of handwriting

Position for writing

This is an aspect of writing teaching which is often overlooked. The position which the pupil adopts for writing can be quite revealing and can induce difficulties. It is important to ensure that the pupil's writing posture is relaxed and controlled. If the furniture is an inappropriate size and style this can place particular stress upon pupils with coordination difficulties and is likely to occur where the pupils are growing rapidly or have to use furniture more suitable for older, bigger pupils. The pupil should sit facing the desk and paper, hold the pen in the standard grip shown in Figure 2.10 and have both feet securely on the floor.

Penhold and paper position

The tripod grip is the standard and most flexible penhold form for English. Any difference in this grip should be investigated. Younger pupils can be helped by being given a plastic grip to put round the pen or given moulding substances which can take on an individual pupil's corrected finger pattern and left to harden. A range of grips may be used by pupils in their efforts to gain better control of their pens.

The next most common grip is the rigid tripod grip with the second finger also on top of the pen; this is a less flexible form. It may have been adopted to gain better control of the pen when in reception. At this early stage children may have bendy finger joints and need to use extra support. However, all other grips need to be analysed and strategies for correction developed at the earliest stage. After this the child has to be willing to change and work at it or no effect will result.

Bladon (2004) examined unusual penhold and school performance. Her pairs of subjects were matched for school achievements in maths and science. She found that those with unusual grips were over represented in set one (high ability groups)

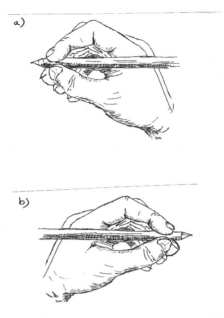

Figure 2.10 Standard flexible handwriting grip for (a) right handers and (b) left handers

but this was not maintained as they went through school. Although the experimental groups had a higher Raven's IQ score than those with whom they were matched, as they went through secondary school they began to underachieve and were moved down to lower sets.

The distance of the fingers from the pen tip should not be too far or too near. For adults the optimum distance lies between 2.5 and 3 cm whereas for primary school pupils it was 2.0 to 2.5 cm (Thomas 1997). Left handers need to keep half a centimetre longer distance from the point so that they can see their writing as they pull the pen towards the mid line. In Thomas's survey most adults taught prior to the 1960s used the flexible tripod grip whereas in the 1990s one-third of children had a four finger grip and one-third a dominant thumb feature. Eighty-two per cent of seven- to nine-year-olds used a near point grip to gain control of the pen but this reduced with age to 74 per cent in secondary school for example. She found very near point grip common amongst her poorest spellers. In addition, the optimal distance of eyes from pen tip (35 cm adults, 30 cm adolescents, 25 cm seven-year-olds) was not evident in 90 per cent of children. Thirty per cent worked at closer distances than 10 cm which could distort the feedback.

The elbow of the writing arm needs to be 'locked' to permit the pen to glide smoothly in an arc across the page. This means that the paper for right handed pupils should be slightly sloped away from the mid line and for left handers it should be more sloped. Pupils should place the non writing hand on the paper to keep it in place. Some left handers need to have the paper rotated by 90 degrees and write down the page. It also helps if left handers have a slightly higher chair and sit on the left side of partners to give their left arm freedom of movement. They also need the teacher to model writing with the left hand.

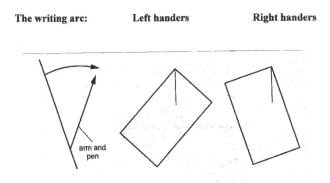

The writing arc: **Left handers**   **Right handers**

arm and
pen

Figure 2.11 Paper position for left handers. The paper for the left handers should have a marked slope in the opposite directtion. It is most unwise to make pupils write with their paper square on to the table's edge

Changing styles?

Of particular importance is the problem of pupils learning infant print and then having to change to cursive at about seven to eight years. This is not achieved without considerable sacrifice in terms of time which at this stage could more usefully be given to the subject curriculum by all the pupils. A significant number of them will find the learning of a whole new set of motor programmes too difficult and may fail to see the relevance of it. Those who have writing difficulties will probably find it too hard to make the transfer as they have hardly acquired a competent writing form in the first place. In addition it is common practice not to allow pupils who cannot write neatly in print to go on to learn cursive; it is withheld from them. This is a particularly punitive measure for it may well be that it is only through learning a full cursive that they will ever conquer their writing and spelling problems.

Once the skill and a style of handwriting has been learnt it is difficult to change. Cognitive control has to be reasserted over the old skill programme and the new programme must not be so similar as to elicit it. It also needs enough practice to make it as fluent and speedy as the programme it replaces. In adults determined to change this process, it can take six months before the original speed and fluency is achieved. The point is that if the pupils are not convinced that the change is worthwhile then they will not make the effort needed to reassert cognitive control and undertake the necessary practice.

The motor programmes once established in the cerebellum operate under minimal cognitive guidance. Thus showing and copying new forms is not going to be effective. The child has to *want to learn* the new style and then be prepared to put in the cognitive effort to learn the new programme and suppress the other. It also has to be overlearnt so that there is no relapse into the earlier form. Print script should be taught after cursive has been well established and only used for form-filling and similar tasks, and especially not be insisted upon in course or project work.

Figure 2.12 Changing writing: before and after unisensory interventions (half size)

a

Before

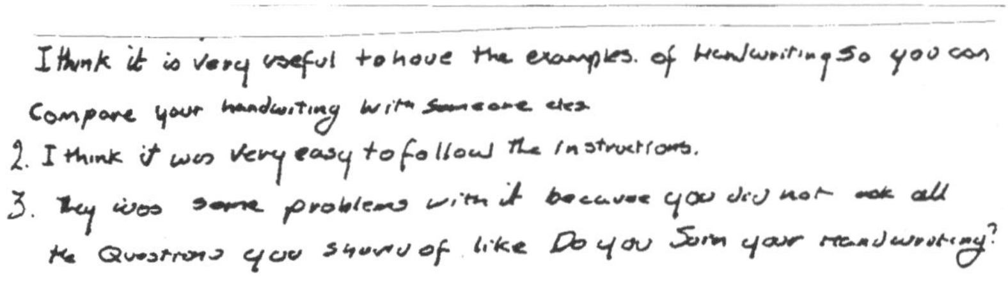

I think it is very useful to have the examples of Handwriting So you can Compare your handwriting with Someone eles.
2. I think it was very easy to follow the Instructions.
3. They was some problems with it because you did not ask all the Questions you should of like Do you Sorn your handwriting?

After

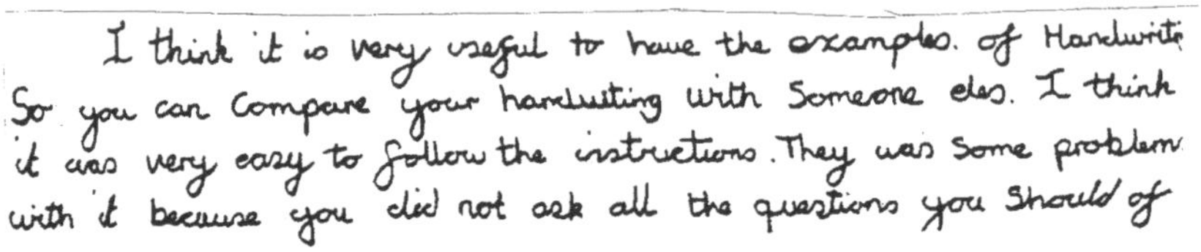

I think it is very useful to have the examples. of Handwrite So you can Compare your handwriting with Someone eles. I think it was very easy to follow the instructions. They was Some problem with it because you did not ask all the questions you should of

b (Mark)

Before

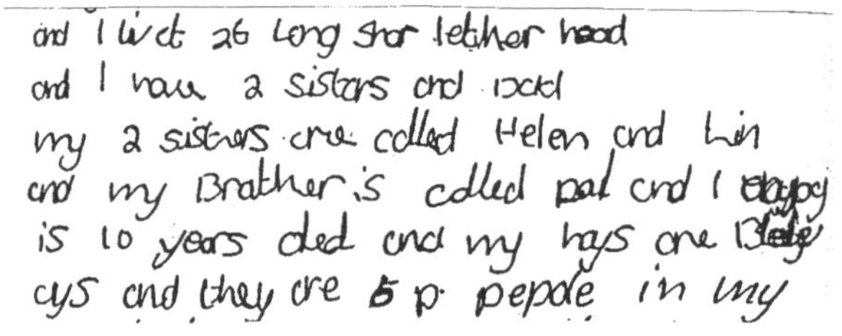

and I livet 26 long stor letther head
and I have a sisters and 1cccl
my 2 sistws are colled Helen and Lin
and my Brather is colled pal and I clopy
is 10 years ded and my has one Blade
cys and they cre 5 p pepole in my

After

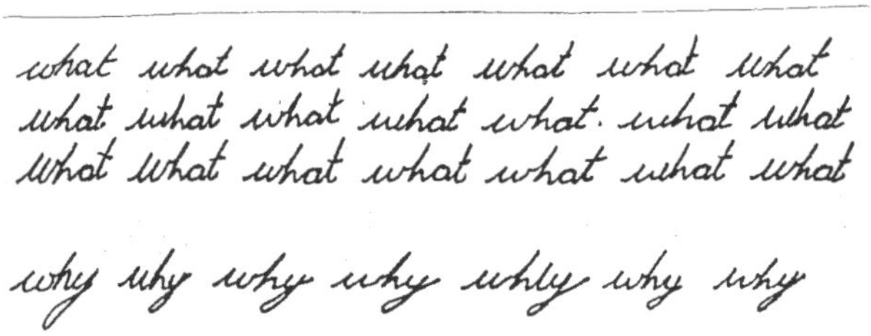

what what what what what what what
what what what what what. what what
What What what what what what what

why why why why whly why why

c

Before

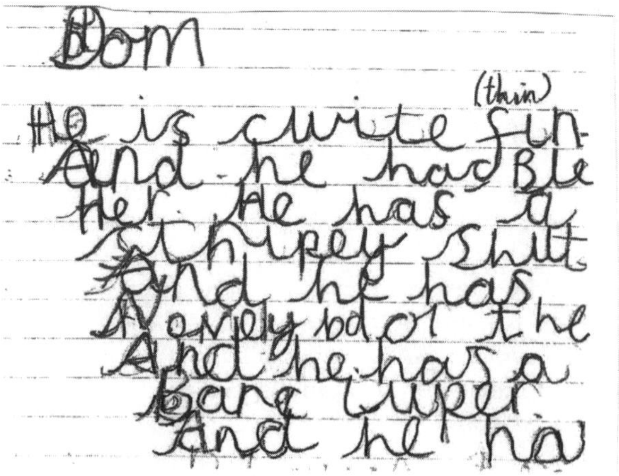

Dom
(thin)
He is cwite fun
And he had Ble
Her. He has a
Stripey Shirt
And he has
lovely bd or the
And he has a
bang wiper
And he ha

Figure 2.12 continued

After

One day Jack was playing in the woods and he
met an old man. The man game hem some beans.
He ran home to his mum and gave her the beans.
She was very pleased with Jack for brenging
the behs to her.

d

Before

One day I was fishing in

Epping Fores I was eating

a appol wen I finesb I made

a how in the grand and

I pot it in it I got

Bake To my fishing I was

After

Kit is a cat she is a cleuler
cat, and she can speak Ehgish.
One day when it was asleep on
my bed kit came up and said
that she had heard two men talking
about killing the a queen so it
went win kit and we listened to
the two men. I went to a phone box
and dialed 999 but the phone was not
working, so kit and iI ran to the
police station. I told the police and
we went in a police car. When we was
holf way the car broke down
so we had to run the rest of of

Mark (Figure 2.12b) was getting into trouble from the class teacher on a regular basis because his writing was illegible and badly spelled. He was becoming depressed and exhibiting behaviour problems at home. He desperately wanted to change his scrappy writing somehow and asked my student if he would teach him to write like him. We made a plan for Mark and every day for a fortnight he spent a few minutes before school practising the word patterns, especially the ones he needed to help with spelling. He was so pleased with the effect he practised at home and at the weekends. Finally he dared to try out his new joined style in his classroom project. His teacher was delighted with the transformation and so was Mark. His work was displayed for others to admire and Mark was out of trouble and a much happier child, looking forward at last to going to secondary school.

Extreme anxiety

There are some children who are suffering distress and who are extremely anxious and this can sometimes be seen in their writing which may be very small or very faint, with words running together and a tiny tremor seen in all the strokes. There are of course some minor hand tremors which run in families which also cause the handwriting to wobble. Other signs of anxiety such as sighing and breathlessness, beads of perspiration on the upper lip, voicelessness and so on will enable the teacher to identify the type of problem.

A school writing policy

A primary school with an effective handwriting policy is expected in the NLS to produce by Year 5 only a few students who may still have problems. The Kingston research using cursive suggested that this can be achieved by the end of Key Stage 1, in Year 3.

The following are some of the recommendations made by Bishop (2002) based on research into 'writing speed and extra time in examinations':

1   Schools can influence handwriting style.
2   Cursive handwriting should be introduced as the initial style at infant school.
3   Subsequent levels of education should encourage cursive writing.

Handwriting has been referred to as the 'Cinderella skill' for the way it has been neglected in education since the 1950s. However, there is more to writing than handwriting alone and so the policy needs to include talking and handwriting as aids to composition, plus an appropriate and connected spelling teaching programme such as discussed in later chapters.

The value of talk as an aid to writing, especially composition, is often overlooked but good practice examples abound. To promote talk we can conceive of a 'talking curriculum' (see pp.4–5) which is threaded through everyday teaching, or should be.

The more children engage in talk as argument, elaboration, description, narrative, exploration and discussion the more fluent their thinking becomes for writing. It is a necessary precursor especially in young children, according to Sharman (2004) among others reporting on the Kent LEA project *Writing in the Air*.

The project succeeded in promoting the talking and writing of underachieving and disadvantaged boys in particular.

Similar effects are found to promote the imaginative and narrative writing of older children when they engage in experiential learning such as in museum and theatre visits, visits to sites of interest, observation and recording of real events, participation in plays, special classes conducted by experts and so on. They become excited, involved and motivated and want to talk and write about their experience.

Scaffolding

When pupils have difficulty in organising their written work the technique of providing scaffolds or structures for writing can be implemented. This can be part of study skills and research in which pupils learn how to write in different text forms and genres. At a simple level they learn that a story must have a beginning, middle and end; that paragraphs may be structured to explain a cause and effect, a sequence of events or give a description of something; that experiments in science have diagrams, methods, results and conclusions and so on.

Summary and conclusions

In this chapter the nature of handwriting teaching, particularly during different phases of the twentieth century, is discussed and related to the impact of the National Curriculum and the National Literacy Strategy. It is suggested, based on the cohort analyses of handwriting and other research, that the evidence points to a neglect of the study and the teaching of handwriting.

Lack of careful teaching together with handwriting difficulties would appear to have contributed to significant levels of underachievement in schools. Studies showed that these difficulties frequently have the effects of lowering motivation and self-esteem and are responsible for a significant amount of disruption. It is argued that the disaffection and decline in standards seen on entry to secondary school are in part a result of the spelling and handwriting difficulties children experience. It also is shown in the research that these difficulties contribute significantly to boys' underachievement in comparison with girls but that girls with difficulties appear to be penalised more. Poor handwriting quality is the overt handicap and slow handwriting the unseen one.

A range of general strategies and styles of handwriting are reviewed and their strengths and weaknesses pointed out. Their relative values are discussed based on research studies. When and when not to teach handwriting is outlined for students who have severe coordination difficulties, and alternative strategies are suggested.

Issues such as form, style, penhold, handedness and speed are explored using research and practice examples from a range of writing. The problem of how, when and if to introduce cursive writing are discussed and the research backing the conclusions is explained. The remedial effects of short paced interventions in improving speed and legibility are illustrated. Comparisons are made with what occurs in other countries and in the UK and lessons are drawn from these examples which could help children here.

It is concluded that all primary school teachers should have more knowledge of and training in handwriting teaching techniques for developmental, preventative and first stage remedial work. Secondary school and college teachers also need to have some basic understanding of and training in corrective strategies, especially related to writing in their disciplines. They need to be able to identify handwriting problems and learn not to harass the pupils about them. They should know how to do first stage intervention and if this is not successful know how to obtain specialist support and advice for the student and to support their own teaching.

Chapter 3

Dyslexia and dyspraxia

Their role in spelling and
handwriting difficulties

Introduction

The term 'dyslexia' is widely used as a shortened version for 'specific developmental dyslexia' for individuals who have an unexpected difficulty in learning symbol
codes at a level in accord with their intellectual ability. It particularly affects reading
and writing but can also cause difficulties with number and musical notation in
some pupils. It is a less popular term in education for a number of reasons, some of
them to do with an aversion to medical sounding words, to potentially stigmatising
labels and to the economics of provision. However, dyslexics and their parents are
often greatly relieved to have this diagnosis given for it helps them feel less at fault.
For brevity the term 'dyslexia' is used in this book.

The term *learning disabilities* is frequently used to refer to dyslexia in the USA and
many other English-speaking countries. In the UK following Warnock's (1978)
attempt to remove stigmatising labels the term *specific learning difficulties in reading*
was preferred in education but it was often shortened to specific learning difficulties (SpLD). But this term includes many other conditions as well as dyslexia such
as attention deficit hyperactivity disorder (ADHD), developmental coordination
difficulties (DCD – dyspraxia), specific language difficulties (SLD – Dysphasia) and
so on. The full correct term should have been 'specific learning difficulties in reading and spelling' as will be seen.

The study of dyslexia has a long history going back to Kussmaul (1877) who first
named it and it has been through many phases ever since without being precisely
defined and finally understood. After a long period of being regarded as 'word
blindness' the most widely held definition which emerged in the dyslexia field
based upon the surveys of Clements (1966) was as follows: 'A disorder manifested
by a difficulty in learning to read despite conventional instruction, adequate intelligence and socio-cultural opportunity. It is dependent upon fundamental cognitive
disabilities which are frequently constitutional in origin'.

There are now seen to be a number of problems with this definition. It is a definition by exclusion where once we have excluded low intelligence, poor teaching,
disadvantaging backgrounds and so on then the problem we have left must be
dyslexia. But dys-lexis simply means a difficulty with words, particularly in their
written form – a circular definition.

The fact that 'words in their written form' is used only to refer to reading difficulties has given reading a primacy over spelling which may not have been justified. It

perhaps reflects the era when the definition was formed and the emphasis on reading in education at that time in the USA. It certainly reflects the situation in the UK both then and now. It has created problems both for teaching and for research and practice. It has directed the focus of remedial provision for five decades. Even the document *Excellence for All Children* (DfEE 1997) states 'Dyslexia, or reading difficulties' (p. 15).

In addition, Clements' use of the word 'disorder' carries with it a whole set of assumptions and attitudes that may not be justified. It suggests that the system from which dyslexia emanates is disordered and dysfunctional, and even that medication might be appropriate, and in the end that it is not remediable but might be patched up or be compensated for. Although some elements of this definition may be accurate, as with all definitions, it needs to be considered within its context. In those days the medical doctor would be the one who diagnosed dyslexia. It only gradually moved to be the concern of psychologists as the educational psychology profession itself developed. At that stage their training and background was in behavioural psychology and so interventions were frequently behaviourally orientated rather than cognitive and educational.

More recently an expert group established to advise the British Psychological Society (1989) offered the following definition of dyslexia:

> A specific difficulty in learning, constitutional in origin, in one or more of reading, spelling and written language which may be accompanied by a difficulty in number work. It is particularly related to mastering and using written language (alphabetic, numerical and musical notation) although often affecting oral language to some degree.

This definition covers the main areas of dyslexic difficulties that research has identified since Clements and tries to give focus to the key issues. Implicitly it tells us now that dyslexia may be found across the ability range and that written language or coded symbols applies to text, number and musical scores.

In the interim we have learned that in some dyslexics there is the implication of deeper language difficulties which can taper to such a mild and subtle degree that they are normally not noticeable. More dyslexics than might at first appear have these subtle difficulties, such as in word retrieval and naming. My main concern with this definition is that it suggests that a dyslexic might be thought to have only *one* of the areas of difficulty i.e. reading or spelling or number and this does not fit with experience of dyslexics. They do have reading *and* spelling difficulties but rarely if ever reading without spelling difficulties although a significant number seem to have spelling with no reading difficulties. The number of difficulties some dyslexics have seem to be more due to their difficulties associated with dyslexia and in the language of maths, plus tendencies in others to mirror write, than to be a separate condition which is called 'dyscalculia'.

The British Dyslexia Association's definition was somewhat similar to that of the BPS but went on to extend it to cover what teachers might observe in their dyslexics, and thus it becomes over inclusive.

> Dyslexia is best described as a combination of abilities and difficulties which affect the learning process in one or more of reading, spelling and writing.

Accompanying weaknesses may be identified in areas of speed of processing, short term memory, sequencing, auditory and/or visual perception, spoken language and motor skills. It is particularly related to mastering and using written language, which may include alphabetic, numeric and musical notation. Some children have outstanding creative skills, others have strong oral skills. Dyslexia occurs despite normal teaching, and is independent of socio-economic background or intelligence. It is, however, more easily detected in those with average or above average intelligence.

(BDA 1999: 61)

Many readers miss the words 'accompanying weaknesses' and regard them as central to the dyslexia. It also reinforces theories of dyslexia causation which Vellutino (1979) had already demonstrated were untenable e.g. limitations in short term or working memory, sequencing problems and visual perceptual and auditory problems.

Introducing the positive side of dyslexia is seen in the BDA definition. Dyslexics often do have other special abilities than literacy and it is good to credit this. But they often have to develop these compensatory strategies and different talents and find achievement in other fields than school subjects. We probably all know someone who would now have been working in the local stores or bank if they had been able to read and write but who had to become a dealer or builder and now run their own big companies. Some very talented dyslexics have been encouraging people to think of the possibility of enhanced creativity in dyslexics unhampered by the sequential processor of the language hemisphere (West 1999).

Reading and spelling difficulties are not causes of dyslexia, they result from it, and are the main educational problems dyslexics face, for they prevent access to the wider curriculum.

Patterns in and associated with dyslexia

There are a number of different patterns surrounding the key aspects of dyslexia which are met in case work. Some dyslexics have all of the patterns and make up the severest end of the distribution e.g. they may have *developmental dyslexia, developmental dysorthographia, developmental dysgraphia, developmental dyspraxia, developmental dysphasia* and *developmental dyscalculia* – in other words they have *complex specific learning difficulties*. This complex condition makes their educational needs difficult to deal with in the mainstream. They are likely to find their way to specialist clinics and research centres and often need full-time dyslexia-focused education at least up to secondary school level. It is also the case that their complex difficulties often define the way research on dyslexia is pursued and the results it obtains.

Comorbidity

Dyslexia is often associated with other specific learning difficulties such as attention deficit hyperactivity disorder (ADHD) and dyspraxia. The overlap in these conditions is estimated to be as high as 30 per cent. The reasons expounded centre on shared genetic material in the conditions (Duane 2002). An association has also been found between specific learning difficulties and allergies as well as immune deficiencies.

Recent terminological trends

Once again in the UK, the use of the term 'dyslexia' is likely to be discouraged and viewed instead as one of the 'barriers to learning' which children with special needs face (DfES, 2004). This is of course a useful educational notion but a more specific label gives an identity which can bring specific provision. Dyslexia being just one of the barriers may mean dyslexics are included in larger groups all receiving a range of non-specific provision. Even with the label this does still happen in some schools.

The history of the study of dyslexia can be seen in its terminology. It is a medical term for an educational condition for if we did not have to go to school and become educated dyslexia would not bother us. In pre-literate societies they do have individuals with the propensity for dyslexia but it does not matter or discriminate against them. Medical diagnosis has often led to the prescription of medicaments and 'treatment' with drugs, and dyslexia has been no exception. Even the term 'diagnosis' was proscribed on occasion and emphasis was given to 'assessment' instead.

In relation to dyspraxia the term now favoured internationally is developmental coordination difficulties (DCD) although there are some questions left over ideational plans. DCD is less medical sounding and suggests that as it is a difficulty and developmental it can be overcome to some extent in most individuals. In children at least we are moving away from the notion of disordered systems to difficulties in the system.

In relation to dysphasia we see the terms specific language disorders (SLD) and specific language impairment (SLI) taking over and no doubt this will move further to specific language difficulties. Unfortunately SLD has already been used in education for the severe learning difficulties of those formerly called 'mentally handicapped'.

In line with this trend it would seem that the term dyslexic spectrum difficulties (DSD) might help keep a wider perspective on dyslexia and suggest that it also may be overcome with the right sort of provision. In DSD we can have different patterns with and without reading difficulties, handwriting and number and language difficulties, but spelling problems are found in all of them.

Incidences of dyslexia worldwide

The differences in incidence in the different countries reflect to some extent the different ages that pupils enter schooling, the difficulties in acquiring the different languages and orthographies as well as the different techniques by which they are taught and assessed. For example, Scotland retained a more formal system of phonics teaching in the early years. In some cultures such as Saudi Arabia the concept of dyslexia is generally unknown and all difficulties are put down to general ineducability, or stupidity. In Norway children begin formal schooling at seven but by 10–11 years old they are ahead, in literacy skills, of British children who begin formal schooling at five and sometimes four years old (Sylva 1998).

In languages that have regular symbol-to-sound correspondence such as Spanish, Turkish and Italian we may expect fewer difficulties in the acquisition of literacy as was reported with the i.t.a. system (Downing 1964) and now by Hanley *et al.* (cited in Goswami 2003: 401) who followed matched groups of Welsh language learners and English ones living in the same area of Wales. Welsh is a language with

Table 3.1 The incidence of dyslexia in different countries

Belgium	5%
Britain	4%
Czech Republic	2–3%
Finland	10% (includes all poor readers)
Greece	5%
Italy	1.3–5%
Japan	6%
Nigeria	11%
Norway	3%
Poland	4%
Russia	10%
Singapore	2–3%
Slovakia	1–2%
USA	8.5%

(England and Wales 4% Rutter *et al.* 1970; 10% BDA 2004 (their current figures for England and Wales); Scotland 1.5% SED 1978)
Source: Smythe 1997: 238

almost one-to-one consistency. The English children were slower in reading acquisition than the Welsh children but faster readers. This was perhaps due to the slower strategy of using sequential letter sound correspondence in Welsh.

Levels of involvement in dyslexia

In addition to patterns it is also necessary to introduce the concept of different levels of permeation of the difficulties due to different levels of neurological involvement or difficulties which as yet have not been unravelled.

Frith (2000) developed a model for understanding dyslexia theory, research and practice which involves three levels. These are the *educational,* the *psychological* and the *biological* levels of the model and dyslexia will be discussed in relation to each of them. Underpinning the educational skills are psychological subskills and processes such as phonological and information-processing skills and abilities. These derive from the biological bases involving neurological levels and gene functioning. Research goes on at all the levels and sometimes a connection between levels can be made which provides an explanatory basis for what we observe or how we define and intervene in dyslexia.

Educational difficulties as barriers to learning

Educational difficulties and dyslexia

Children who have *general learning difficulties* may also have dyslexia. Most without dyslexia will develop both reading and spelling skills consistent with their slower profile of development across a range of skills and abilities. However, they may have good reading and copying skills. The key factor is in their much poorer comprehension of what they read. An intelligence quotient is not a stable predictor of reading ability, for groups of subjects with IQs as low as 40 have been taught to read fluently. They fail however to comprehend what they read. Fifty per cent of slower learners have language difficulties and frequently have coordination difficulties; both contribute to poor spelling development.

Some poor spellers and readers have been subject to poor teaching, have missed key aspects of early schooling, or have suffered from a range of different teachers or transfers from one school to another (SED 1978). These factors have disrupted some but not all pupils' literacy learning and they need opportunities to catch up or to receive the teaching, if somewhat compacted, that they may have missed. The NLS improved the transfer prospects but has proved to move too fast for many dyslexic pupils and did not provide sufficient opportunities for catching up. For the most able readers and spellers it moved too slowly.

There are also a small number of pupils who have failed to read and spell by any method and who have severe difficulties often in the presence of average or above average intellectual abilities. They may have experienced very good teaching provision in reception class and Year 1, they may also have been given in-class remedial support for their reading and spelling which has failed, they may then have been referred for specialist withdrawal provision as well as in-class support, and over a three to five year period they may have made little or no progress. It is this group who are referred to as 'dyslexic'.

It is typical to read that the diagnosis of their difficulties must wait upon the failure to learn to read and that dyslexia cannot ordinarily be diagnosed until the age of eight to eleven years (Robertson 2000). This is not correct. Dyslexia can be identified by reception class teachers (lightly trained) within a week or two of children entering formal education (Torgeson 1995) and the potential for dyslexia can also now be identified in the pre-school period (Fawcett and Nicolson 1999).

Failure to help dyslexics means that they will be unable to achieve recognised qualifications which are consistent with their intellectual abilities in the so-called academic areas. They experience a loss of self-esteem and of success and there is also a loss of their contribution in the workforce. Compensation can be provided by having readers and taped presentations but much of school work still involves reading and writing and so the dyslexic is doubly disadvantaged in all areas of the curriculum involving these skills. Remedial help is essential to bring them up to at least grade level as soon as possible. Often associated with the failure to help dyslexic pupils are the secondary emotional and behavioural difficulties (Montgomery 1995; Edwards 1994). Bullying is also often a factor, in which pupils and some teachers bully and demean the dyslexic, or the fact that remedial withdrawal or learning support is given brings about bullying.

In addition to the reading and spelling difficulties the dyslexic may have a range of secondary or associated difficulties such as problems in learning the alphabet and alphabetical order, the days of the week and months of the year, identifying right and left, and remembering a list of digits in the correct order (digit span). It is often concluded from this that they have sequencing and ordering problems and a problem with auditory memory but this is not so. The names of alphabet letters, days and months, and digits are arbitrary and dyslexics have difficulties with naming and laying down the phonological codes involved in the registration and retrieval of this type of information. In other words they are secondary to the dyslexic condition. What they all have are literacy difficulties; as these clear up so do the secondary problems (Koppitz 1977).

Educational difficulties and dysorthographia

Dysorthographia is mainly an unrecognised specific verbal learning difficulty. It consists of a mild to severe spelling difficulty but in the presence of average or even excellent ability to read. Misspellings of easy words make people think quite wrongly that the child is not very bright. The problem may go deeper than this and may affect not only spelling but also the ability to organise and create a coherent account or argument in text. The major signs of an earlier reading difficulty will be in slow reading particularly with the more complex texts in the sixth form and in higher education. The residual effect of dyslexia in many adults is the spelling problem. The incidence as yet is unknown but seems higher than that of dyslexia perhaps in the order of a further 10 per cent.

Spelling disability was particularly common in my gifted undergraduate teachers who underachieved. They had often taught themselves to read well before school, and because they were good readers their problems did not emerge until about the age of eight years when the vocabulary they needed to use became much more extensive. Many were very clever at concealing their problems until exams for they used proofreaders and spell checkers. At GCSE and undergraduate level the barrier is often only reached when they meet new technical vocabulary or have to write rapidly in examinations.

Educational difficulties and dyscalculia

In addition to the reading and spelling difficulties the dyslexic may have associated number difficulties sometimes called *dyscalculia*. However, analysis of the number difficulties shows that often it is very much to do with vocabulary, naming and reading problems, reciting tables, and mental arithmetic (Miles 1993). This is because they all involve verbal or subvocal verbalisation, rather than a problem with understanding numbers per se.

Recent research by Butterworth (2006) has found that 6 per cent of the population appear to be 'dyscalculic'. They can determine whether there is more or less of a colour in computerised squares but fail with items requiring absolute knowledge e.g. threes or fives. We need to question whether this is related to the naming of '3' and '5' or with the concept itself.

Educational difficulties and dysgraphia

There is a significant minority of pupils who will have handwriting coordination difficulties in the absence of any other motor coordination problems. Their problems and how to overcome them have been discussed in Chapter 2 as 'handwriting difficulties'. They are the dysgraphics and boys appear to be affected more than girls in the ratio of two to one.

Younger, more able pupils think rapidly but frequently do not have the handwriting coordination skills to write the thoughts down. This can prove extremely frustrating and teachers become disappointed at the disparities between verbal and written performance. The pupils will be criticised and content can be ignored. It is only when a piece of work arrives word processed and deeply thoughtful that the busy teacher may realise the potential there. Sadly it may be assumed that the lengthy thesis has been copied from the internet or is a parent's work and it is back to handwriting again.

In schools in particular the needs of pupils with these non-verbal learning difficulties have not been understood. Difficulties such as in handwriting (dysgraphia) attract a great deal of criticism and bullying, prevent access to the curriculum, and handicap spelling. They appear to contribute significantly to underachievement at all levels of education (Connelly and Hurst 2001).

Educational difficulties and DCD

Movement difficulties in children have been documented since the turn of the twentieth century and it has long been acknowledged in the medical and educational world that movement difficulties are a significant problem in child development. Whilst many observable behaviours of the difficulties may be evident in the pre-school years, 'dyspraxic youngsters are not referred ... until they reach 6 or 7 years' (Portwood 1999: 35) when their problems begin to impact upon learning in the wider curriculum.

DCDs range from general clumsiness in running and walking to specific fine motor coordination difficulties in handwriting, bead threading, shoelace tying, and buttoning. A pupil with DCD might lurch out of the classroom door, speed down the corridor veering to one side, grazing the wall, losing books and pens on the way, burst into the next classroom and send desks and others' property flying, arrive sprawling in their own seat dumping the contents of their school bag on the floor, and looking as though he (usually he) has been pulled through a hedge backwards. Food is spilled and exercise books are filled with scruffy, scrappy work loaded with crossings out and erasures.

Such pupils are not picked in team games and are frequently seriously bullied and become the butt of jokes and blame. The difficulties may affect not only general coordination but deeper neurocerebral levels and pathways (Kokot 2003). Despite a range of seemingly stupid behaviours, and perhaps a lack of control of emotional and social responses, the individual may be highly intelligent but trapped in a body which will not do as desired unless specific training is given to help establish these controls. Chesson et al. (1991) found that in their sample of children with coordination difficulties, over 50 per cent had had speech therapy, and some of the group were identified only on entry to school. Half their sample were doing well at maths but the rest had spelling and handwriting problems which were hampering their progress in school. Some children identified as 'clumsy' at an early age may grow out of it but most do not.

The Diagnostic and Statistical Manual (DSM-IV) of the American Psychiatric Association (APA 1994) states the following as diagnostic criteria in DCD:

- Impairment in the development of motor-coordination.
- Significant impairment interfering with academic achievement or activities of daily living.
- Coordination difficulties not due to a general medical condition, e.g. cerebral palsy, hemiplegia.
- It is not a pervasive developmental disorder.
- If developmental delay is evident, then motor difficulties are usually in excess of those associated with it.

There are also other associated behaviour features that may be observed along with the coordination problems, such as difficulties with articulation, limited concentration, and an inability to follow instructions.

The significance of DCD as a contributing factor in underachievement is too often overlooked. It often brings about bullying and derision because of the lack of movement and ball skills, but it also involves poor social skills and attentional problems. These together with the poor coordination lead to the lowering of literacy skills and can particularly affect handwriting and spelling. Macintyre (2001) found that 50 per cent of dyslexics had some form of dyspraxia, that is gross movement or fine motor coordination difficulties. In the cohort studies (see Chapter 2) it appeared that one-third of dyslexics had dysgraphic difficulties.

Another aspect which may be found in some pupils is visuo-spatial difficulties in the absence of more overt signs of coordination problems. These pupils will have problems in far and/or near point copying i.e. from the board or from the adjacent page, even from the same page; difficulties in drawing representational forms and constructional activities and in directional and orienteering tasks. In the severest cases they will tend 'to get lost in Woolworths'.

Children with severe coordination difficulties in handwriting should not be forced to wield a pen; they may need several years' extra developmental time before they are really able to learn to write more than their own name. A careful assessment of need would reveal that such a pupil would be far better occupied in learning to word process in reception class or use a voice activation system and transfer to some handwriting later or not at all.

The child who has the relatively rare disorder, *cerebellar dyspraxia*, which disrupts the control over handwriting and other movements, will have very shaky, scribbly handwriting which no amount of cursive handwriting training can remediate. This pupil must also have access to word processing at home and at school if the difficulty is not to be made into a handicap. Even this may prove too difficult and voice activation systems will be needed.

Educational difficulties and specific language difficulties

The incidence of SLD appears to be 1 to 3 per cent. These children need specific and structured language teaching from the earliest stages but mild conditions may go undiscovered well into school age. Typical behaviours are that they are monosyllabic and unresponsive in lessons, unable to express ideas clearly either verbally or in writing. They fall further and further behind in all the language-based curriculum areas. They need a language-enriched curriculum which promotes talking and listening whilst those with the severest problems need highly structured special language teaching (AFASIC 2006).

Psychological difficulties as barriers to learning

Psychological functions consist of memory, perceptual, behavioural, emotional, motivational and cognitive processes. Memory, perception and cognition form the underpinnings of all the higher mental functions we use in education. In dyslexia psychological difficulties in some ways both cause dyslexia and result from it. The psychological causes remain hypothetical because we cannot see the processes but can only infer them from behaviour and tests.

Sometimes inferences from the data have been incorrect although they seemed true at the time. For example, for nearly 100 years dyslexia was thought to be 'word blindness', then a visual perceptual problem, and later it became both a visual and an auditory processing problem. Now in the majority of cases it is regarded as a verbal processing problem particularly in relation to phonological difficulties after the extensive analysis of Vellutino (1979). This was a major paradigm change in the psychological research field and only penetrated the education field in the the mid 1990s.

Speed of auditory processing hypothesis

This work has come to prominence in the past ten years although research has been going on for much longer. In essence, Tallal and Piercy (1973) and Tallal (1994) suggest that the dyslexic problem lies in an inability to process sensory input rapidly, particularly the auditory information contained in speech. The deficit is in the millisecond range and could be due to cell size differences in the left language hemisphere which are smaller in dyslexics (Holmes 1994: 27). The difficulty would create problems in 'b' and 'd' perception for example which lasts only 40 milliseconds. When the sounds were separated by 100 milliseconds, discrimination was possible for the dyslexics. Galaburda (1993) has argued that this deficit does not indicate a cause of dyslexia but is a secondary effect associated with a deeper cause.

The question we need to ask is why, when pupils are taught sounds of the letters in isolation, they hear, see and write them in reception and dyslexics fail to learn them, is speed an issue? It becomes an issue in fluent reading and only if we teach by 'look and say' or the top-down sentence-reading methods alone.

The discrimination of 'b' and 'd' for reading or spelling does not just depend upon our ability to distinguish the differences auditorily, nor is speed of processing a critical factor in learning to read or spell, *the acquisition stage*. It may be more relevant in learning to speak or to read in some teaching regimes but not to spell.

Although young children have a better ability than adults to discriminate between sounds, what we do know, according to Liberman *et al.* (1967), is that the human ear is incapable of distinguishing the sounds in syllables. Most often the initial sound is accompanied by a stronger burst of energy and thus is easier than the rest of the syllable to become aware of (for reading) than to segment (for spelling). The rest of the letters are shingled on top of each other, making them impossible to separate out. Thus teaching 'c-a-t', 'cat' is set for failure. But teaching onset and rime 'c-at' makes sense, especially when we have a picture clue to help us. The I Spy game is thus a very important part of early learning in school.

The phonological processing hypothesis – verbal processing theory

In this theory the majority of cases of dyslexia are thought to be due to an underlying *verbal processing difficulty* particularly in the *phonological area*, which can give rise to:

- inability to appreciate rhyme
- lack of phonemic awareness
- poor development of alphabetic knowledge
- lack of development of symbol-to-sound correspondence
- lack of development of phoneme segmentation skills
- lack of spelling development at the higher levels
- lack of metacognitive awareness of spelling
                    (Chomsky 1971; Liberman 1973; Golinkoff 1978; Vellutino 1979; Frith
                    1980; Bryant and Bradley 1985; Brown and Ellis 1994; Snowling 2000)

These skills and abilities underlie the development of good spelling and reading and appear to develop incidentally in most pupils during reading and writing. Phonemic awareness and appreciation of rhyme are more closely associated with reading skills. Alphabetic knowledge, symbol–sound correspondence and phoneme segmentation are more associated with spelling. However, even with direct teaching of phonics the dyslexic may not be able to acquire early alphabetic and segmentation skills. Thus it is that these can be used as a primary indicator of dyslexia and dysorthographia in reception classes.

If the dyslexia goes unremediated what we find is that in severe cases very little alphabetic knowledge and phonemic skills are shown in the spelling. However, by about the age of eight years many dyslexics do begin to appear to 'crack the alphabetic code'. This is especially so where great efforts are made with multisensory phonics. By now however the child is three years behind peers in literacy development and as each year goes by the gap widens because the literacy teaching environment of the junior school is geared to subject teaching using literacy skills.

When we look at scripts from dyslexics it is puzzling to think why they seem unable to learn a few basic phonic or phonemic skills in the infant school which would support their reading and writing. The alphabet system is elegant, efficient and simple. Thus we have to ask why some very bright children are dyslexic; can the phonological processing deficit alone explain this? In languages which are more regular phonically, such as Italian, dyslexics still exist, at a level of 1.3–5 per cent. Thus phonics teaching alone is unlikely to solve the dyslexic problem. Claims instead are made for phonological interventions, but are they justified?

We know that pupils will be able to decipher syllable beats by ear if they can hear and understand speech. But phoneme tapping is different; for example, when asked to tap 'seven', 'write' and 'bad', dyslexics tapped three and four times, three times and three times. Controls tapped five times, five and four times and three times. In a series of such experiments (Montgomery 1997a) it became clear that phoneme tapping was only accurate if the dyslexics and controls could spell the word in the first place. Similarly, phoneme segmentation involving cutting off the initial sound of *c -at* was facilitated by knowledge of the letter sound 'c'. In other words these exercises were subskills of spelling and dependent upon it. Careful case work with individuals can reveal such information whereas as adults we often draw incorrect inferences from group research data.

Articulation awareness hypothesis – an intersensory integration theory

The easy association between the arbitrary symbols of the alphabet and their sounds which most beginners pick up incidentally during reading is lost on dyslexics. Even in classrooms where sounds are being said slowly and the connections between them and the graphemes are made explicit, dyslexics fail to learn them. They do not learn to segment the sound 'c' from 'cat' for example as other children do. Ehri (1979) has suggested that this is because the sound is an *abstract perceptual unit* which has to be linked to the arbitrary graphemic unit. It occurred to me that such abstraction could be the core of the problem in learning sounds and alphabetic information.

Studies of the alphabet lead to some significant facts. The alphabet was only invented once. It was invented within the context of a semitic language by the Phoenicians. Their semitic language was consonantal without vowels and consisted of 22 sounds, the clue. If the originator had used the articulatory feel of each of the 22 consonants by which to assign a symbol, an alphabetic system had been invented. Any one could learn it, except perhaps dyslexics? The articulatory pattern would indeed be the only concrete clue between the arbitrary and abstract sound and the arbitrary and abstract visual symbol. The three of them would make a kinaesthetic multisensory triangle, to which we add the writing component, a four-way relationship.

If the dyslexic does not have the awareness of the articulatory feel of a particular phoneme it will make the sound–symbol association particularly problematic to acquire (Montgomery 1981). As sounds with the same symbols appear in different forms – *allophones* in syllables, this can quickly become confusing. Graphemes represent phonemes not allophones and so do not distinguish between different pronunciations. It is the articulatory pattern which is *concrete* and remains roughly the same and which can be used to connect the sound and symbol. By using articulatory cues a pupil should be able to decode the consonantal structure of a syllable or a word even though vowels might be missed. This could account for the scaffold or skeletal phonics seen such as in *mstr, ws, bd* and so on when beginning spellers and dyslexics have begun to break the alphabetic code.

Treiman *et al.* (1995) showed that the consistency of spelling to sound in English of initial consonants is not at all consistent as it is in other languages. For example, for the initial sound 's' in 'seal' 'sun' and 'sing' the consistency is 96 per cent. For the vowel 'u' in 'sun' 'bud' and 'pull' it is 51 per cent. For the final consonant 'p' in 'soap' 'cup' and 'rip' it is 91 per cent. In CV-segmentation 'ca' as in 'cap' 'call' and 'car' it is 52 per cent and in VC-segmentation 'un' as in 'bun' 'fun' and 'run' it is 77 per cent. Thus the concrete articulatory feel of a consonant or cluster can help considerably to support the learning of the associations even for non-dyslexic learners.

Steven, six years six months

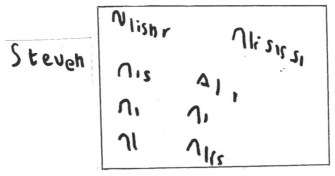

Caroline, seven years: 'My name is Caroline and I am 7 years old. I have 3 brothers and 3 sisters. Some of them live at home and some of them do not. My mum and dad live at home and so do my goldfish. Paul, Brenda and Mark still live at home. They are a lot older than me. Paul is 21, Breda is 21 and Mark is 22. My other brothers and sisters are a lot older than them.'

David, eight years: 'Tiny was a big animal and slept a lot at night and in the morning I have to keep waking him up. I have to keep waking him up to have his breakfast. When I go to the shops I have to drag him with me.'

Figure 3.1 Examples of the spelling of dyslexics before they have cracked the alphabetic code and have difficulties with phonics (half size)

Gavin, 10 years, spelling test. Item 13 was the word 'parcel'.

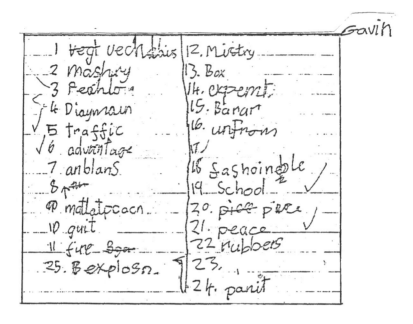

Roger, 10.5 years

Figure 3.2 Examples of the spellings of dyslexics after they have cracked the alphabetic code and have difficulties with orthographics

In a series of pilot studies, then controlled experiments, this articulation awareness hypothesis was tested. It was found that dyslexics in comparison with spelling-age-matched controls had significantly poorer articulation awareness skills even though they were two-and-a-half years older. In order to help remediate these difficulties and improve their basic spelling skills a number of strategies termed 'multisensory mouth training' for spelling were developed. This is exactly what Edith Norrie (1917) must have done when she developed the letter case and taught herself to spell.

Table 3.2 Results of the main articulation awareness investigation

	Numbers	Reading age	Spelling age	PS (15)	AA (10)	IQ	Chronological age
Controls	84	8.61	8.02	11.94	7.75	110.03	7.94
Dyslexics	114	7.95	7.62	10.27	4.31	110.43	12.90
Dyslexics (waiting)	30	6.71	6.00	4.13	5.87	112.67	8.97

Key: 15/10 = items on tests; PS = phoneme segmentation; AA = articulation awareness; Dyslexics (waiting) not on APSL programme; Dyslexics at least 1 term on APSL programme

When a word is pronounced by a careful speaker most of its key constituent phonemes can be heard or felt. It is this 'citation' form that spellers need to use to support their spelling until a word is learned and can be written automatically by direct reference to the lexicon.

Learning to feel the initial sound can also give strong concrete support to the onset and rime strategy by helping segment the initial sound for reading as well as spelling. When Peter, aged ten, was given four 20-minute 'multisensory mouth training' support sessions he made two years' reading and spelling progress in a fortnight. This is of course unusual but it provided the clue he needed to gain metacognitive insight into the whole process of spelling.

It will first of all be the consonants and consonant blends which can be identified by 'feel'. The vowels do not cause the articulators to make contacts; they are open-mouthed non-contacting 'voiced' sounds varied by the position of the tongue and the shape of the lips and are particularly difficult to notice in medial positions.

Beginners may often be seen mouthing their words for spelling both aloud and subvocally and earlier researchers such as Monroe (1932) and Schonell (1942) were most insistent about the articulatory aspect of learning to spell.

The reason for delay in development of this refined form of sensitivity or integration of information above the level required not to bite the tongue is not entirely clear. It is a form of metalinguistic awareness which dyslexics may fail to acquire in reception class but may gradually do so at a later stage. Training in this area could well enable the reception class dyslexic to overcome the phonological disability. It may then make the acquisition of the higher order aspects of the language far easier for them to learn and they may not become disabled at all.

What has been known for many decades is that visual, auditory and articulatory elements *must be firmly cemented in writing* (Schonell 1942). In writing the attention is focused and helps reinforce the articulatory and kinaesthetic bridge between the visual and auditory symbols. This makes the four-way relationship between *auditory, visual, articulatory* and *manual kinaesthetic*.

A check of knowledge of lower case alphabet letters by 200 children in ten reception classes in urban and suburban settings showed that after three weeks in school the majority of pupils knew between five and ten names or sounds. Those who knew none fell into several groups: one or two were developmentally immature and seemed unable to grasp what they needed to do, one or two were unable to concentrate on the task and had very disturbed backgrounds, the rest tried and made

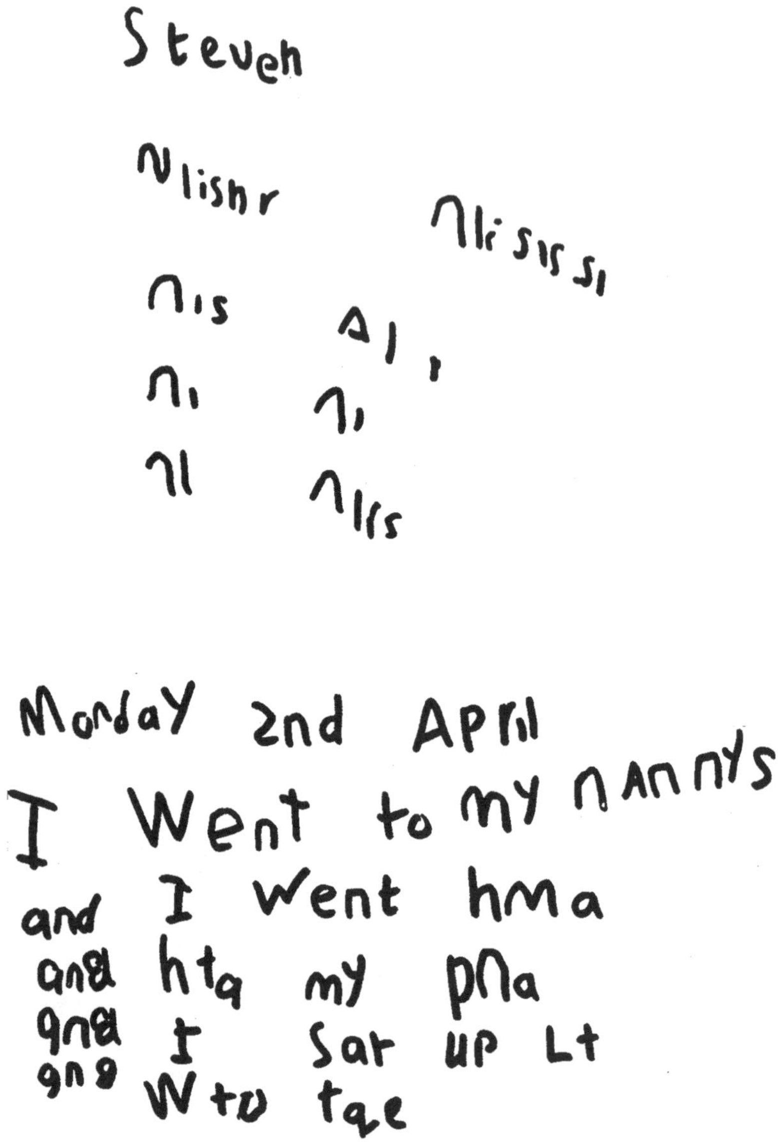

Steven

Nlishr   Nli sis si

Nis   Al ,

Ni   Ni

Nl   Nlrs

MondaY 2nd April
I Went to my nAnnys
and I Went hma
and hta my pna
gna I Sat up Lt
gng W to tae

Figure 3.3 Steven's spelling before and after six 20-minute interventions with articulatory phonics

random associations and were unaware how they were making sounds such as: l t d a s f in their mouths. Forsyth (1988) followed up a cohort for two years given LEA screening in three reception classes and found that failure to develop alphabetic knowledge was the best predictor of later reading and spelling ability at seven (although this was not originally included in the LEA screening inventory).

Although Vellutino (1979) discounted the intersensory integration theory of Birch (1962) and Birch and Belmont (1964), the evidence upon which he did so was slight in comparison with his work on the other theories. This was mainly due to a problem arising from the difficulties in devising test items which would serve the purpose. Most of them were contaminated by naming or verbal processing. However, the articulation awareness difficulty fits best into this dyslexia theory area and there does appear to be *neurological evidence* emerging which suggests that there could be a disconnection problem in the area of the left angular gyrus (Geschwind 1979; Horwitz *et al.* 1998) where auditory, visual and kinaesthetic information is integrated. It is suggested that this system may not be functioning adequately and this might account for the awareness difficulties observed. If there is a disconnection then multisensory training would be an important feature in remediation, encouraging other local brain areas to take over the function – hard work to establish at first but easy thereafter.

Biological bases for barriers to learning

The biological bases of learning include a complex range of neurological, anatomical, physiological and genetic factors, some of which have gained wide recognition and are outlined below.

As each new hypothesis emerges the store of dyslexic brains is checked to try to confirm or disconfirm the hypotheses. For example, the structure of the cerebral cortex in the visual areas of the left hemispheres seems to be more diffuse in dyslexics (Geschwind 1979; Galaburda 1985, 1993). Some neurons in male dyslexics appear to have migrated to the outside cortical layer in the brain; in females there appears to be neuron death. Both phenomena appeared to occur before six months gestation (Sherman 1995). More cases are still needed to confirm these findings but are of course difficult to come by. Geschwind (1979) first identified these phenomena and proposed that this could cause the dyslexics to be deficient in processing and connecting graphemic symbols to their sounds. It may cause them to switch processing to the other hemisphere (Witelson 1977) which is not so well set up for verbal processing.

Brunswick *et al.* (1999) showed that young dyslexic adults, when reading aloud and using non-word recognition tests, had less activation in the left posterior cortex than controls. A deficit in the left 'brain' was said to be implicated, but once again we can argue that this may well be a result and not a cause of their dyslexia. Their phonological processing was not secure. In fact when the dyslexic difficulties are given remediation and begin to clear up then the brain activation changes towards resembling that of controls (Kappers 1990).

Primary reflex hypothesis

The work of Blythe and McGlown (1979) at the Chester Centre was among the first in the UK to promote the study of the persistence of infant reflexes and their relationship to learning difficulties.

More recently McPhillips *et al.* (2000) studied foetal scans and found that the foetuses engaged in more stereotyped primary reflex movement patterns than newborns. They concluded that the functions served to facilitate the development of the cytoarchitecture of the central nervous system. After birth and by about one year most individuals transform the primary reflexes into different movements. The primary reflex hypothesis suggests that there is considerable evidence to show that in dyslexia this transformation is incomplete.

As the infant becomes upright a different system takes over: this is the cerebellar-vestibular system, which organises and controls balance and coordination. In order to cope with the upright gravitational world it is hypothesised that humans develop a three-dimensional grid system within which they operate but this cannot fully develop in the presence of the persistence of the primary reflex system geared to movement in fluid in the womb.

Remediation involves reactivating the primary reflexes in order to switch them off. The exercises are deliberate and slow, mimicking the pattern of the primary reflexes. In the double-blind trial, eight- to eleven-year-old pupils with dyslexia were selected on the basis of their condition being resistant to change and their negative attitudes to the remediation they had already experienced. One assessment measure involved getting the children to hold their hands out in front of them and then the examiner moved their heads. If the children's arms moved then this was a strong indication of the presence of a primary reflex. Strength of the primary reflexes was measured as well as eye tracking movements in the assessments.

After intervention the dyslexics' reading had significantly improved and they reported that objects had stopped moving about. Their worlds had become stable and their self-esteem had grown. Following words on a page and holding and moving a pencil in writing and copying were the skills affected. Boys had more problems than girls in a ratio of three to one. McPhillips *et al.* concluded that the primary reflex issue could be easily addressed in school-age children through special exercises in P.E.

The cerebellar-vestibular dysfunction hypothesis

The seat of balance in the human body lies in the semicircular canals or vestibular system which lies on top of the inner ears, the cochlea. The three canals contain fluid and tiny bony elements called 'otoliths' which settle in the differently facing canals when at rest. They excite sensory hairs and cells in the canals which tell us via the vestibular nerve collecting information from each canal which way up we are. Of course we have to learn to interpret this information and are reminded of the importance of this area when a virus infection gets in (labyrinthitis) and causes a problem in one or all of the canals. It is impossible if all are affected to stand up or even lie down without the whole world whirling round and causing nausea.

The cerebellum is the hind brain, two small lobed organs lying under the visual or occipital cortex and to the rear. It is the centre for the storage of all the learned motor programmes. Damage to the cerebellum will cause a staggering gait and the well-known Korsakov's syndrome of alcoholics. It also integrates the movement with the balance information coming from the vestibular system. The cerebellar-vestibular hypothesis implies that there is some developmental dysfunction in the cerebellum and/or in the pathways feeding it information which certain types of training might help it overcome.

Over a period of 35 years Judith Bluestone has been treating children with complex learning difficulties using a system she calls the Holistic Approach to

NeuroDevelopment and Learning Efficiency (HANDLE). She maintains that the neurological system is a hierarchically organised system of integrated and interdependent subsystems. Higher level functions depend on lower level systems. For example, it is claimed that reading or maths difficulties may be traced all the way back to a dysfunctional vestibular system. The therapist would therefore sequence and prioritise exercise activities according to where the individual's weaknesses show up on the hierarchy. The lowest level system would be addressed first so that when strengthened it supports the functions at the higher levels.

To address higher level functions before strengthening weaker foundational skills is, according to the HANDLE paradigm, an exercise in futility. It might improve the 'splinter' skill at the time but gives minimal gain and does not address the causal issue. An assessment is made of the individual by the trained observer and this includes: identifying what distracts attention from the task in hand; finding what requires energy for the task in hand; identifying what physical/environmental changes affect learning such as allergens, diet and so on; and finding which learning modalities are most successful.

The interactive, non-standardised evaluation protocol identifies, according to Kokot (2003: 14) the following features:

- distraction due to tactile or auditory sensitivity;
- vestibular inadequacy to support muscle tone, visual tracking and linguistic/phonetic awareness simultaneously;
- irregular interhemispheric integration interfering with auditory-visual integration, parts-to-whole configuration as well as problems with central auditory processing due to an inability to integrate the word/language component with the picture/meaning of the word;
- light sensitivity and visual motor dysfunctions that cause irregular visual/visual-motor feedback.

From the evaluation a therapeutic individualised programme is devised to strengthen the weak functions and resolve learning difficulties at their roots.

Kokot (2003) then goes on to describe two example case studies in which she uses the HANDLE programme to help resolve the individual difficulties. The vestibular functioning in one case was strengthened by exercises involving rolling backwards from a sitting position to the floor and then up again and from one side to the other. A weak sucking reflex was resolved by getting the child to drink water with eyes closed from a straw manufactured with three loops in it, to 'promote sucking in order to help gently and naturally practise eye convergence as well as to integrate her two brain hemispheres' (p.19). In addition, the parents were taught specific massage techniques 'related to neurodevelopment ... to help her tactile sensitivity and improve her proprioception' (p.19).

The key principle established by Bluestone is that of 'gentle enhancement'. This involves designing a home-based programme that only takes a few minutes per day to complete. This is carefully monitored so that any signs of stress such as change of facial colour, reddening of the ears, discomfort and so on causes the activity to be discontinued. Therapeutic equipment is not used as it may conceal the stress levels involved.

In the above example the original diagnosis was that of 'dyslexia' but in fact it was far more complex, as Kokot pointed out. It consisted mainly of developmental coordination difficulties with specific handwriting problems and some associated visuo-motor and perceptual difficulties.

It is not surprising in this case that a programme designed to support the weak vestibular system was more effective than a dyslexia remediation programme. The diagnosis and the remediation must coincide and both be fit for purpose. To simply state that reading and maths can be traced back to the functioning of the vestibular system is also concerning for it would seem reasonable that only certain functions in reading and maths attach to this area or route. These might include activities such as those involving coordinated movement, eye tracking in reading, switching gaze in copying from board to page, and coordinating movements when learning to write, but not in skilled writing.

Rae *et al.* (2002) suggested that there are cerebellar anomalies in developmental dyslexia and that cerebellar-vestibular dysfunction has been found to be involved in 96 per cent of a large dyslexic sample. This does of course depend upon how we define and identify dyslexia in these samples. We could be looking at a biased sample who find their way to specialist treatment centres and who receive statements of SEN at school. In other words they are at the severe end of the dyslexic spectrum and it could be argued that they are likely therefore to have complex specific learning difficulties involving dyslexia and DCD. We might also have a training function where the slow development in spelling and handwriting has not yet established a fluent pathway and set of connections.

The involvement of cerebellar dysfunction in dyslexia cases has been known in the literature for several decades. Frank and Levinson (1973) with the aid of Supportive Reading Teachers, identified 115 English-speaking dyslexic students in Years 1 to 6 in the New York City public school system. Forty second to sixth graders were found who had responded poorly and made slow progress in two one-hour remedial reading programme sessions per week over a year. Fifteen second to fifth graders were referred on the basis of being two years behind in their reading; and 60 first graders were selected for referral for investigation because of poor performance on an initial screening test and the Supportive Reading Teacher's opinion that they had made slow progress. The sample only included those subjects with average or above intellectual abilities and no diffuse brain dysfunction, and they were a subset of a larger group of 803 subjects all receiving remedial reading teaching.

In a later screening survey of first graders Frank and Levinson estimated that the incidence of what they called *dysmetric dyslexia* was 2 per cent of the school population. Nicolson and Fawcett, in 1994, also reported a high correlation between dyslexia and cerebellar impairments. In a task involving putting arms out straight in front and allowing the hands to dangle from the wrists they found a 10 per cent difference in the position of the right and left hands of dyslexics. These subjects also showed difficulties with balance when blindfolded, which correlated with their deficits in reading, spelling and phonological skills. Nicolson and Fawcett found that the two balance tests classified 90 per cent of dyslexics correctly and incorporated these items into their Dyslexia Early Screening Test (DEST) (1996), the Dyslexia Screening Test (DST) (Fawcett and Nicolson 1999) and the Dyslexia Adult Screening Test (DAST) (Fawcett and Nicolson 1999). All these tests are useable by 'lightly trained' professionals.

In 2004, the Dyslexia, Dyspraxia and Attention Treatment (DDAT) Centre at Kenilworth in a report put forward the view that dyslexia is a neurological difficulty caused by deficiencies in the links between the visual, vestibular and sensosomatory (related to the muscles and joints) areas. It was claimed that the DDAT exercise programme was similar to that given to returning astronauts by NASA to help reintroduce stability after weightlessness and it cured the temporary dyslexic symptoms which had developed after space flights. (NASA on its website has denied that their astronauts exhibit any symptoms of dyslexia whilst involved in training or in space flight).

It is claimed by Dove and Rutherford, DDAT founders, that the DDAT programme trains the cerebellum to respond in a normal way to information from the vestibular system. Vestibular stimulation affects learning in four ways according to Goddard Blythe (2004): when the vestibular pathways mature they form inhibitors; it helps improve postural reactions not affected by balance; it integrates the different sensory systems; and retinal image stability is produced when the vestibular-ocular system matures, resulting in stable eye movements. The vestibular system is also linked via the reticular activating system (RAS) to the limbic system which controls emotions. The RAS sprays the cortex with increased electrical activity making it ready to receive and attend to information so its connection with the limbic system may serve the same purpose.

The staff at DDAT had developed a remedial physical exercise programme that focused on balance, posture and eye control. The exercises included balancing on a wobble board, standing one-legged on a cushion while throwing a bean bag from one hand to the other above eye level and reciting a times table. Before children are started on a five-stage exercise programme they are given both an eye-tracking test and a NASA-style computerised 'sensory organisation test'. In one study, children on this programme made 67 per cent more progress in reading than the national average for all children, which includes children who do not have learning difficulties. This would mean they made about 19 months' progress in one year. We have to ask whether this is enough for a remedial intervention.

A group of 36 Key Stage 2 children were screened, using DEST (Nicolson and Fawcett 1996) before entering the DDAT programme and then again after six months. They were also tested for cerebellar-vestibular function and eye movement before and after the programme. They were then randomly divided into two groups, matched by age and test score. All children received the same educational content at school but the experimental group also used the exercise programme daily at home. The tests showed significant improvement for those children who had been following the exercise treatment, whereas there were no significant changes for the control group. These significant improvements included postural stability, dexterity, phonological skill, naming fluency, verbal fluency, semantic fluency, visual tracking, reading fluency and nonsense passage reading.

The percentage of children on the exercise programme who were identified as being in the 'strong risk' category on the dyslexia screening test reduced from 33 per cent to 11 per cent. The performance of this group on national tests of literacy showed acceleration of progress, allowing them to catch up with their peers. This seems an important finding and we must await further studies to identify who amongst the dyslexic population obtained most benefit and exactly what was the cause of these effects. Can dysorthographics benefit as much and what happens to dyslexics without DCD symptoms? What were the diagnostic differences between the 90 per cent with and the 10 per cent without cerebellar-vestibular difficulties? The fact that there were 10 per cent without such difficulties suggests that the c-v difficulties might not be core problems.

The benefits of the DDAT exercise treatment are said to lead to improvements in the areas of the cognitive skills underlying literacy, the reading process, standardised national literacy attainment, balance, dexterity and eye movement.

In a year-long programme Goddard Blythe (2004) tested subjects' reading and spelling skills on the Draw a Person test plus balance, coordination, maturity of reflexes and verbal processing. Daily exercises were instituted involving finger exercises, and slow motion movements to music involving turning in space and lying on the floor. A metronome beat was used to develop more complex levels of these skills to rhythm. Improvements were found in all the tested areas, especially in drawing and handwriting. This is not surprising as over a year all of the areas would be expected to improve and especially drawing and handwriting as these were particularly targeted in the finger and movement exercises. The latter would also develop conceptions of body image essential to the DAPT.

In DCD the signs are similar (Polatajko *et al.* 1995); however the progress made by children with DCD is small or nil after motor-based training. Humphries *et al.* (1993) used sensory integration and perceptual motor therapy in one-hour sessions but no significant effects were found. In an earlier period Frostig and Horn (1964) produced a visuo-motor test and training procedure for remediation in dyslexia and under controlled conditions it was found by Smith and Marx (1972) that there was no transfer to reading but the subjects' drawing and writing skills did improve. Once again this is not surprising as it was indeed the sensorimotor aspects of these, and not reading, which had really been the target of the training. This of course was a result of the misconception about the underlying subskills of reading and what results in reading difficulty. The key factor was that the training materials and processes did not have ecological validity (Montgomery 1977) with reading. It is this validity concept which we also need to consider when examining each of the dyslexia hypotheses. Three questions arise from it.

- Is the research based upon a fit-for-purpose definition of reading and spelling?
- Is the process of acquisition defined and different from processes more fluent readers use?
- Has the literacy teaching environment been taken into account in the analysis?

The magnocellular deficit hypothesis

The magnocellular deficit hypothesis holds that there is an inability to perceive or distinguish rapidly changing visual stimuli in dyslexia (Lovegrove 1996). There are two parallel pathways involved: the magnocellular (large cells) and the parvocellular (small cells) which transmit information from the retina in the eyes to the visual cortex via the thalamus. The magnocellular system responds to fast moving, low contrast images. The parvocellular system is sensitive to colour and fine spatial detail. It is suggested that each system is stimulated at different times in the reading process and that visual search mechanisms are compromised in dyslexics when a scene is cluttered because the magnocellular system turns on the spotlight or focus needed for reading. These and similar findings do not tell us whether these are cause, correlate or consequence (Bishop 2002).

On autopsy the magnocellular cells of dyslexics have been found to be small. This would affect conduction and their thinner neurons would conduct signals more slowly. It has been inferred that this could cause signals to arrive at the cortex out of sequence. In fact Lehmkule *et al.* (1993) found in their EEG studies that disabled readers' responses showed long time intervals when the stimuli changed rapidly. Robertson (2000: 29) concluded from these studies that there was a temporal order issue in dyslexia. We might also suggest that what is observed at autopsy is the long result of time spent as a dyslexic.

We need to question also whether speed, clutter and temporal order are involved in the initial stages of learning to read; they certainly are not in any simple or direct way involved in learning to write. It is perhaps only in reading development and fluent reading that such systems are more influential, rather than in acquisition processes. For example, the span of apprehension when reading is usually over about three letters (Rozin and Gleitman 1977), a syllable size. This span can be extended and one small eye movement can easily take in a two-syllabled word. As a beginning reader engages in word-by-word reading at first with many pauses, *random eye movements* (Pavlidis 1981) and rapidly oscillating black and white patterns may not play such a significant part.

In fact Rayner (1986) was unable to replicate Pavlidis' original findings. Here we might suggest that by the time dyslexics are conventionally identified, the random eye movements seen are a *result* of their confusion and inability to read adequately, and not a cause.

Other visual-perceptual deficit hypotheses

Scotopic sensitivity syndrome (Irlen and Lass 1989)

This was previously known as the Irlen Syndrome and now as the Mears-Irlen Syndrome in which coloured overlays can cut down visual confusion and help with reading in some dyslexics. It may also be connected to the pathway deficits but it is difficult to see how it causes the dyslexia seen in beginners, although it may well be associated with it in some cases and cause confusion and further learning problems in the later stages. SSS is said to result from the overstimulation of the retinal receptors. The polarised tinted overlays cut down the highly contrastive effects of black print on a white background.

In a controlled research study Francis *et al.* (1992) used Dex frames to hold the tinted strips (not polarised) and the experimental group of poor readers wore them for reading for a whole term. At the end of the period there were no significant gains in comparison with controls. What was significant however was that 20 per cent of the children screened had undetected refractive or muscular/vergence problems and had to be excluded from the study. Teachers questioned before the results were given felt that only one in ten of their poor readers might benefit. It would seem that there are even fewer than this who might benefit.

Saccadic eye movements

These are the tiny eye movements made as the eyes track over text. They jump and focus, jump and focus. It is important that the focus occurs in the rest period of the saccade, and not whilst the eye is moving. Of course it is always possible that there will be a small, possibly tiny number of dyslexics who have a problem with coordination of focus and saccadic movements. Again it should not affect single word reading or spelling and writing.

Fixed reference eye

When we learn to see we develop one eye which is dominant, for looking particularly when reading and writing. This is called the fixed reference eye (FRE). Some individuals are thought to fail to develop FRE and so both sides of the brain try to process the information and this is why (it is inferred) they make reversals errors and have difficulty in acquiring literacy in the competition between the hemispheres over data handling. Occluding vision in the left eye during reading is the strategy developed for establishing FREs. Children who appear to be affected sometimes seek to establish their own FRE by shutting one eye whilst reading, and laying the head on an arm and looking along it when writing.

The diet hypotheses

There is circumstantial evidence of a positive relationship between a generally balanced diet and raised attainment. Breakfast clubs serving a cereal breakfast before school are claimed to have improved concentration in class. Nutritious, cooked school dinners rather than pre-prepared 'fast foods' have also been reported by teachers to have improved children's concentration and behaviour. This suggests a metabolic relationship between attention and inhibition but not dyslexia.

Omega-3 fatty acid (linolenic acid), and omega-6 (linoleic acid) cannot be made in the body and are essential in the diet. They are found in fish oil and some vegetable oils. Richardson et al. (1998) used a small double-blind, placebo-controlled treatment trial of 29 dyslexic children, who all took either the placebo or the fatty acid supplement for three months. Assessments of reading and spelling were carried out both before and after treatment. The dyslexic children who received fatty acids showed greater progress in reading but not spelling. In further testing (Richardson et al. 2001) of 41 special school children aged eight to twelve, supplements were given in a double-blind trial to children who were chosen because of their specific reading difficulties. The placebo was olive oil. 'Stark' differences were reported in children's relaxation levels, attention spans, shyness and emotional outbursts after taking omega-3.

In Middlesbrough and Durham LEAs during 2005, trials with hundreds of children taking a fish oil and primrose oil combination have confirmed marked improvements in hyperactivity, inattention and impulsivity plus significant improvements in short-term auditory memory.

As can be seen, taking fish oil supplements impacts mostly on attention and behavioural issues which may affect reading. The levels of improvement may well be 'significant' but do they enable pupils to catch up to grade level?

Low blood pressure

A group of dyslexic children and a control group of non-dyslexic children were studied by Stein and Taylor (2002). They found that a high percentage of the non-dyslexic children had some history of high blood pressure in their families, but the dyslexic children had a much smaller incidence of any high blood pressure in the family. The dyslexic children themselves had a greater incidence of low blood pressure. A chemical called phospholipid platelet activating factor is thought to be present in higher amounts in dyslexics than in children not 'at risk' of dyslexia. This fatty acid has a vital role in chemical signalling between cells. The study awaits replication and some attempt to show how it may impact upon dyslexia.

Dyslexia and genetic inheritance

Dyslexia appears to run in families and so it has been proposed that there is a genetic basis for it. Gilger *et al.* (1991) estimated that the probability of a dyslexic father having a dyslexic son was 40 per cent. Thus it is not a simple dominant or recessive gene inheritance pattern. Chromosomes 15, 6 and 18 have all been identified as locations for 'dyslexic genes'. These genes are also thought to be in the same region as genes for the auto-immune diseases which have been found to be co-morbid with dyslexia (Duane, 2002).

Subtypes in dyslexia?

A unitary theory or subtypes in dyslexia?

The unitary theory proposes that there is one major underlying deficiency or problem in dyslexia which causes the range of deficits seen, as opposed to there being several causes of dyslexia and a number of distinct subtypes resulting from these. Since the paradigm shift with the publication of Vellutino's (1979) analysis, a unitary theory has held sway, and that is that dyslexia results from a verbal processing difficulty particularly in the phonological area. This has been challenged by a small group led by Stein (Stein and Fowler 1981; Stein 2000) who hold that there are visual perceptual processing difficulties in some dyslexics due to magnocellular dysfunction ad not accounted for by the phonological deficit hypothesis. In addition, Tallal et al. (1980) and Tallal et al. (1994) have accumulated evidence which they suggest shows that dyslexics may have a problem in processing auditory aspects of speech presented at speed, but the causative link has not been established.

In fact before the phonological processing deficit held sway it was common to regard dyslexia as caused by either a visual perceptual and visual memory problem or an auditory perceptual and memory problem, the dual hypothesis (de Hirsch and Jansky 1972; Johnson and Myklebust 1967), or a sequencing problem due to temporal order deficits (Bakker 1972; Birch 1962; Birch and Belmont 1964).

Bakker (1992) has suggested that there are two distinct types of dyslexia mediated by the left and right cerebral hemispheres. The 'L group' appear to read impulsively and are searching for meaning and guessing from minimal cues. The 'R group' engage in laborious bottom-up processing using phonological knowledge they have struggled to acquire and meaning is often lost in the heavy processing work.

In both groups spelling remains poor with whole word knowledge more evident in the former and phonemic spelling in the latter. Whilst Bakker accounts for these differences by the differing facility in using left and right hemisphere processing, we could equally argue this has been as a result of the teaching regime and presumably the personality characteristics of the child.

Lisa at seven years was an 'L type'. She had few or no word attack skills and tried to read quickly and fluently guessing at meaning from whole word knowledge and context. Robert at seven was an 'R type' and tried to sound out all the words as if they were regular within the limited phonics knowledge that he had. He read laboriously word by word and was poor at abstracting meaning from texts. His spelling was phonetic and at the same poor level as his reading.

It is questionable that their difficulties reflect different types of dyslexia. They may reflect the different strategies and teaching regimes to which they have been exposed, or different levels of processing. Perhaps the preferences in processing style reflect a deeper penetration of the difficulties in one or other hemisphere, or it could be that Lisa has more severe problems than Robert and these are reflected in her inability to develop word attack (phonogram knowledge) whereas he has just done this and is stuck in early alphabetic stage.

Boder (1973) was able to classify dyslexic errors on spelling tests as either *dyseidetic* (visual perceptual errors) or *dysphonetic* (problems in phonic representation). The proportion of dysphonetics to dyseidetic dyslexics was roughly 70 to 20 with the rest 'mixed'. However, when the errors she classified as 'good phonetic equivalents' (GFEs) are examined with the dyseidetic errors they do not appear as distinct categories but lie more easily on a developmental continuum showing spelling ranging from lack of alphabetic and phonic knowledge, through to some such knowledge, plus some whole word knowledge, to nearly correct orthography. When examples of such dyslexic spellings are compared with those of spelling-age-matched controls there are no significant differences (see Chapter 5).

Another popular theory arose after the 'word blind' period and is still held by some teachers and researchers today. It seems confirmed by the digit span results of dyslexics who generally show a poorer level. This is then taken as evidence that they have a short-term memory problem affecting reading and spelling and is linked with Baddeley's 1986 working memory deficit hypothesis. However, Vellutino (1979, 1987) showed that when the items were presented visually or auditorily but without it being possible to name them then no deficit could be identified. It was in fact the naming of the digits or verbal processing of items that caused the dyslexic the difficulties and lowered the performance. My research with dyslexics and controls on visual and verbal items spoken or written/drawn showed the same phenomenon

(Montgomery 1997a). It also revealed that the dyslexics' levels on the verbal items were consistent with their reading and spelling ages, not their abilities and age levels. A similar result was found by Koppitz (1977) using her visual aural digit span (VADS) Test. The Wechsler Intelligence Scale for Children (WISC) now has a subset of tests used to assess 'working memory' and this can contribute to the confusion of correlation with causation when poor results are obtained by dyslexics. At the educational level this can lead teachers to engage in extensive memory training games and activities with no transfer to improved literacy skills.

The dyseidetic errors in which letter order might be reversed or muddled in a word, plus digits out of sequence in the digit span test and dyslexics' inability to sequence the alphabet, days of the week or months of the year, seemed to some to give evidence of sequencing deficits in dyslexia. In fact it is the arbitrary nature of the symbols and the names attached to them that create the difficulties for dyslexics *because* they have verbal processing problems. Again, Vellutino was not able to find evidence from research to support the sequencing hypothesis.

Finally, does dyslexia exist?

The question of whether dyslexia exists is one that regularly comes up for debate. The last major period was in the 1970s when it was regarded by some as merely a 'middle-class' disease and the product of having neurotic mothers. The debate has arisen again in the UK with the suggestion by Professor Elliot of Durham University (BBC 2005) that we should 'dispense' with the very term dyslexia as it 'offers little of clinical or educational value'.

This suggestion not unexpectedly caused much debate, with many rejecting it and some (e.g. British Dyslexia Association) arguing that Professor Elliot's view was far too narrow and seemed to be viewing dyslexia just in terms of poor reading skills rather than as a complex disorder which often affects other areas, not just problems with words.

Ultimately, the government rejected Elliott's view that dyslexia does not exist, in the ministerial statement by Lord Adonis:

> Let me state, clearly and categorically, ... that dyslexia is a complex neurological condition and that people with dyslexia do need proper support to develop the reading, writing and comprehension skills essential to succeeding in school, in life and in work.
>
> (Adonis 2005)

In her response to Elliot, Professor Snowling (2005) argued that even if appropriate procedures for the 'identification, assessment and intervention of children at risk of reading problems were put into place in all schools', dyslexia would still not be diminished as it is a brain-based disorder. She added that the above interventions and practices would, however, help to alleviate the difficulties faced by these children. Note the use of 'reading problems' as still synonymous with dyslexia and the view that the difficulties cannot be overcome. 'The only thing they [dyslexics] share in common is the difficulty in achieving reading and writing skills commensurate with their age and ability level and a weakness in phonic skills' (Westwood 2004: 36). I think I nearly agree with Westwood except that not all dyslexics have reading problems!

Summary and conclusions

In this chapter the fundamental educational problems in dyslexia are identified as both reading and spelling difficulties in the school-age child. It is these which deny pupils access to the wider curriculum and cause many to underachieve by hampering compositional skills. Separate problems with handwriting coordination can exacerbate these literacy difficulties or may appear on their own without dyslexia and hamper spelling development and composition. It is spelling difficulty which has proved the most resistant to remediation and which it is argued here is the core difficulty in dyslexia.

Dyslexic difficulties are then discussed in relation to psychological processes and biological factors. Key current psychological theories of causation are examined, especially verbal processing problems leading to phonological difficulties which appear to be present in the majority of cases. However, the support for the phonological dysfunction hypothesis is of limited value for it still remains to be specified how the phonological skills affect the acquisition of alphabetic skills. In this chapter the key connection suggested is an articulation awareness difficulty arising from an intersensory integration deficit at the neurological level.

Working memory deficits, phonological discrimination (hearing the sounds in words), sound order and sequencing deficits are challenged as causes of dyslexia and it is suggested they may be the result of the failure to learn to read and spell. The impact of DCD in dyslexia is discussed as a co-morbid condition rather than as part of the dyslexia.

In the neurological sphere the primary reflex, cerebellar-vestibular dysfunction and the magnocellular hypothesis are discussed and links are made as far as possible between the three levels – educational, psychological and neurological/biological.

The recent controversy on whether dyslexia exists or not is outlined, as well as other issues such as the possible existence or otherwise of subtypes in dyslexia.

Finally it is suggested that many of the difficulties in dyslexia could be overcome during early in-school intervention by nursery and reception teachers if they were suitably trained and this would be more cost effective than the current huge bureaucracy devised to remediate these failures.

In Chapter 4 intervention methods will be examined for their capacity to remediate dyslexia and consideration will be given to the notion of effectiveness. As a preface to Part II on intervention methods some current identification and assessment techniques will be outlined.

Part II

Intervention techniques

Assessment and identification instruments

Identification and assessment of literacy difficulties

Identification and assessment instruments are outlined as a preface to examining intervention programmes. There are of course a number of options available and some for the future. For example, should the identification involve neurological/biological, psychological or educational assessments? As yet the neurological indicators are controversial, such as 'random eye movements', 'fixed reference eye' and 'soft neurological signs', and then expensive, involving scanners and tomography. At the psychological level, IQ and cognitive abilities testing may be included as well as phonological batteries and profiles, and tests of working memory, perception and sequential ordering assumed to underpin literacy skills.

At the educational level we are on firmer ground. As dyslexia is defined as difficulties with reading and spelling we must give a reading *and* a spelling test. Associated writing difficulties would warrant giving writing, spelling and compositional tests; these will measure attainment.

Early identification

In reception age children, classroom observation of performance on writing, spelling, reading and movement tasks as already described in Chapters 1 and 2 are more appropriate than tests. Once a concern is raised in the general classroom observation then diagnostic investigation can take place. This should include collecting samples of writing for analysis and giving a test of randomly presented letters to find which sounds and names of the alphabet are known, if any. For the reading assessment an informal hearing reading inventory (IHRI) is most useful. See Appendix for a photocopiable example IHRI (p.180).

Early screening

After reception the teacher will need to screen all the pupils to look at the pattern of their achievements using easily and quickly administered group tests. This screening should include a reading test (word recognition and prose reading) to obtain comparative accuracy, speed and comprehension data; a spelling test; and a sample of story writing. If concerns are raised about individual children then a more detailed analysis can be undertaken.

Individual diagnosis

At this stage a test of ability is needed to gain an estimate of the assumed level of competence to be expected in literacy learning. If there is a significant discrepancy, e.g. between higher ability and lower attainment in literacy skills, then concerns are in order. In the average learner reading should be expected to run a few months ahead of ability and spelling be at about the age level. In more able pupils poor literacy performance may go unnoticed if it is at the same level as that of age when it should be closer to the ability level. Slower learners may have good mechanical literacy skills but fall behind in their comprehension and quality of composition. They may also be dyslexic with literacy skills well below the expected level for their ability.

At this stage knowledge of the names and sounds of letters of the alphabet should be checked as well as common blends and digraphs. This according to a wide range of research is the best early predictor of later literacy achievement.

There are many teacher administered and standardised ability tests available from the National Foundation for Educational Research (NFER) and other test corporations such as Harcourt Assessment and publishers such as Learning Development Aids (LDA). These include tests of verbal reasoning, cognitive abilities tests (Thorndike *et al.* 1986), picture vocabulary tests, and Raven's progressive matrice (Raven 1985). Raven's tests non-verbal abilities and is particularly useful with potential dyslexics and pupils with limited or no grasp of English.

Dyslexia tests

The Aston Index (Newton and Thomson 1976)

This is a compilation of tests at the educational and psychological levels. At the educational level it includes: Schonell word reading test; Schonell spelling test; a letter naming test or phoneme–grapheme correspondence; free writing; and graphomotor test. At the psychological level it includes: visual sequential memory test (symbolic); visual sequential memory (pictorial); auditory sequential memory; sound blending; sound discrimination; sequencing of days and months.

Other tests included the Goodenough Draw a Person test, copying designs (these assess drawing and cognitive ability), and a vocabulary test (to give an indication of verbal ability).

Also recorded are laterality and some family history.

The Bangor Dyslexia Test (Miles and Miles 1992)

The test items consist of: left–right body parts; polysyllables; subtraction; tables – three sets, usually the six, seven and eight times tables; months of the year forward; months reversed; digits forward; digits reversed; b–d confusion; familial incidence.

The test would have to be accompanied by reading, spelling and IQ data. Older dyslexics often do not have problems which can be identified on reading and spelling tests and so the Bangor indicants are often used to reveal residual problems.

Phonological Assessment Battery (PhAB) (Frederickson et al. 1997)

This test is made up from eight subtests and two supplementaries. These are:

*   alliteration (segment initial sound inc. consonant digraph);
*   rhyme – identify same-end segments of words 'rime' e.g. -ed as in bed, fed and peg;
*   spoonerisms (Part 1 – 'cat' with a 'f' gives? 'fat') (Part 2 – 'King John' gives 'Jing Kong');
*   non-word reading;
*   naming speed (pictures);
*   naming speed (digits);
*   fluency (alliteration) e.g. generate /k-/ words cat, cap, can, etc.;
*   fluency (rhyme) e.g. generate -/at/ words bat, sat, cat, etc.

*   Supplementary test (alliteration with pictures)
*   Non-phonological test (fluency test semantic))

From these items a profile of the pupil's performance is obtained and the number of highlighted PhAB scores is identified. We have to think what the results might show, for example LW at 11.3 years (reading age 8.0 years; spelling age 7.7 years) shows weaknesses in naming speed with pictures and digits, and in the fluency in alliteration test. As his reading and spelling ages show, he has cracked the alphabetic code and has achieved some basic literacy skills but are 'phonological abilities' just another word for spelling abilities except for the naming test?

Phonological assessment batteries have been designed to assess assumed phonological processing subskills. At the end of such a test which may take 40 minutes to administer we may know little more than if we gave the pupil a reading and spelling test, followed by some attempt at open-ended writing.

Cognitive Profiling System (CoPS) (Singleton 1996)

This is a computerised administered test and eight components contribute to the profile as follows.

*   Rabbits: measures visual sequential memory (using temporal and spatial position)
*   Zoid's friends: measures visual sequential memory (using temporal position and colour)
*   Toybox: measures visual associative memory using shape-colour or for older pupils shape-pattern association
*   Letters: measures visual sequential memory based on symbol sequence
*   Letter names: measures visual-verbal associative memory (sound-symbol correspondence)
*   Races: measures auditory/verbal sequential memory (using animal names)
*   Rhymes: measures phonological awareness using detection of rhyme and for older pupils alliteration
*   Wock: measures phonological discrimination

(Clown is used to identify pupils with poor colour discrimination and is not included in the profile.)

Nathan in Chapter 4 showed low scores on Rabbits and Rhymes; was average on Letters; above average on Wock; and good on Friends, Toybox and Races. On Letter names his score was between Risk and Concern. Thus he could discriminate the sounds but had problems in letter naming and any items which might include verbal processing even where the task appeared to be visual. Again a reading and spelling test could have told us this and we would also have learnt about the writing capabilities. There are an increasing number of computerised tests becoming available on the Web but they all rest on similar principles.

The Dyslexia Early Screening Test (DEST) (Nicolson and Fawcett 1996)

The test is one of a series including older children and adults by the same authors. DEST is designed to identify dyslexia in children aged 4.6 to 6.5 years.

The DEST consist of ten subtests which give a profile of performance and enable 'at risk' pupils to be identified. The subtests are: rapid naming; bead threading; phonological discrimination; postural stability; rhyme detection/first letter sound; forwards digit span; digit naming; letter naming; sound order; shape copying.

This test aims at identification of dyslexia before and as literacy begins to develop or fails to do so. The items will identify potential literacy difficulties with the naming tests including digit span and phonological discrimination and segmentation and rhyme. The copying, bead threading and postural stability will pick up the potential for DCD.

Informal dyslexia identification

Teachers are able to diagnose potential dyslexia by asking the reception class pupil to write a story as the five-year-olds did in Chapter 1 and as those at risk who could not in Chapter 3. Concerns identified can be followed up with further diagnostic testing.

Individual IQ tests administered by psychologists

The test used by psychologists worldwide is the individually administered IQ test WISC-III and now WISC-IV. For a long time WISC was used in the diagnosis of dyslexia without reading and spelling tests; now they have their own literacy tests (WORD – Wechsler Objective Reading Dimensions). The principle behind the use of any of these tests is first to find a discrepancy between scores, IQ and reading (including spelling), then between the IQ types of test – verbal items (VQ), and performance items (PQ). To these have been added another subset – working memory (WM). However, we need to remember that digit span, arithmetic, coding and much sequencing are all dependent on naming and phonological coding which poor literacy skills hamper.

VQ and PQ scores in the majority of normal people are expected to lie within a few points of each other but even discrepancies of 8–10 points lie within the error region of the tests' own construction. A discrepancy of 11 or more points e.g. in the verbal scale shows that the pupil has significantly greater difficulties in this area, but is that pupil likely to be dyslexic? A sample of 132 dyslexics in my research showed 12 per cent had significant performance scale deficits, and 26 per cent had significant verbal scale deficits; the rest did not have either. All of them had severe reading and spelling difficulties of well over two years' deficit. The spelling ages of those with VQ deficits were 7 points higher on average than those with PQ deficits. Those with the performance deficits were likely to have more organisational difficulties perhaps associated with DCD and thereby had less spelling practice.

In the UK many psychologists use the British Ability Scales (Elliot 1996) in place of WISC which are individually administered and also require specialist interpretation by trained personnel.

At the end of hours of testing and drawing up of a detailed and expensive psychological profile all we learn is that the pupil is not reading and writing as well as he or she should, given the level of ability which is usually what s/he was referred for in the first place. More adequate teacher training could ensure that teachers were qualified to assess young children's literacy development and schools could be funded to ensure there is time for it to be done. Then it remains to select an appropriate form of intervention.

Intellectual or cognitive skills?

Intellectual skills are about knowing 'that' and knowing 'how'. They include converting printed words into meaning, fractions into decimals, knowing about classes, groups and categories, laws of mechanics and genetics, forming sentences and pictures. They enable us to deal with the world 'out there'. Mostly these are taught in schools within subjects and also make up items on IQ tests.

Cognitive skills are internally organised capabilities which we make use of in guiding our attention, learning, thinking and remembering. They are executive control processes which activate and direct other learning processes. We use them when we think about our learning, plan a course of action and evaluate learning outcomes. These are seldom taught in schools or given value there. They form the basis of wisdom and are seldom tested except in real life situations.

The reasons for using these distinctions first suggested by Gagne (1973) is to indicate that IQ is not only about capacity but also the extent to which skills and knowledge have been taught or absorbed from the contact with the environment, i.e. products of memory. Cognitive skills are different from this and calling IQ and phonological tests 'cognitive' could be a misinterpretation.

Chapter 4

Overcoming dyslexia
Dyslexia remedial programmes

Introduction

A remedial programme must fulfil a number of criteria according to the expert group of the British Dyslexia Association (BDA) established to review the provision and the available teaching programmes which had proved successful with dyslexics. The criteria were that programmes should be *phonic, structural, cumulative, thorough* and *multisensory.*

> On this theoretical basis are built sympathetic, stimulating and enjoyable lessons, employing all possible aids such as card, phonic work books, suitably graded readers, etc. to ensure that the teaching results in solid progress as well as entertainment. Such methods have in fact been shown to be effective.
> (BDA Expert Group minutes 1981)

After 25 years this advice has not substantially changed and dyslexia teaching programmes do follow these guidelines. However, what we find is that some programmes are more effective than others and this suggests that either the guidelines fall short or the methods by which they are implemented are incomplete.

When the programmes used or designed by this expert group are examined they can be seen to be structured, cumulative, sequential, *multisensory* and thorough phonics programmes, but most are much more than this. They all introduce *alphabet* training. At an appropriate stage they teach the sequence of the alphabet, alphabet skills and the upper and lower case letters, names and sounds. They teach both analytic and synthetic *phonics* and the letter symbols or graphemes which are associated with the sound structure of words in a structured and cumulative order. They teach about *syllables,* their structure and the rules which apply to them in relation to their structures and their affixes. Within this integrated programme they also introduce some knowledge of *linguistics,* the rules and structures, and the morphemics, the meanings and origins which change the basic patterns. Hence the abbreviated form of referring to these programmes and their derivatives is APSL (*alphabetic – phonic – syllabic – linguistic*) programmes. The BDA guidelines are to some extent misleading in that they only refer to phonics and this may well have caused some remediators to construct programmes based only on phonics. These have been shown to be necessary but not sufficient for teaching dyslexics especially if the problems arise at two different levels – alphabetic and orthographic, as Frith (1985) has suggested.

The multisensory APSL approach is based upon the original design of Gillingham *et al.* (1940) and was introduced into this country from the United States by Sally Childs in 1963. As a result Kathleen Hickey, Frula Shear and Beve Hornsby went to America on a study visit to the Scottish Rites Hospital to learn the details of the programme and produced Anglicised versions of it (Hickey Language Programme/DILP and Alpha to Omega) which are still widely used.

The title 'remedial' suggests that an intervention will be successful and bring the reading and spelling back up to grade level, consistent with age and/or ability, i.e. it is a remedy. Analysis of case histories of dyslexics as a background to this book showed that they had not been brought up to grade level by the end of Key Stage 2. They had been offered extra help with reading in the infant school, 'remedial' support in class, and in withdrawal groups usually for phonics and reading at the School Action stage. At the School Action Plus stage (see Code of Practice, DfEE 2001b) specialist remedial tuition was given, frequently on a one-to-one basis by a trained dyslexia teacher. Despite something like four years or more of regular intervention based on a series of individual education plans (IEPs) the reading and spelling scores of most dyslexics remained more than two years below their grade level. When they entered secondary schools they tended to slip further and further behind, particularly in spelling, so that some 15-year-olds finished up with the spelling abilities of six-year-olds.

The impact of the NLS does not appear to have changed this situation. In fact in the Year 7 cohort analyses of spelling in Chapter 1 the 'dyslexia' figures seem to have risen and the numbers of pupils with some form of spelling difficulties hover around 30 per cent after a full seven years of the NLS. It is not therefore surprising that employers and now universities are complaining about literacy levels of new entrants.

The methods offered by schools prior to the NLS followed a seemingly logical pattern from extra help of the same kind at first; then a different reading scheme usually emphasising phonics, remedial teaching of sounds for blending and use in reading and spelling in withdrawal groups or on an individual basis; and finally the use of a scheme such as Spelling Made Easy (Brand 1998) or Alpha to Omega (Hornsby and Shear 1995). The NLS with its Literacy Hour was expected to obviate the need for these options. Even though phonics has been put into all primary school programmes it has not cleared up the problems. Instead we appear to have an even longer tail of literacy underachievement.

How is this failure to be explained? Just as the earlier interventions had not appeared to make any significant difference, a result which Tansley and Pankhurst (1981), Ysseldyke (1987) and Pumfrey and Reason (1991) in their surveys of remedial teaching had reported, now we have a similar situation with the NLS in 2006. Thus the formal structure has been scrapped but teachers must teach phonics first, fast and alone (Rose 2005). Will it too fail our dyslexics?

Certainly if nothing is done to support those who cannot learn fast and furious it will fail them just as Ashman (1995) found when nothing was done. Of 200 students in Grade 1 who were tested in 1989, half of them had learning difficulties. Of the 100 with learning difficulties in Grade 1, only four to six could be considered not to have them by Grade 7. The teachers were committed and enthusiastic but not proficient in the necessary remedial techniques which would target the deficits. It was concluded that the research on effective programmes was not transferring to the classroom.

We have the situation where doing nothing does not allow the literacy problems to clear up by themselves, doing something called 'remedial' does not always work, and if it does work it may not continue to do so.

Possible reasons for failure to remediate

Many teachers in the past who were giving learning support may have had no additional training in the dyslexia field other than the occasional in-service training day or short course. It is only over the past two decades that the BDA and the RSA (now OCR) have certified an increasing number of approved courses of dyslexia training which colleges and 'dyslexia centres' run. A few institutions of higher education run and validate their own courses. There are also other specialist centres running certificated programmes such as Hornsby and Helen Arkell.

Training courses however do not all teach quite the same principles and practices and there has been a dearth of research funding to evaluate their different outcomes. However, one factor seems to be to be important. In the mid 1970s soon after the BDA was established it tried to get a training curriculum based on Hickey's programme validated by the CNAA (Council for National Academic Awards) at certificate level. The CNAA refused to validate this programme unless it was revised to provide an eclectic perspective on remedial tuition in dyslexia; the highly specific model presented was said not to be 'academically sound'. The people CNAA recruited to evaluate the dyslexia programme were of course expert teachers in reading teaching in higher education and the LEAs. They were shocked by the specificity of the programmes on offer such as in the Hickey version of Gillingham and Stillman (1956). They disliked the overlearning techniques, the cursive writing, the alphabetics, the phonics at the outset, the lack of a reading scheme, the lack of a whole language and meaning approach, the dictations and the lack of creativity. Approval was withheld unless an eclectic training was offered on lines more consistent with current 'good practice' for the teaching of reading.

Whilst the BDA opted to move with the flow the Dyslexia Institute established by Kathleen Hickey, then at Staines, refused to do so. It offered its own certification and still maintains its programmes closely based upon Hickey's original training course. Beve Hornsby likewise opened up her own teaching centre in Wandsworth and courses run there are based on her programme and certification. My distance learning MA programmes (MA SEN and MA SpLD) teach a Hickey variant called TRTS (*Teaching Reading Through spelling*), developed by Cowdery *et al.* (1994) who trained with Hickey.

As many teachers come from the BDA/OCR programmes to my MAs I have had the opportunity to review their training in some detail. Often an attitude has been developed against APSL programmes because they are repetitive and prescriptive. Teachers are encouraged towards individualised selection of methods and materials. As they are in training they often lack the experience and knowledge to do this and need to learn to follow a structured programme first designed by experts who have made all the mistakes over time and learned from them. Once they gain this experience they can begin to know how to individualise a programme. They also learn how slow the first stages need to be and how to let the student direct the pace.

The following is a typical quote from such a teacher:

When I knew I finally had to use an APSL programme I was dreading it. They have a reputation for being boring and highly prescriptive. I chose to work with a student who had been on our remedial programmes for over a year and had made no discernible progress. This would be a real test of the method.

(The APSL method worked – within a few sessions real progress had been made and they were both overjoyed.)

Over time, and since the identification of phonological difficulties in dyslexia permeated education in the 1990s, all the dyslexia teaching programmes have become more similar and more like the Gillingham and Stillman (1956) original.

A second and related reason for failure was identified by Snowling (2000) in a critical evaluation of a range of researches on success in intervention and remediation. She found that it was only those training methods which made explicit the link between the phoneme and grapheme in the phonological training that were successful and retained the student gains over time.

A further important consideration is whether the remediation deals directly with the skills of reading, spelling and writing at the educational level or whether they target the subskills underpinning them, such as phonological skills and processes. The issue that then becomes crucial is 'ecological validity' in the subskills training. The training must be a valid subset of the targets towards which it is directed. Often prima facie evidence and current theory suggest there is ecological validity but in the 1950s there was a decade of research and training in oculomotor control in dyslexia which failed (Goldberg and Schiffman 1972). There then followed a decade or more of visual perceptual subskills testing and training but these also failed to give transfer to reading (Smith and Marx 1972). Now we have the era of phonological testing and training and I am concerned that this too might fail. We know that there is some transfer with phonological skills training (Wilson and Frederickson 1995), but need to question whether it is as much as could be achieved by more direct methods which address the skills deficits themselves at the educational level. Is there a mystique attached to testing, psychological processes and cognitive profiles which is not wholly justified? Because many of the skills approaches have failed dyslexics we seek other methods when perhaps we should analyse why there are failures. Case work can be very revealing in this respect and learners know when something is successful and remember it rather than just recalling that nice person who played the games.

What constitutes effective remedial tuition?

Effective remedial tuition may have several parameters. For example, a child who is not reading at six years begins to learn and this may be regarded as a success. Another may be able to read and write a little at age eight years and after a year has made six months' progress in reading and spelling to the 6.5 year level. In the first case the news is good but by seven years he or she may still only have a reading and spelling age approaching six years and now is like case two. For case two the news is bad. He or she has only made six months' progress in a year when progress of at least one year was needed so as not to fall further behind. In fact the progress needed was 18 months and a further 18 months in the next year in order to catch up to grade level in infant school. Later when assessing the effectiveness of a programme we need to see at least *two years' progress in each year* after the infant school years. It can then be concluded and a top-up term of spelling support be given at a later stage if necessary.

Too often remedial success is measured in months' progress, not in months' progress after the developmental age has been deducted. On average after two years' remediation of two sessions per week the dyslexic should have been brought up to grade level by an effective programme. If this is not achieved, then something is wrong with the programme: it may not be being taught effectively, or it is not a suitable dyslexia remedial programme. In addition the positive effects must be seen to *transfer* to the rest of the curriculum work, not just occur in the remedial sessions and they must persist over time. If this does not happen then the programme, teacher or policy needs to be changed.

Brooks (1999) and Brooks *et al.* (1998) recommended that as reading ages are not particularly good as measures of gain, ratio gains are better. Ratio gains are calculated by dividing the average gain made by the children by the number of months over which the gains were made. Brooks argued however that effect size is the best measure. Effect size is calculated by deducting the average gain made by the control group from the average gain made by the experimental group and dividing the result by the standard deviation. This of course only applies where there are control groups and subjects are randomly assigned to treatments. For transparency months' progress per year will be reported here.

Another criterion to be established is that remedial provision is of necessity a compacted programme of upskilling and it is not always suitable in the remedial withdrawal format for slower learners with dyslexia. Usually an IQ below 90 suggests that a developmental remedial programme is needed. This is one which is built into the full daily curriculum in school so that there are extensive opportunities for reinforcement and practice over the primary period. This type of provision is also necessary for children who have *complex specific learning difficulties* and often only specialist schools can provide this.

In addition because a remedial programme is a compacted 'catch up' programme it is not feasible to run it during another lesson as some people have tried to do. These criteria are not plucked from the air. Experience with the TRTS team and observing Miss Hickey and other expert trainers plus the review of research has suggested them.

Table 4.1 Results of two years' remedial intervention in 10,000 cases

Learning disability diagnosed in grades	Success rate after two years
Grade 2 (7 years)	82%
Grade 3 (8 years)	46%
Grade 4 (9 years)	42%
Grade 5 (10 years)	15%
Grade 6 (11 years)	8%
Grade 7 (12 years)	10%
Grade 8 (13 years)	11%
Grade 9 (14 years)	6%

Source: Goldberg and Schiffman 1972: 32

The data in Table 4.1 were based upon a follow-up study two years later of 10,000 cases of dyslexia by Schiffman. The initial diagnosis of dyslexia included a two year or more decrement in reading and spelling skills in relation to chronological age. It can be seen that even though this is USA data and some decades ago, it shows the urgency of identifying and intervening in dyslexia as early as possible to get the best effects.

The peak period for statementing and referral of pupils for specialist help prior to the Code of Practice (DfE 1994) in an LEA which did recognise dyslexia was between 10 and 11 years of age (Montgomery 1997a). The girls were found to be referred on average 11 months later than boys and their problems tended to be more severe. There were well over 400 dyslexic pupil records examined and the ratio of boys to girls was five to one. What we see here is a gender bias in referral processes and perhaps a difference in response overall between boys and girls to their difficulties, with boys tending to 'act out' their problems more and girls perhaps developing more compensatory strategies and being prepared to sit quietly at work and rote learn and copy write for longer.

It was expected that the Code of Practice and its revision (DfEE 2001b) would have improved this situation but this was not the case. Instead what happened was that the delays in diagnosis and implementation of specialist tuition were institutionalised. Instead of identifying potential dyslexics in the first month in reception and taking preventative steps children were allowed to fail and then have an IEP. They would then develop the classic dyslexic profile and move to School Action. This provision would invariably fail and after a year or more they would be put on School Action Plus and if they were lucky would finally gain the services of a specialist four years too late. By this stage they are three- and four-time failures and have a lot of 'baggage' and a lot to 'unlearn'. If only this was possible!

Some more recent research findings

Although the ratio of dyslexic boys to girls nationally is said to be four to one based on the Isle of Wight survey by Rutter *et al.* (1970) the cohort studies of Year 7s suggest it may be closer to 1.5 to one, or two to one for underachievement found for boys in literacy (Rutter *et al.* 2004).

Although it is now thought possible to identify the potential for dyslexia in preschool the indicants become much clearer in reception class and the need for preventative measures becomes urgent. Torgeson (1995) for example found that 98 per cent of phonological based reading disabilities can be accurately identified in kindergarten. He said that these were the children who at second grade would have been in the bottom set if nothing had been done for them and whose reading problems at eight years would have become refractory to treatment. He investigated the relative effectiveness of three different forms of intervention with the kindergarteners: *alphabetic phonics* using a synthetic phonics method; *Recipe for Reading*, an onset and rime method; and *Edmark*, a whole word method. He found that there was a change in phonological processing abilities in all the groups but there was a significantly higher performance overall from the onset and rime method. He recommended that instead of testing all kindergarten children the curriculum should be changed to incorporate this form of teaching.

It has to be noted that Torgeson's research was focused on reading not spelling. Thus a method using onset and rime (c-at; l-ook) tuition would favour reading whereas synthetic phonics favours spelling (Watson and Johnson 1998). However, teaching the segmentation of initial sounds in onsets could be the most important prerequisite skill for both reading and spelling in kindergarten and may well give the best results in developing phonological skills at this stage. The strategy matches what can be observed in reception class beginning readers and spellers as they mouth words for spelling and use initial sounds to decode words in context in reading. Thus, as Torgeson found, all the groups developed some phonological skills. At the next stage it may be that synthetic phonics is the most appropriate strategy once the 'alphabetic code' (Montgomery 1977) has been cracked. This fits with Frith's (1985) model in which reading is the pacemaker at certain stages. However, for dyslexics the synthetic phonic method would appear to be essential from the outset.

There was a failure in one-third of Bryant and Bradley's (1985) subjects to appreciate rhyme. Later at seven, they were failing in reading. Again we see the emphasis on reading only and the importance of rime and rhyme for reading.

James at eight years six months (no reading or spelling score at eight years), just started on TRTS

James at nine years ten months writing from dictation, now with a reading age and a spelling age of eight years

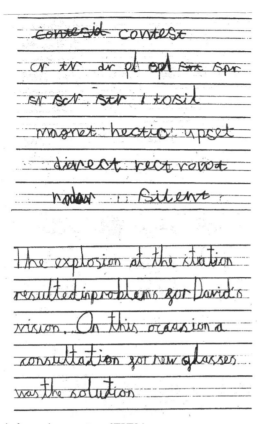

Edward before and after a short series of TRTS lessons

Figure 4.1 Examples of the writing of two dyslexics before and after APSL intervention (half size)

In dyslexics in general there is a failure to show alphabet knowledge in emergent writing and a failure to demonstrate phoneme awareness in reading and phoneme segmentation skills in spelling (Liberman 1973; Golinkoff 1978; Vellutino 1979, 1987; Montgomery 1997a). This failure is despite a home background in which books are read to them and despite direct teaching of initial sounds and phonics.

> [I]t has become customary to delay the institution of corrective programmes until third grade or later when the dyslexic will have segregated himself from the 'late bloomer'. This undoubtedly effects an economy from the standpoint of the administrator ... but this economy is accomplished at a heavy cost to the dyslexic child. For by the time the remedial programme is offered to him, he has had several years of failure, with consequent development of aversion to reading and related activities as well as of emotional problems related to feelings of inadequacy.
>
> (Eisenberg 1962: 4–5)

Nearly 50 years later we are still in the same position. Is it too much to expect that this time round dyslexics can expect to get a fair deal in the new millennium?

Table 4.2 Outcomes from different effective programmes

APSL dyslexia programmes: progress in one year			Non-APSL programmes: progress in one year		
	Reading progress	Spelling progress	Reading progress	Spelling progress	Researcher
A to O	1.93	1.95	0.53	0.32	Hornsby and
N = 107			N = ?		Farrar (1990)
TRTS	2.45	2.01	1.06	0.16	Montgomery (1997a)
N = 38			N = 15 (Eclectic mix by teacher)		
(H and A to O)	1.21	0.96	0.69	0.65	Ridehalgh (1999)
N = 50			N = 50 (SME)		
TRTS	3.31	1.85	2.2	1.14	Webb (2000)
N = 12			N = 12 (SME/TRTS)		

In Table 4.2 are some outcome results to show the relative effects of particular programmes.

The crucial factor in effective early years teaching and in remediation of dyslexics' difficulties as Snowling (2000) has pointed out is that the relationship between
phoneme and grapheme must be made explicit. The first lessons of the Hickey and
TRTS APSL programmes do this very carefully and specifically. This enables the
breakthrough so that dyslexics acquire the alphabetic principle – they 'crack the
code'. It is this aspect that teachers find tedious but the learner must not be rushed.
It is a laborious multisensory training function to educate new areas of the brain – in
the angular gyrus? – to take over or reconnect the dysfunctional areas.

Ridehalgh (1999) examined the results from teachers who had undertaken
dyslexia training courses for a number of factors such as length of remediation, frequency of sessions and size of tutorial groups in dyslexic subjects taught by three
different schemes: Alpha to Omega, Dyslexia Institute Language Programme
(DILP/Hickey), and Spelling Made Easy (SME). She found that when all the factors
were held constant the only programme in which the dyslexics gained significantly
in skills above their increasing age was Alpha to Omega. However, in a follow-up
Ridehalgh found that the users of the Hickey programme in her sample had found it
more convenient to leave out the spelling pack work and the dictations! The data
also showed that in paired tuition the dyslexics made greater gains than when working alone with the teacher.

It could be argued that one-on-one is too 'in your face' and too intensive for a
dyslexic who needs consolidation of thinking and processing time. The teacher
often talks too much and pressurises the pupil too much to permit this time.
Transcripts and evaluation of one-on-one teaching have illustrated these problems
in our MA programme. Once a teacher is experienced, two matched pupils can get
over some of these problems and this successfully operated in the teaching sessions
with the TRTS team.

Webb (2000) on the other hand was doing the research and the teaching herself.
When questioned about the exceptional SME results she said that as she was

teaching the two groups she could see the shortcomings in the SME programme as the pupils failed to make the same progress and felt obliged on ethical grounds to supplement SME with elements of the multisensory articulatory phonics of TRTS so that the children made progress. The lack of very good progress in spelling with TRTS she put down to having to curtail the spelling pack work and omit the dictations because the lesson lengths were not long enough in the school timetable which she had to follow.

As can be seen, cutting the spelling work and the dictation fitted with the prevailing orthodoxy about reading, reading, reading. It also makes a difference if the time for the tutorial lesson is squeezed, as the spelling and dictations come at the end of the sessions and can too easily be left out.

In comparison, the group of 15 pupils aged eight to nine years followed by Montgomery (1997a), diagnosed as dyslexic by a school, were given individual teaching by the SEN coordinator (SENCo) mainly based upon phonics worksheets and reading miscues rather than a specific programme. After six months of one session per week and one hour of in-class support they showed a mean gain of 0.53 months in reading, they kept pace with age but did not catch up. Within-group differences cancelled each other out, for example seven subjects improved their reading over the six month period by a mean of 8.43 months, while eight subjects' scores decreased by 7.4 months in the same period. One subject's reading age was now above age level by one year and three months. The rest remained below chronological age by a mean of 2.1 years. In spelling, five subjects gained 8.4 months and eight subjects regressed by 3.9 months. Total progress made by the group was 0.08 months and they were still 1.7 years behind in spelling. Those who had not made progress over increasing chronological age by a ratio in the order of two to one would be unlikely ever to catch up under the teaching regime offered.

In a follow-up study of dyslexics on Alpha to Omega, Hornsby and Farrar (1990) in Table 4.2 concluded that 91 out of the 107 dyslexics had more than kept up with the age clock during the remediation period. In fact the group progress was close to two years per year and it is this kind of progress somewhere near a ratio of two to one that is needed to rehabilitate dyslexics. However, simply adopting a programme and following it does not guarantee success. The skill and experience of the tutor also appears to be an important factor in matching method to need, and knowing when to go slowly and when to speed up, taking the lead from the learner.

Thomson (1989) and Thomson and Watkins (1993) also found evidence for the success of the APSL approach. They showed that progress in reading and spelling can be boosted to compensate for increased delay which occurs as dyslexics grow older but that spelling is more resistant than reading to remediation. Thomson (1989) found that there appeared to be an alphabetic barrier in the reading and spelling of regular words at around the eight year reading age level which provided a platform for 'take off' for written language learning.

He showed that the problems of irregular words were more difficult to remediate. He went on to state that one specific technique, that of syllable analysis using the categorising of syllables based on vowel sounds, can be of considerable help in the spelling of two- and three-syllabled regular words and seemed to circumvent some of the dyslexic's problems in phonemic awareness and phoneme segmentation.

Some case study research findings

Batya was 9.4 years old, reading a year below this level and with a Schonell spelling age of 7.7 years. Her IQ was in the average range but with a marked discrepancy (VQ 104, PQ 80 and full scale 92), and she had organisational difficulties. She read hesitantly from her reading book *The Mum Hunt* by Gwyneth Rees. She was able to name the letters of the alphabet but knew only six sounds. From her free writing it was clear she had little phonic knowledge to help her read or spell although she could spell some CVC words. During interview she mispronounced words and confirmed she did need help with her spelling and cursive writing. The teacher decided to use the Hickey programme with her over a period of seven weeks and then the SENCo would take over the work. Batya participated in nine lessons.

Reading was not included in the sessions although at the end of the intervention she had been given the first seven phonemes *i t p n s a* and *d* and the reading cards for those letters. She was able to progress in the alphabet work after the initial sound with several letters at a time. When working with the spelling cards she did not like the tracing part and wanted to rush ahead to the writing with her eyes closed. In the first two sessions working with *i* and *t* it needed many different ways to get her to listen to the initial sound. It seemed as if the sound really was locked away to her. When working on *t* it took a long time to get her to understand she should not say the intrusive 'scwha' sound with it because it would make her misspell the word. It also took a long time to get her to feel the consonant sound in her mouth. Helene (2004) reports:

> It seemed that having spent time at the beginning to make the connection between sound and symbol this finally clicked in her brain and all of a sudden it was easy. When introducing the other letters we chose the keyword, she drew the picture and just said the sound straight away.
>
> (p. 17)

When introduced to the other letters she also stopped using the 'schwa' sound. Whilst Batya's class teacher had not noticed any changes in her spelling she had been surprised by a big change in her attitude to reading. She was no longer nervous when reading aloud, tried to sound difficult words and was usually successful. She now also followed the meaning of the text.

The SENCo did the post-intervention testing and was also surprised because now instead of making wild guesses at words Batya had some word attack skills. The post-intervention results showed some progress although different tests had to be used because of the short interval between tests. Her age equivalent scores were 8.3 years for reading, 7.3 for comprehension, and 8.0 for spelling (Wechsler Objective Reading Dimensions, WORD 2006). More important however is the progress not picked up by the tests which suggests she will now be able to move forward, having cracked the code at last. If only this help had been there for her at six. The initial difficulties shown with 'i' and 't' are typical and it was crucial that nothing else was introduced until she had mastered them for the reasons already outlined.

Some key dyslexia programmes used in the UK

The Hickey Language Course (Hickey 1977; Augur and Briggs 1991; Combley 2000) and Dyslexia Institute Language Programme (DILP)

Kathleen Hickey began her interest in the area when she found a way to teach a group of young cerebral palsied children, who had previously been thought to be ineducable, to read and write. Later she became head of the Clayhill Centre for remedial education in Epsom. She was helped in her work by Jean Augur who ran the local authority remedial centre and who later became director of the BDA. Of all the groups who most interested 'Miss Hickey', as she was always called, were those pupils who, even after they had achieved a high level of reading achievement, still showed failure in spelling and fluency of written expression. For them she developed a system of teaching spelling through writing, based on the work of Aylett Cox and Lucius Waites, the course directors at the Scottish Rites Hospital. Their detailed, systematic and cumulative remedial programme was based upon the original programme of Gillingham *et al.* (1940) and Gillingham and Stillman (1956). Miss Hickey decided to adapt this programme for teachers in the UK. She substituted English terms for the American ones, revised the spelling to British from American English, and anglicised the pronunciation and diacritical marking. Her multisensory techniques for learning the regular part of the language adapted from the teacher-centred techniques of Gillingham *et al.* to her child-centred ones. For learning the irregular words she introduced the Fernald (1943) multisensory tracing techniques. Hickey's emphasis in the programme was for the learners to become self-directed and so be able to play a part in their own recovery. She maintained that if the method was adapted for use in schools, the dyslexic's problems could actually be prevented.

It was Hickey's experience that not all pupils attending remedial education would need this specialist approach but that many would benefit from it, particularly in the early stages. She found that those pupils who were late in reading would make progress with extra practice with the usual school approach of the 'look and say' reading schemes and some supporting use of phonics suited to their age and maturity. The dyslexics however needed to be identified at an early stage and the systematic, cumulative language training approach used so that they never experienced failure. For diagnosis, she recommended the Schonell reading and spelling tests and, in addition, the Schonell Silent Reading Test A for reading speed and comprehension. An outline of her programme follows.

Multisensory phonogram training

Each new phonogram is introduced by a stimulus-response training routine. It is the beginning of the process of establishing automaticity. It can take a large amount of time to establish the first few phonograms and then the procedure, which only proceeds at the child's pace, will suddenly speed up.

- The teacher begins by presenting reading pack card 'i'. The pupil learns to respond and say /i/.
- The teacher shows the clueword card igloo and asks for the sound beginning the word. The pupil responds /i/.

- The teacher says and shows the name of the letter on the reading pack card, I. The pupil responds igloo /i/.
- The teacher says /i/ and asks for the clue word and name of the letter.
- The teacher says 'igloo' and asks for the initial letter's sound and name.
- The teacher says /i/ and asks the pupil to repeat the sound and give the I name and now also write the letter.
- The teacher writes the letter 'i' in the air, on a surface, or on the pupil's back and asks for the clueword, sound and name of the letter. The pupil responds.

When this first phonogram has been securely learnt, the second reading card is introduced in the same way until the response to the card is automatic and the written form has been reduced to a normal handwriting size. The introduction of the first letters is in order of their frequency of occurrence in children's writing (Fry 1964) leaving aside 'd' because of its potential for confusion with 'b'. After learning the phonogram in this way it is only necessary for step 3 to be rehearsed for the reading pack i.e. the learner is shown the reading pack I card and asked for the clue word and the sound. When working with the spelling pack the start is at step 6 i.e. make the sound /i/, ask the learner to repeat sound and name of the letter and write it down.

The *Reading Pack* consists of 84 small pocket-sized cards. On the face of each card is a phonogram (a symbol representing a spoken sound) printed in lower case. At the bottom right of the card is its capital letter form. On the reverse side of each card are the keywords for sound and name, plus a picture. All vowel cards have two lines drawn across the top to distinguish them from other phonograms. It is recommended that the learner also uses the reading pack once a day in spare moments when alone.

The *Spelling Pack* comprises 51 cards. The written sound is presented, read by the teacher or learner, then repeated by the learner. It is then spelled by naming the letter(s) 'I' . The letters are then written and each one is named just before writing. Later irregular spellings of 'i' are added to the 'I' card e.g. -igh and ie as they are learnt.

The reading and spelling packs are crucial parts of the programme and are presented in detail with letters, cluewords and pictures. It is this element which enables the dyslexic to break the alphabetic code as the relationships between phoneme and grapheme are made explicit. The first 16 letters of the programme are: i, t, p, n, s, a, d, h, e, c, k, ck, b, r, m, y. Word building begins as soon as two letters have been learnt – synthetic phonics: i t (it); i t p (pit, tip, tit, pit); i t p n (nip, pin, tin, tint). These regular words are presented for both reading and spelling from dictation. In addition to synthetic phonic word building with phonograms, the position in a word is taught and the pupil is trained to expect to find a particular phonogram at the beginning, middle or end of a word.

The *Alphabet Work* is introduced for five minutes at the beginning of each lesson. This is so that the pupil can learn to use a dictionary and add to word knowledge and understanding. First, two-inch high wooden capital letters are presented randomly to be laid out in an arc from A to Z for multisensory training in naming, feeling shape and sequential ordering. It is quite startling to discover that the majority of dyslexics, even those who can read and spell somewhat falter and fail at first in this task and have to receive training. They are also taught to find the quartile into which a dictionary word falls: A–D; E–M; N–R; S–Z, and exercises in looking up words in three, four or five moves are practised. Alphabet games are devised and practised.

The *Handwriting Scheme* training system is based upon that of Anna Gillingham and alternatives to the form recommended are accepted provided that the letter is made all in one movement and has *a lead-in and follow-up* stroke, a full remedial cursive. The pupil is encouraged to verbalise the directions in the letters as they are made, e.g. 'over and back'. Lines are recommended for writing upon, with a faint line above to indicate the size of the main body of the letter in the early stages. Fluency and speed of writing are developed and practised often with a timer to 'beat the clock'.

Thus far the system can be seen to be *multisensory alphabetic synthetic phonics*. After the first 16 phonograms, 'i-e' as in 'pipe' and vowel 'y' (number 20) are introduced and Hickey suggests that, at this point, when the long vowel sounds have been introduced more sensible reading material can be studied. She suggests that by the time the thirty-ninth phonogram in the course has been introduced, the pupil will have a large number of regular and irregular words in the reading vocabulary. At this stage, a published scheme can be introduced: Hickey recommended that one of the best in her view was *The Royal Road Readers* by Daniels and Diack (published by Philip and Tacey, 1954–1971) because it had a phonic emphasis and gave systematic practice when introducing a new word.

Syllable structures are explained by Hickey and the six common types are detailed and their order in introduction is specified. The six types are as follows.

1   syllables which are also words: big and pet
2   closed syllables: mas/ter, car/rot
3   open syllables: o/pen
4   regular final syllables: -le, -ic
5   suffixes (usually a syllable): -ing, -ment
6   prefixes: pre-, op-

To these are added the spelling rules for adding affixes e.g. when to add (flying); double (hopping); drop (hoping); change (pay/paid).

Composition recommendations are made in section 8 on how to assist pupils with continuous prose writing and the use of story schema or scaffolds are shown including the simple notions of beginnings, middles and ends, and cartoon sequences with captions to illustrate story ideas. Section 9 of the training pack shows games which can be made and used to illustrate particular teaching points. Many of these are drawn from Childs (1968) and also the teachers on her early courses. All of them had to make a game as one of the course requirements.

Hickey's contribution was to bring the Gillingham and Stillman (1956) programme to this country and introduce her own modest improvements and additions to what was already a well-tried and well-structured programme. It extends well beyond phonics to syllable and linguistic structures and meaning and origins. This is why Hickey called it an alphabetic – phonic – structural – linguistic programme.

In 1991 a second and revised edition was published, edited by Jean Augur and Sue Briggs. Both had dyslexic children and had only finally found help for them when they found Miss Hickey. The second edition was to be more user-friendly.

The Augur and Briggs edition divides the programme into three sections. Part 1 contains chapters on the theory and background to the multisensory approach to teaching and the basic techniques of the programme such as how to introduce the phonograms using the stimulus-response routine in 9 steps; the first 12 phonograms are detailed as follows: i, t, p, n, s, a, d, h, e, c, (k), k, and -ck (k). To these are added concepts, spelling rules and vocabulary, the basic language programme, alphabet work, cursive handwriting training, reading and spelling, story writing and self-directed learning activities. These chapters are essential reading before embarking on the teaching programme. The copyright holder did not permit new insights from research to be included and so the book remains true to the ideas and principles of its originator.

Parts 2 and 3 are both divided into three sections and demonstrate in a carefully ordered sequence the teaching of the 84 phonograms which make up the programme and the associated rules and structures. A range of teaching games are presented with ideas for others given and each section is carefully cross-referenced for ease of use. Teachers with an interest in the area could well follow the programme even if they had not had the benefit of training.

The third edition update by Combley (2000) introduces early work on phonological skills. But this work on sub-skills may contribute to confusion for dyslexics; Miss Hickey would not have been pleased.

Dyslexia Institute Language Programme (DILP)

This programme is produced in a two-folder format and is only available to those who have attended one of the Institute's training courses. It is not surprising that it is fundamentally based upon the original Hickey language training programme and the courses she ran at Staines, which is acknowledged in the manual. The programme has been extended in folder two to include more example work sheets, games, study skills and language training.

Rack and Walker (1994) followed 145 pupils in Sheffield attending the Dyslexia Institute over a two-year period. The reading and spelling progress ranged from six months to two years in each calendar year. The mean is not quite the progress we would want but most of these pupils would, if left to the schools, have made no progress at all. In a later study Rack and Rudduck (2002) monitored the progress over one year of 113 pupils attending three dyslexia centres. All the pupils made standard score gains. Those in the 'severe' dyslexic group made 9 point gains (equivalent to one year's progress) in reading and 6 point gains (equivalent to eight months' progress) in spelling. The less severe group made from 3.5 to 5 point gains in reading and spelling, equivalent to four months' progress. This suggests that after the initial spurt, resulting from having the sound–symbol correspondences made explicit and using this for decoding and encoding, progress slows down and it is more difficult to move students forward even on APSL programmes. Perhaps after one year they should be withdrawn from the programme and time allowed for consolidation and extended practice whilst careful monitoring takes place to ensure they do not slip backwards. An alternative explanation was that the Sheffield centre was using the programme correctly whereas the other three were not.

In Ridehalgh's study (1999) it was found that where DILP was used the rate was 1.06 years' progress in the first six months, dropping to 0.54 in the next six months. The long summer holiday may have had some influence in studies that were year-long rather than counted in months ignoring holidays. Alternatively the initial spurt was predictable as they gained alphabetic/phonic skills and then consolidated them.

Teaching Reading Through Spelling (TRTS) (Cowdery et al. 1994)

The TRTS programme is presented in a series of slim A4 books now published by TRTS Publishing, Clywd. Book 2A details the process of making an assessment and compiling a case profile under the title of *Diagnosis*. The profile contains interview data from the parents and the pupil, criterion-referenced and norm-referenced, and diagnostic data from tests and information from the psychologist's report and speech therapist if available. Now of course the profile would be supplemented by data from the Statement. Much of the book is about showing how to gain a direct insight into the young person's needs and difficulties from direct observation, with the test data as a background.

In Book 2B, *Foundations of the Programme*, the four essential elements of the programme are described: *alphabet work*, the *reading and spelling packs* and the *cursive handwriting* style and training method. The *alphabet* work (Cowdery) is similar to that found in Hickey and other APSL derivatives, using wooden capital letters which the pupil has to lay out in alphabetical order in an arc. The procedures involve tracing, naming, visualising and verbalising three times before they are put away. A range of games is included on alphabet mazes, 'soup', dominoes, battle, crosswords and codes. More advanced work centres upon dictionary use and the four quartiles.

In Section 2 the *reading and spelling* packs (Prince-Bruce) are introduced. The multisensory format follows that of Hickey except that the pupils write their own cards. The main linguistic terms are explained and the first five single letters of the scheme which are introduced are *i, t, p, n, s* as in the Hickey programme. Thereafter the order differs significantly and is based upon an earlier publication by Prince-Bruce (1978) for Kingston LEA. The reading pack is introduced and has red coloured borders on vowel cards so that those with experience of Norrie's letter case can carry their knowledge forward and others will have theirs supported by this extra clue. Some diacritical marking is used to aid pronunciation with the macron denoting the long vowel sound and the breve the short one.

The spelling pack is built up in a similar fashion. The teacher articulates the sound, the pupil repeats it and *notes the articulatory 'feel'*, writes the appropriate grapheme down from memory, reads what has been written and then checks by looking at the card whether this is correct. 'The use and practice of the Spelling pack is the key to the programme' (Cowdery *et al.* 1994: 25). Suffixes are written in green. If a key word is needed this is written on the back in pencil. The articulatory component is crucial in this part of the work. It is a major contribution to making the phoneme–grapheme connection explicit.

In the third section the cursive *handwriting* (Morse) training system is described; it is the round upright 'Kingston' cursive style. In Section 4 there is guidance for those pupils who have wider difficulties in motor coordination. These include strategies for writing patterns, notes on the use of lines and some examples.

Section 5 contains records of pupils' written progress through the scheme and the final section describes *multisensory mouth training* (Montgomery), the articulation component, which is the essential link between phoneme and grapheme. Mirrors are not used.

The next three books in the series are *The Early Stages of the Programme 2C* (Prince-Bruce and Morse, 1986), *The Programme: The Later Stages, 2D Part One* and *2D Part Two* (Prince-Bruce and Morse, 1986). Book 2C gives an overview of the whole programme, the structure, the terms used, and example lessons, and explains the linguistics of the early stages, sound pictures, how English words are constructed, syllable division rules, the meanings of prefixes and suffixes, plurals, simultaneous oral spelling, the l-f-s rule and then provides a range of games to reinforce points made. The final section provides 16 pages of dictations to enable the teacher to check that the sounds and structures have been learned. In Book 2D1, the full set of diacritical marks are explained but only the breve and macron are for pupil's use. The rest of the phonograms are introduced, with the rules and generalisations associated with them, related vocabulary and dictations and more exercises and games. Book 2D2 contains the higher order end of linguistics teaching, silent letters, word families and stable final syllables with example lesson plans. Finally, accented syllables, accents in English and related games are given.

What becomes apparent is the tightly structured nature of the Hickey/TRTS teaching session. It is highly intensive and demanding of both pupil and teacher. Sessions of 50–60 minutes are conducted with pairs of pupils matched for sociability and in terms of skills and needs. A typical session has the following pattern: alphabet work, reading pack, spelling pack, words for reading, words for spelling, dictation, pupil uses new words in own open ended writing, games and activities to reinforce learning.

The TRTS order of introduction, based upon their teaching experience of what pupils need and can best cope with if skills are being built upon in sequential order, is as follows:

> i t p n -nt s sp- sn- a -sp st- l pl- sl- d spl- f -ll -ff -ss -nd h -kt fl- -ft g gl- -ng -ing
> o -st m -mp sm- r dr- fr- gr- y pr- e tr- spr- str- u c cr- cl- sc- scr- -ct k sk- -sk -lk
> -nk -ck b bl br j w sw- tw- dw- qu- v squ- x z

At any point after i t p n s, a particular letter or blend can be introduced if the pupil especially needs to learn it but then a return to the order is advised.

There are three final books in the series – *The Handwriting Copy Book* (Morse 1986), the *Infant Handwriting Copy Book* (Morse 1988) and *The Spelling Notebook* (Cowdery 1987). The latter is a reference work and contains a summary of all the linguistic rules and teaching points governing English spelling which a teacher and pupil might conceivably need. It is an indispensable companion to the series but also useful as a general reference and source book for anyone interested in spelling.

STRANDS: Spelling then reading, approaching the needs of dyslexic students

This is a loose-leaf file of worksheets produced by a team of Hampshire teachers led by the then adviser Gill Tester who had moved there from Kingston where she had become familiar with TRTS. STRANDS was only available to teachers who had followed the Hampshire training course and was a worksheet version of much of TRTS without the rationale and detailed structure. This means it can be degraded to random selection of individual sheets by busy teachers for an LSA to monitor.

Alpha to Omega (Hornsby and Shear 1976 et seq.)

Updates and reprints of the original book and newer related materials have continued to be produced throughout the decades. According to Hornsby (1994), a structured phonetic-linguistic method of remediation is used in all centres where dyslexia is taken seriously. She argues that, unfortunately, phonics approaches are frequently misunderstood and often involve teaching association of letter shapes with single sounds without using their names. She insists that letter names need to be taught in order to describe how a word such as 'betting' is spelled, for b-e-t can be sounded out and makes sense but betting cannot. Letter names are constants whereas sounds change according to context in a word. It is notable that all APSL variants teach the letter names and sounds together by a system of phonogram training.

The order of introduction of Hornsby and Shear's consonants

- 1st: b p m w h
- 2nd: d t n g k n
- 3rd: f s z
- 4th: v th (voiced) sh l ch j
- 5th: y qu r th (unvoiced) x
- 6th: consonant blends

The vowels are taught as a group by names and sounds at the outset. In the first series the pupil learns to write the letters in print script and only later is cursive suggested as an option. This was no doubt to fit in with schools' expectations as none at that period permitted cursive until a neat print had been established. Hickey's work first with the cerebral palsied children showed her the benefits of cursive and she insisted upon it. Hornsby suggests that there are no hard and fast rules about handwriting form. The authors of A to O do insist that the pupils must be taught to form the letters correctly and be shown where each letter should start.

In the order of letter introduction Hornsby and Shear add a final activity, 'pupil writes letter eyes closed' and this is indeed a good idea and can be added to any training programme. It is usually done in the development stage of writing the letters in TRTS as is writing on the back but is not a formal part of the programme.

Alpha to Omega according to its authors is a highly structured, multisensory and cumulative reading, writing and spelling programme moving from single letters through to single-syllabled and multisyllabled words using cards in a reading and spelling pack as previously described for Hickey's programme. It is suggested that the reading cards can show more advanced patterns, for reading accelerates faster than spelling and it will also serve to familiarise the pupils with the spelling patterns by the time they are expected to spell them.

The linguistic basis of A to O is also detailed. Dictations are recommended to begin early, to help structure the language, and examples of sentence structures are given beginning with SAAD, the simple active affirmative declarative sentences e.g. 'The man ran to the red van'. This is given as an early example of a dictation using regular words. A later more advanced level is exemplified in 'A black cat jumped on the table'. The procedure for the dictation is a multisensory one: sentence is dictated – pupil repeats it – teacher dictates it again slowly and clearly – pupil writes it down – pupil reads it aloud – self corrects and teacher corrects if necessary – pupil reads again 'with expression'.

The sentence structure taught is also structured and cumulative leading from affirmatives to negative passive constructions. The claims of Alpha to Omega to be phonetic-linguistic are well founded but the claims to be structured and sequential by comparisons with the other schemes are less so and dyslexics can become confused when taught five vowel sounds and names as a group followed quickly by vowel 'y'.

In TRTS the teaching of the short and long vowel sounds is well separated as they can also confuse the dyslexic when put together. James aged seven was a case in point: he had failed to learn in class and was having private remedial tuition from a teacher using A to O. She had given him each vowel to draw in turn and a clue picture to illustrate the sound which he also had to draw. In the labour of all this and with his handwriting coordination problem he recalled nothing though he had practised it all many times.

Edith Norrie letter case (Norrie 1917, 1973)

Edith Norrie was a Danish dyslexic, born in 1888, who at the age of 20 taught herself to read and spell by making a set of letters of the Danish alphabet which she ordered and systematised so that she could read her fiance's letters from the First World War. In 1939 she established the Word Blind Institute in Copenhagen and later institutes were set up in many countries including the UK.

An English version of the letter case is produced and marketed by the Helen Arkell Centre at Farnham, Surrey. It is primarily an aid to spelling and consists of a box made up of three sections containing the letters of the alphabet. Each compartment contains either a letter or a consonant digraph. The letters are grouped according to the *place of articulation* of the sound most frequently associated with it. There are several examples of each lower case letter and two upper case in the compartments. There is also a small mirror in which only the mouth can be viewed.

When the pupil attempts to spell a word, it is necessary first to work out how the sound is made in the mouth. This, according to Goulandris (1986), increases the awareness of speech sounds and the relationship between phonemes and graphemes, and it is most beneficial to pupils with difficulties in this area. The *vowels are all coloured red* so that the pupil can check that there is one in every syllable. The black and green coloured consonants help sort out the differences between voiced and unvoiced consonants. The emphasis is thus very much upon the 'speech therapy' element in the early stages. The mirror is to enable the pupils to see where and how they are making the sounds.

As can be seen, the system emphasises both phonological and articulation training associated with word building with the cards which can then be read. The pupils are said to enjoy the word building with the letters as they can ensure they have the correct spelling before they copy it down. However, there are some limitations to this as a full remedial scheme as it only deals with the 'cracking of the alphabetic code' and the early stages of regular word building but it could usefully be imported into reception classes.

With a reading age of about eight years many dyslexics have passed that stage and need more technical syllabic and linguistic help. The letter case deals with the alphabetic-phonics and not the syllabic-linguistics. It also promotes the use of print script as the pupils copy the letters from the cards.

Helen Arkell Centre Training

Joy Pollack and Elizabeth Waller (1994, 2001) were former teachers at the Helen Arkell Centre and in their book *Day to Day Dyslexia in the Classroom* described their approach to remedial work. There are substantial chapters on spelling and handwriting. On spelling they give nine spelling guides covering work on initial sounds; the order of teaching spelling conventions; silent 'e'; 'murmuring' vowels and digraphs; short vowels and doubling consonants following vowels; -ed endings and -le words following short and long vowels; spelling guidelines for -dge, -tch -ck, c and k; plurals and when to change y to i and add -es; syllable structure, syllable tapping, syllable division; and finally stems (roots), prefixes and suffixes. The order given is very different from the APSL programmes and there is less detail of structure and fewer methods of training but the emphasis upon language and speech problems is characteristic of the Helen Arkell Centre as is the use of the Edith Norrie letter case in place of the multisensory phonogram training.

The authors strongly recommend the use of the Edith Norrie letter case and the Hickey Multisensory Language course, Letterland, Alpha to Omega and TRTS, all of which they state (p. 34) set out a structured approach. They advocate selecting from a structured programme material to suit the needs of a particular child. While this is a sensible strategy for these skilled and experienced remediators this strategy *is not recommended* for teachers beginning work in the area nor for those who have never followed an APSL programme.

Beat Dyslexia (Stone et al. 1993)

This is an APSL/TRTS derivative presented as a series of booklets. It teaches multisensory alphabetics and phonics, uses spelling and reading cards and cursive writing, and introduces a record page for the pupils to complete as they progress. The standard printed cards can be laid over each other so that words can be built and there are photocopiable worksheets. The order of presentation is as follows:

- Book 1: i t p n s sp st d a c o r dr cr tr pr spr scr str
- Book 2: m mp e h nd nt b br ss l sl pl cl bl ll f fl fr g gl gr u k sk

- Book 3: ng nk th ck v w sw tw sh j y qu x z -ff ch
- Book 4: ee ar or -y i-e a-e ay ce ci cy er oo ge gi gy -dge o-e u-e
- Book 5: -ic u-e (oo) ture ea -tion ou our/are igh o(u) -ice(is) age (ij) -ough al ow oa e-e ir -tch
- Book 6: - ur ir/er/ur oi oy ir au ph aw -ew -sion ue ear ch(k) ch(sh) ous us/ous -cian sion/tion/cian or -y ei our ar ul/ey/eu/oe

An example from a work sheet illustrates the general APSL approach:

More about letter 'd'
- Find it Say it Hear it Write it
- Put a ring round every letter that says 'd'. You should find 4.
- Write 'd' under the pictures which begin with 'd'.
- Write 'd' in the box if you hear the sound 'd'.
- Trace over the letters, filling in 'd' to end the word.
- Now use these words for - - -
- Read and copy these words in your exercise book.
- Practise your reading and spelling cards. Find and trace d in your record book.
- The facing page presents alphabet work on 'D' and copying and tracing 'd' in full upright round (Kingston) cursive.

A case example of its effect in use suggests it would be worthy of testing in a research study: Vallence (2002) reported that by the end of reception year Nicholas had failed to make any progress in reading, writing and spelling although he had received a lot of one-on-one help. He had only reliably remembered numbers one to five. His teacher was reluctant to push him and his parents said he was too young for them to reinforce work done at school. Various approaches were tried such as Precision Teaching and Letterland without success.

After 12 weeks of two half-hour sessions per week using 'Beat Dyslexia' he was able to recognise all the letter sounds in his reading pack, and able to write all the sounds in the sound/spelling pack that had been covered. He completed the first book in the programme and could read any words using any combination of letters covered. He could also spell any three- or four-letter word in the same way. The initial phases were very slow but by the time he had learned i, t, p, n, s he no longer needed the clue word for each one. 'His joy at his success was wonderful to see.'

What was important for Nicholas was the cumulative aspect of the programme. In the past he had learned letters in the lesson, or during the week they were focused upon, but when the class moved on to new letters the ones from the previous week were lost. This was not the case with the 'Beat Dyslexia' programme.

A crucial point to consider here as well as the success of the programme is the attitude of the teacher to any direct intervention. This is particularly common in reception and early years from my observation and training work with teachers. In a study of teachers' ability to predict literacy success and failure, Feiler and Webster (1998) found that reception teachers' informal judgements do identify children in need of additional literacy support but were 'generally not convinced that intervention for the weaker children was appropriate' (p. 193)', or advised the next year teacher to do so. Concerns about labelling, incorrectly predicting and the children being too young acted against them initiating early formal intervention. It was their view that this was a critical issue and more attention needed to be directed to it to gain professional consensus on when it is suitable to intervene with children at risk of failing. My view is that we should upskill reception teachers to intervene as soon as they identify a child at risk is failing. For example, LSAs could then be delegated to work with them and use the 'Beat Dyslexia' or other similar programme for a trial period.

Step by Step (Broomfield and Combley 1997)

This is another Hickey/TRTS derivative presented in their book *Overcoming Dyslexia*. It is a reduced version of the originals but still starts with multisensory training on *i t p n s*, then *st sp sn a d h e c k sk b r br cr dr pr tr m sm y l bl cl pl sl f fl fr o g gl gr u j v w sw tw x z qu th sh ch wh ng nk*. Of note is that the synthetic element with *i t p n s* is delayed.

Level two consists of *ar or ou ow ce ge ir ur igh oi au aw ie ph ch tion sion*. It uses round 'Kingston' cursive, one set of letter cards for both spelling and reading, mirrors to watch the mouth when making the sounds, and uses 'listen, look, write and say' as its format for every phoneme/grapheme combination. It is structurally alphabetic and phonic, a phonogram training system, not syllabic-linguistic or morphemic. Combley (2000) edited the third edition of *The Hickey Multisensory Language Course*.

Bangor Dyslexia Teaching Scheme (Miles 1978; Miles and Miles 1992; Cooke, 1992)

The basic system is a phonological-linguistics one according to its originator Elaine Miles. The original teaching manual was produced in 1978 for teachers at the dyslexia unit, University College of North Wales, Bangor. She and her husband Professor T. R. Miles are well known for their extensive work in the dyslexia field.

Part 1 of the newer version is intended for teaching in primary age pupils and Part 2 is for the secondary stage, although Miles states that some secondary stage pupils may need to be started on Part 1 as their skills are so poor. She recommends that as dyslexics have a problem with the phonological aspects of language or what she calls 'phoneme deafness' then the remedial programme needs to address this. She also recommends multisensory teaching using any of the Alpha to Omega or Hickey phoneme-grapheme cards, or the Edith Norrie letter case. The handwriting style illustrated is print script (Miles and Miles 1992: 40) although it is stated that dyslexic pupils may be taught cursive from the outset because they can become confused at the changeover stage. The essence of the scheme is that the pupils must have a book in which to record the spelling patterns that they have learnt, and they need another for practices and dictations. Miles recommends an emphasis upon patterns rather than rules, plenty of practice, using mnemonics where necessary, and teaching reading and spelling together as decoding and encoding activities. She advocates using phonic reading books for the first six months, and encouraging plenty of oral work trying words aloud and saying sentences before writing them down.

Part 1 is organised in six sections as follows:

1   Single letter sounds and single syllabled words with short vowel sounds. At the end of this section -ar, -or and -er are introduced.
2   The commonest long vowel patterns including final (silent 'e', vowel digraphs especially 'oo'; and vowel 'w' or 'y'.
3   A checklist of common irregular words to be learnt by rote.
4   More patterns to be learnt such as -ight, -ir, -ur, and ought, aught, and ough.
5   Silent consonant patterns.
6   Word endings, common grammatical endings and changes to base words when affixing.

The teacher is advised to check all the consonants and their second sounds; knowledge of names at this stage is optional. The five short vowels are to be taught gradually in the order a, i, o, u, e and the short sound is marked as a breve (˘) as in the Hickey and TRTS systems. Work on the alphabet and dictionary skills can start 'quite soon'. Singing the alphabet in letter groups is recommended and the display of the whole alphabet, 'as in a rainbow formation or some similar arrangement is a useful way for pupils to become more proficient in its use' (Miles and Miles 1992: 40). Learning the quartiles is mentioned in this volume and alphabet tracking exercises are advocated. As these recommendations on handwriting and alphabet work are in an appendix they appear not to be integral in the scheme. In the same edition it was recommended (p. 26) that letters should be grouped for handwriting according to their starting points as follows:

*   those starting on the right *a c d g o q s*
*   those starting on the left *r m n p i j v w x y z u*
*   those at the top of the 'stick' *l h b k t f*
*   starts in the middle *e*

The building of the personal dictionary is considered to be paramount. The advice begins with 'Begin by checking that your pupil knows most of the usual sounds of all the consonants including y qu and the hard sounds of c and g (Miles and Miles 1992: 9) and, 'Knowledge of sound can be optional at this stage' (ibid.). This knowledge is to be recorded on the first page of the dictionary, the inside cover, and then three-letter words with short vowels are taught and recorded. This is followed by tracing of consonant digraphs and consonant blends, followed by doubling with l-f-s; then -ck, -ld and dge; doubling with polysyllables, e.g. hop/hopping; silent e; stress and much more.

The pupil's dictionary should contain all vowels, consonants and blends, digraphs and -ng and -nk. Page 1 of the dictionary lists all the single vowel words; all combinations of beginning and ending blends including three-letter blends. A sample page 2 (Miles and Miles, 1992: 19) includes the long vowel sounds, final 'e' patterns; silent 'w' as in 'write', and final 'e' patterns as in -ee, -ie, -oe, -ue, and appropriate lists. Hard and soft 'c' and 'g' are included here.

As can be seen the Bangor system is very different from that of the APSL programmes. It resembles more the orthodoxy of the day in that it relies on a top-down approach, a great deal of visual training, a word book, and rote learning of patterns and strings. Reading and spelling are taught together and handwriting is a minor consideration in the process rather than a crucial part of it. The speed and complexity of the process and order of introduction if followed by an inexperienced teacher could lead to confusion.

A companion volume *Tackling Dyslexia the Bangor Way* by Cooke (1992) is essential reading for those wishing to use the system. Cooke explains that the Bangor system is basically phonological, not visual or linguistic. It is not linguistic but does emphasise many of the popular visual approaches. She details ways in which Miles and Miles' (1992) recommendations are operationalised, and it becomes clear that the alphabet work and multisensory learning are still secondary to the main thrust of the programme. There is still a choice to be made on print over cursive and all the children's examples are in print. There is a chapter on the use of computers in lessons with dyslexics and an appendix on materials, games and books for teaching.

MSL: The complete structured literacy course (MSL 1998)

MSL claims to be the complete structured literacy course with everything necessary for teaching dyslexic children. It includes 200 integrated worksheets, games, story books, dictations, spelling, reading, spelling and memory packs, sequencing exercises, blank cards, and wooden upper and lower case letters and feely bags.

The programme is divided into four units, each of five modules. It introduces 83 separate phonograms. The order in Module 1 is i-t-p-n-s-a which tells us that it is based upon the Gillingham *et al.*/Hickey programmes and format, teaching names and sounds using clue words and cards. At 's' the second sound 'z' is introduced and plural 's' and then initial blends sp, st, sn. Word building patterns are not introduced until Unit 2 with VC/CV.

The programme appears to contain all the elements of multisensory phonogram training teachers might expect to see but no research evaluation of their effectiveness other than nice quotes from teachers who have used it and like the attractiveness of the worksheets and the range of tasks.

MTSR: Multisensory Training System for Reading (Taylor-Smith 1993; Johnson et al. 1993)

MTSR, the original, is actually based upon the Gillingham and Stillman (1956) programme and begins by presenting the letters in the same order: i, t, p, n, s. The UK MTSR was developed as the result of a DfEE-funded project by Manchester Metropolitan University and the British Dyslexia Association. 'The aim was to investigate ways in which classroom teachers in mainstream primary schools could develop reading skills of pupils with specific learning difficulties including mild to moderate dyslexia'. (Johnson *et al.* 1999: ix).

The key elements are the books of course lessons which teachers can literally read out to the children:

* picture cards pack, a set of cards showing graphemes and pictures representing key words;

- letter cards pack, a set of cards showing graphemes to be taught – the letters;
- reading concept cards pack, a set of cards with a symbol representing a reading concept on the card front and a statement of the concept on the back;
- MTSR suffix cards, a set of cards with a suffix on the front and information about the meaning and pronunciation on the back;
- MTSR irregular words cards, a set of cards with irregular words that cannot be decoded using the rules introduced;
- small mirrors for use when introducing graphemes, one for the teacher and one for each pupil.

Because the NLS had just been introduced the advice the team was given by LEA advisers was that any resource must be compatible with it and include multisensory teaching and require minimal professional development. Despite these restrictions the main feature of the original MTS – synthetic phonics – was preserved as distinct from the usual analytic phonics of UK schools. As soon as i and t are taught the pupil learns to read 'it'. But the writing system is print script.

The scheme teaches the systematic study of syllable types, suffixes and prefixes. 'Later MTS books include syllable division, Latin stems and Greek word parts. These are available from EDMAR in the USA' (p. 3).

MTS and the UK version MTSR 'are based on the direct instruction model and are faster paced than the original Gillingham and Stillman course and concentrate only on reading' (p. 1).

Therein lie the problems for dyslexics. The authors admit that there will be pupils who do not benefit from the scheme and who should be referred on as soon as possible. However, speeding up is not what dyslexics need, they need the first stages slowed down, they need to learn to write the graphemes in cursive, they need to have an emphasis on spelling development, and they need to have syllable structures and rules built in as they go. The plethora of cards will also be a problem and the pupils would be better to scribe their own.

A typical MTSR grapheme/phoneme teaching session runs on the principle of 'guided discovery' (p. 40). An example follows from lesson 5.

- A list of key words is read with the target sound in it e.g. it, if, in, is, ill.
- Pupils repeat each word after the teacher says it.
- 'Which sound did you hear at the beginning of each word?'
- 'Is this sound open, with nothing blocking the air?' Yes.
- 'Touch your vocal cords with your finger tips' – teacher helps them identify the sound as a vowel or a consonant after these have been taught.
- The pupils are shown the letter card I and are told the name and about voicing of vowels, short and long vowel sounds, and the key word 'igloo' through a set of sentences presented as a riddle. Beginning: 'I am a kind of house. You might see me in very cold places ... I am an igloo, etc.'

The pupils repeat the main parts of the procedure watching their mouths in the mirrors. They are taught the breve mark for the short vowel sound (lesson 19). Each lesson such as this is scheduled to take about 20 minutes.

One irregular word is introduced at lesson 32. It is *said*. We learn that it is not pronounced *sa-id* as it is spelled and there are other words which act like this. The
pupils note that *s* and *d* are pronounced as expected and the teacher circles 'ai'. The
pupils then study the Reading Concept Card 33 which has 'ai' on the front and on
the back is the rule 'irregular sounds have an unexpected pronunciation. Circle
irregular words when coding for reading'. They then add this card to their Reading
Concepts Review Pack.

With all the verbiage and at this speed it is to be expected that by now our average dyslexic is totally confused. In addition, can the word 'said' really be regarded
as irregular? For example in our distant past we would probably have pronounced
the word 'said' as 'sayed'. This form was still used in Suffolk rural areas into the
twentieth century. All we have to do is tell the story, 'he say' (says) in Suffolk is still
heard now versus he 'ses' (says) in the rest of the country. So if we teach the suffix
rule 'change y to i' then we can show how 'sayed' changes to 'said'. Compare it with
'paid' and 'laid' which have retained the original sound. Reinforce the spelling by
writing the word as a whole unit 'said' in cursive three times from memory. Give a
dictation later to see if it has been retained. Further examples of this 'strategic'
approach are in Chapter 6.

What is puzzling is that the DfEE and the BDA had to go abroad to seek a partial
variant of a well tried system which has had English versions for the past 30 years.

Spelling Made Easy (Brand 1998)

Spelling Made Easy is a scheme of worksheets and stories devised by Violet Brand
and first published in 1987 by Egon. It was in its fourteenth impression by 1998
which attests to its popularity at least until the NLS was published. Pupils especially loved the *Fat Sam* stories.

Brand established the Watford Dyslexia Centre and promoted the understanding
and teaching of dyslexic children in a time when there was great hostility in many
quarters to the whole concept. Over a number of years she had devoted her time to
help these children and their teachers and was awarded an MBE in recognition.

Spelling Made Easy can be used as individual, group and class materials and is
presented as a multisensory structured spelling scheme suitable for children from
six years of age through to university students. The central principle is that *word
families* should be the basis of teaching at every level.

There is an Introductory Book, *Fat Sam*; then Level 1, *Sam and the Train*; Level 2,
The Adventures of Augustus; and Level 3, *Making and Taking Notes from Text*. There are
copy masters for each of the books and a *Teachers' Book on Remedial Spelling* giving
the rationale and details of how to use the materials. The order of introduction of
the key aspects of the scheme is as follows:

*   basic vowel sounds, not in alphabetical order – teach 'a' then 'o' because those
    with speech problems often have difficulty hearing the difference between 'a'
    and 'e';
*   common words needed early on;
*   common principles:
    doubling of vowels (ee)

combinations of vowel and consonant (ar)
combination of two consonants (sh)
effect of silent 'e' on a vowel (cake)
- combinations of two vowels (ai);
- groupings of two or more letters to produce one sound (-igh, -air);
- ir, ur, er.

General recommendations to the teacher are that spellers should be taught to listen to the voice and feel the shape of the mouth when making the sounds. Only one *word family* should be introduced per week, irrespective of age group. When learning basic words the pupil should be shown how to finger trace over the letters on the word card *saying* the whole word (not sounding it out). This needs to be done six times. The cards are then turned face down and the pupil has to write the word correctly without looking. The card is turned back and the spelling checked. If it is correct the pupil hands in the card, if it is not then the procedure is gone through again and they have to keep on practising until it is correct. This method of *whole word tracing* is based upon that of Fernald (1943) and the *phonogram approach* on that of Spalding and Spalding (1967). Both sources are acknowledged in the text. The order of introduction of the phonic aspects of the scheme is as follows:

a o i e u ck ee oo ar or sh ch
th a-e i-e o-e u-e ai oa ir ou
ea /e/ ing ur aw oi er all y /e/
ea /e/ ow igh a (ar / a) o / u / y / i / ow

Some details of the worksheets will illustrate the fundamental approach of the scheme.

Introductory level: Fat Sam

In this there are said to be 'thinking activities' which will hopefully form useful *automatic habits* for the future. Thinking activities and automatic habits are however mutually exclusive and thus this interpretation would seem to be contradictory. The first story is typical and it can be seen why children like them:

Gran is sad
The bad cat sat on her hat
It is flat

The worksheets which accompany this story are arranged as six activities.

1   Choose a colour. Draw a line under the words in the 'a' family.
2   Can you draw a picture of Sad gran?
3   Can you draw a picture of the bad cat and the flat hat?
4   Can you write about the hat?
     (There are then six line drawings of the objects and six words: tap jar bag flag bat hand.)
5   Write the words under the pictures.

6   What is wrong with the following sentence?
     The man has the flag the bag and the tap in his hat.

On each subsequent page there is a similar format as each new word family is introduced. On page 21 question 6 asks what is wrong with the following: a b e f c d h g i.

Levels one, two and three

These workbooks follow the same format with stories and follow-up activities. At each level the text becomes more complex and the tasks more difficult. Level One begins with a six-line story about Granddad's van and the exercises which follow set the pattern for the rest of the book.

1   Draw a line under words in the 'a' family – 'was' and 'gave' look the same but sound different ...
2   Can you write 4 words ending in -amp?
3   Can you write 4 ending in -and?
4   What's wrong? A jumbled sentence is given: 'the man had cramp ...'
5   Make your own comic – finish the story in pictures and write a sentence under each picture. (There are two pictures of Granddad's van in sequential boxes and two empty ones to draw in.)

At Level Two a set of similar but more advanced worksheets are provided, and again a range of activities are suggested, for example: 'Here is the news' presents text from which stories have to be extended, followed by facts, spellings, and elements such as 'o' words, and jumbled sentences.

Level Three helps students write text and take notes from text. A page of detailed and informative text is presented concerning a range of subjects such as Wales, Ireland, temperature, the Thames, oboe and saxophone etc., then pupils have to engage with the text and develop a range of study skills. Aspects of spelling are still included.

•   Look for familiar word families or families in new words.
•   Decide on the tricky part of a spelling. Look (and think about it) then cover, write, and check. Cover again, write and check.

Level three is intended for pupils in their final year in primary school but the worksheets can be selected and adapted for secondary school pupils and adults.

The list of spellings was supplied by Watford Grammar School from those found difficult by the girls entering the school. In the later versions the LCWC strategy was changed to 'say – look – cover – write – check' as research endorsed this old SOS process from Gillingham and Stillman (1956).

The SME scheme is easy to use and is enjoyed by primary pupils, but there are reservations about its use with dyslexics. It is possible for a severe dyslexic who is eight years old but who can neither read nor write to become quickly confused at the Sad Gran stage. He can choose a colour and draw a line under words with 'a' in them once he has been shown an 'a' word. He then matches all the words with 'a' from visual representation. His pictures of gran and the cat and the hat look vaguely similar but the instructions have to be read to him several times. He cannot write about the hat or the cat. He randomly matches the words tap, jar, bag, etc. to the line drawings and he cannot read the final sentence to discover what is wrong with it. When it is read to him he still does not know the answer. He is not an unintelligent boy and he has a reasonable grasp of English as a second language learner.

All the picture drawing and sentences and words distract from the central problem that he has which is learning the sound-to-symbol correspondence for 'a' and then writing it in a reasonable form and size. In fact he would be better started on the letter 'i' as in TRTS as it is easier than 'a' to make.

Summary and conclusions

In this chapter the Gillingham and Stillman (1956) APSL dyslexia programmes and their modern UK derivatives and other variants are described, including the BDA-sponsored MSRT. Those using full alphabetic – phonic – syllabic – linguistic (APSL) programming appear to be the most effective especially when the phonogram teaching is articulatory and multisensory and these connections are made explicit. Some main effects are evaluated in relation to research outcomes and compared with outcomes from other remedial strategies.

It is a BDA recommendation that dyslexia teaching programmes are structured, cumulative and sequentially ordered. However, this is often where many programmes fail, as they are not so well structured regarding students' needs, not cumulative and rely too much upon rote learning at all levels rather than just the basic levels. The remediator often tends to move the student too fast in the earliest stages and presents a programme of inputs thought to be useful and relevant by adult standards and perceptions.

Because of the detailed nature of the remedial work it can be concluded that dyslexics should be taught in a separate tutorial environment, for the intense catch-up curriculum cannot successfully be followed within other lessons. However, withdrawal from lessons is a problematic issue and after-school provision needs to be considered.

It is quite clear that there is a wealth of knowledge and tested and effective programmes in this country. Investment in practice-related remediation research in England and Wales however is still needed. This would establish clear evidence for the most appropriate specialist methodology and the most effective methods of training for the teachers. Reading research and reading teaching has dominated this field and it is concluded that it is time this balance was redressed particularly in the dyslexia field to cover spelling.

The main theme in the dyslexia programmes reviewed is that the problem should be addressed at the educational skills level. In the next two chapters a wider framework for intervention will be reviewed, including subskills approaches and strategies in general for pupils with and without specific literacy difficulties.

Chapter 5

Overcoming barriers to learning

Multisensory phonics and phonological training

Introduction

In this chapter an examination of phonics and an evaluation of phonic schemes follows. After this, phonological training schemes are examined. These include training in phoneme awareness and phoneme segmentation. These subskills of the literacy processes are considered by some to be the precursors of literacy development. However, they might as easily be regarded as the result of developing literacy skills. Ehri (1979, 1984) for example showed that the improvement in phonological awareness on which the acquisition of alphabet reading is based is itself a consequence of learning how sound segments in words are spelled conventionally.

It is expected that schools following the NLS up to 2006 will have taught some basic phonics, rote learning of letter strings and a basic sight vocabulary of 200 words, making mnemonics and using some simple rules. If they hold the view that spelling is mainly acquired through reading and that exposure to a variety of language experiences will automatically improve spelling, this will have influenced their literacy hour work with the whole language approach. They would have used both phonics and look and say approaches structured into the NLS format. Most will now teach a print script with ligatures as suggested in the NLS but copying and tracing will still predominate. However, OfSTED (1998) reported that in 18 schools, 50 per cent of teachers boycotted the phonics part of the NLS and that in 250 schools, some children learned all the letter sounds in eight weeks, while others took three years. A tradition of some 50 years is hard to eradicate.

The following is a quote from a report by a teacher in an independent primary school in 2004 and is not an untypical situation.

> Over the last 5 years my school has frequently changed the methods of teaching spelling. The school has trialled a variety of programmes and strategies, from methods of rote learning, writing the word 5 times, to structured spelling programmes such as, Spelling Made Easy and Keywords Spelling, to using the strategy, Look, Say, Cover, Write and Check and it is now the main strategy used for teaching spelling. This year we adopted the Collins Handwriting Programme. The school policy emphasises the importance of teaching spelling and handwriting together, but teachers find the actual application of this in the classroom difficult to implement.

Phonics is not such a simple teaching vehicle as might be supposed. Nor is the phonic system that simple; for example in English there are 26 letters to represent 44 sounds. There are also 28 initial blends, 48 end blends, and three blends which can appear in both positions (sk, sp, st). There are 15 different vowel and consonant combinations all of which add up to 1260 possible rhyme endings and 1493 sound units to learn (McGuinness 1997). Even single initial sounds in English vary in words (Treiman *et al.* 1995). It is not surprising therefore that a range of phonics programmes have been developed to try to simplify this for beginners rather than teach them all the possible letter patterns by sight. To add to the confusion the DfES (2006) has provided its own list of 45 sounds as shown in Table 5.1.

If we were to teach the sounds as presented here with their different examples of spellings confusion would quickly result for beginners. It gives rise to claims that English language spelling is very difficult to learn and quite irregular. It is the role

Table 5.1 The sounds of English

Vowels	Representative words	Consonants	Representative words
a	cat	b	baby
e	peg, bread	d	dog
i	pig, wanted	f	field, photo
o	log, want	g	game
u	plug, love	h	hat
ae	pain, day, gate, station	j	judge, giant, barge
ee	sweet, heat, thief, these	k	cook, quick, mix, Chris
ie	tried, light, my, shine	l	lamb
oe	road, blow, bone, cold	m	monkey, comb
ue	moon, blue, grew, tune	n	nut, knife, gnat
oo	look, would, put	p	paper
ar	cart, fast	r	rabbit, wrongs
ur	burn, first, term, heard	s	sun, mouse, city, science
or	torn, door, warn	t	tap
au	haul, law, call	v	van
er	wooden, circus, sister	w	was
ow	down, shout	wh	where
oi	coin, boy	y	yes
air	stairs, bear, hare	z	zebra
ear	fear, beer, here	th	then
		th	thin
		ch	chin
		sh	ship, mission, chef
		zh	treasure
		ng	ring, sink

Source: DfES 2006

of a phonic scheme to introduce regularity and simplicity in a structured and cumulative fashion so that beginners can acquire spelling knowledge easily. Some systems do this much better than others.

As a result of the Rose Review (2005) teachers will need to judge children's readiness for synthetic phonics; plan and implement a high-quality phonics programme; use multisensory activities and a mix of resources including ICT in the 20-minute phonics sessions; praise and encourage achievement at every opportunity; and judge how to organise teaching groups to provide optimum conditions for learning. There are, according to the review, four core elements of reading (!) that children should be taught:

- the links between sounds and letters in a clearly defined, incremental sequence;
- the skill of blending sounds all through the word in order to read it e.g. S-T-R-EE-T (!);
- to split words into sounds in order to spell them;
- that blending and splitting are reversible processes.

Teachers are warned that once a scheme is selected they should stick with it and not use a 'pick and mix' approach. Judging readiness will mean that for some, phonics will be too long delayed. The changes were implemented in September 2006.

Some issues for phonics teaching

The preventative role of phonics in dyslexia

Research surveys of the results of particular forms of literacy teaching by Chall (1967, 1985) showed that phonics teaching should be introduced for word decoding *from the very first* reading and spelling sessions. It was important not to wait until a sight vocabulary had been built as phonics teaching should be used from the outset to support word learning. Despite this well known USA survey it had no impact upon research and teaching in the UK. The 'look and say' method, and building a sight vocabulary of 50 words first before phonics, carried on regardless. It is this feature which seems to lead to confusions and subsequent dyslexic difficulties. However, even with the introduction of phonics and phonological training from the outset we can still expect 1.0 to 1.5 per cent of pupils to have dyslexic difficulties (Chall 1967, 1985; Clark 1970; SED 1978; Clay 1979; Hurry *et al.* 1996). For this group multisensory articulatory phonics needs to be built into the teaching, for the phoneme and grapheme link must be made explicit.

The teacher's influence

A wide body of research has pointed to the fact that the majority of pupils will learn to read and write by any method which the teacher or the school selects, as long as it is systematic and well structured. Graded reading schemes and structured programmes of various kinds attest to this. Of five reception teachers observed over two years, the most successful teacher of reading was the most organised and structured in her approach to look and say with the graded reading scheme. However, dyslexics still failed to learn to read and write in this well-ordered regime and more became vulnerable to difficulties as the situations moved towards the chaotic.

Although the methods of reading teaching have been developed to a high degree of sophistication this is not true for spelling. It helps if the methods we use to teach it are varied according to the demands of spelling and not simply directed by reading teaching.

Another factor influencing pupil success is teacher attitude. The overemphasis on reading has already been criticised, but commitment to a system or method also has its Hawthorne Effect. When classroom teachers try the special interventions they tend to be more effective than when a remedial tutor or researcher does it (Torgeson *et al.* 1999). This means the classroom teacher needs to support and reinforce the remedial work if it is to be effective.

Underlying theory

There is a vast array of teaching schemes which include phonics and also a range of schemes which are specifically phonics based and can be used for developmental or remedial work. However, some of the schemes and some of the methods do not actually enable the learners to learn the phonic skills they need, thus any scheme needs to be carefully assessed for its validity. A popular resource for teaching phonics and listing of phonic resources was written by teachers and edited by Hinson and Smith (1993). In explaining their philosophy in the book they state:

> As already discussed, not every child will need to be taught phonics. Nevertheless, the majority will benefit from help at some point in learning to read. The actual teaching of phonics should not therefore be introduced too early. However, do not lose sight of the fact that much valuable pre-school preparation for learning to read will have been going on at home from the time children are very young.
>
> (Hinson and Smith 1993: 11)

This embodies the orthodoxy of the time and is particularly damaging for dyslexics. All children benefit from being introduced to phonics from the outset, even those who arrive already literate at pre-school. They may not need systematic beginners' phonics but they can learn to use phonics to support reading and spelling at their own levels as one of a range of strategies.

'The acquisition of phonics is essentially an oral skill which depends for its success upon well developed auditory discrimination ...' (ibid.). This also needs to be challenged. Whilst the information contained in the rest of Hinson and Smith's book is factual and valuable these two extracts can be regarded as inappropriate to children with spelling difficulties. If they mean that phonic drills and systematic phonics teaching for the majority is unnecessary then this is one thing, but all children need to acquire knowledge of initial word sounds *as they meet print.* Their phonic knowledge needs to be very carefully monitored and direct teaching input given at the first signs if they begin to falter. This will mean that as well as general class teaching of alphabet sound knowledge there should be individually tailored inputs on a need-to-use basis. It also has to be recognised that in many homes there are no pre-reading activities going on.

Phonics is not just an oral skill

The claim that phonics is essentially an oral skill depending for its success upon auditory discrimination must be examined further; it does not seem to be quite as simple as this. Dyslexics and other poor spellers who have not developed sound-to-symbol correspondence rarely seem to have any auditory discrimination difficulties. If they are offered a 'sweet or sweep' they instantly know which one to choose. What a wide body of research has shown is that they do have problems associated with *phoneme segmentation,* very often mistakenly called 'auditory discrimination', activities. Test items frequently reinforce this misconception, for example as shown in Figure 5.1.

A child with ordinary hearing and memory has to compare 'k' in cup with p or pl, s or sp and 'k' in comb. Surprisingly, listeners cannot do this easily by ear. The reason is because the sound frequencies in syllables are shingled on top of each other (Liberman *et al.* 1967) and cannot be separated out by the human ear, even a young one.

Phonics and initial sounds

Initial sounds are a bit more decipherable as *onsets*: extra bursts of energy fractionally in advance of the rest of the buzz of sound frequencies. Most children seem to learn this onset strategy when confronted with print in a systematic way. But children who cannot process fast sounds (Tallal 1994) would be at a distinct disadvantage if left to their own devices and if early learning was only by look and say. Direct teaching of these key features would be essential. One of the ways teachers do this is in 'I Spy' games by overemphasising the initial sound. Even so, dyslexics most often fail by this method and need another.

Phonemes in the syllable

The phoneme is said to be an 'abstract perceptual unit' (Ehri 1979) and has to be linked to an arbitrary and abstract visual symbol, the grapheme. For a five-year-old, abstractions are somewhat difficult to deal with. In addition, some teachers also require children to 'sound out' the letters in a syllable e.g. c - a - t. It is *not* possible for us to do this. Syllables cannot be segmented by ear (Liberman *et al.* 1967). Thus

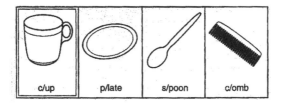

Figure 5.1 Task demonstrating phoneme segmentation rather than auditory discrimination

the only way to segment the 'cat' syllable is to be able to spell it in the first place! This is also true of phoneme tapping tasks in syllables e.g. seven (sevn). We 'hear' four not five phonemes. If we just use the articulatory cues then separating the initial sound is easy by feel, we miss the vowel as there are no articulatory contacts, and then feel the end consonant and write 'svn'. That is if we know our phonics and can word build with them.

Intrusive schwa

Schwa is the 'uh' sound as in 'banana' ('buh - nah - nuh'). In spelling it is often the sound of the medial vowel in a syllable. Diagnosticians often refer to pupils as having 'a problem with the medial vowels'. The result usually is that they are retaught the vowels which of course they already know, but not how to deal with the unaccented vowel in the medial position which sounds like 'uh'. Most teachers know about this 'uh' when saying a word for spelling but classroom helpers must be trained to avoid it or they can wreck any programme.

Phonics teaching in the open air, 10 June 1997 Maldon Quay

Year 1 pupils with clipboards and questionnaires at the ready were writing. A Learning Support Assistant worked with a group of three children presumably with learning difficulties. She said, 'No you spell it like this: 'RUH – OH – PUH – EH, rope'. To another pupil she then turned and said, 'Yes it starts with LUH, LUH – IH – NUH – EH, line'.

  This brand of crazy phonics with intrusive schwa and overemphasised consonants was delivered in a loud important tone. The children were quiet and subdued and seemed, not surprisingly, mystified by the task of spelling.

Phonics in the Post Office, a parent advises a 6–7 year old (2005)

'Yes, you spell Amanda, AH - MUH - AH - NUH - DUH - AH.' She looked puzzled after this but her child duly wrote letters down on the card.

Figure 5.2 Examples of beginning spellers using the phonemes in the syllable

Faye: five years two months: 'my little sister is in bed because she is having her tonsils out'

mi littl sid is in bed bkos se is hafi hi tosis aot

William: five years two months: 'the tree fell on top of the telephone pole wire'

teh tre fel on to f teh telfn pol riu

Unsupervised worksheets and completion activities

This is inherent in many schemes, for example a text might say: 'This is an apple. Look at the picture. Say the word "apple". What sound does it start with? Here are some words with the "a" sound in them. See if you can read them: an, and, am, fat, man, cat, Pat. They all have the a sound in them. They all belong to the same family.' Exercise One: Find the a family words and write them in your book:

1 am and little cat fat
2 Pat gas has him had

In the brief introduction by the teacher or LSA the pupil may not have time to establish the phoneme–grapheme link. If so, the subsequent exercise is little more than searching for a particular shape and then copying the configuration that it is in. When this occurs and the letter is later presented out of context the pupils will be found not to have learned the sound for they can do the task entirely visually. If there is a sound–symbol teaching input the relationship can still be lost in the labour of copying all the other letters, although the exercise is completed accurately in the book.

Draw a picture?

In Exercise Two we may see: 'Draw a picture of a fat man with his hat and bag.' There is no significant association of phoneme and grapheme here and it can be considered to be a way of spending (wasting) the pupil's time. It can be inferred that the methods used in books full of colouring and worksheet completion activities *may* elicit phonics responses but do not teach them, making them just another exercise in wrist movements using different coloured pencils.

Irrational orders for the introduction of phonics

Orders of introduction may be based on the order of the alphabet, hypothesised ease of construction in writing, day-to-day need, serendipity, vowels first, following what a scheme provides without question and so on. In the APSL schemes letters for spelling are introduced in frequency of use order beginning with *i t p n s*. The sounds *and names* for spelling are introduced together in a remedial programme; in teaching beginners this may not always be appropriate at the outset.

Teach a sound and use it

As soon as two sounds have been learnt they should immediately be used to show the pupils how words can be built for spelling and used in word attack and word search in reading e.g. it ti tit, and then it tit pit tip ip ti. This is the basis of 'synthetic phonics'. It is important that real and nonsense words are made up and spelled to dictation. After this with the use of joining words such as 'the' simple sentences can be constructed e.g. Tip it in the pit.

Compile a phonic vocabulary

Many programmes contain errors. Digraphs are called blends, blends are split, diphthongs are called vowel digraphs and so on. A list of the correct meanings of each of these terms should be compiled and translated into words which pupils can understand as this vocabulary is gradually introduced to them. In addition, schemes should be evaluated to check for these errors. Key concepts after vowels, consonants and syllables are:

*   A **consonant digraph** – a combination of two consonants making one sound which is different from either of them. There are six consonant digraphs: ch, sh, ph, wh, and th (voiced and unvoiced).
*   A **vowel digraph/double vowels** – this is a combination of two vowels in one syllable but there is only one resulting sound. One of the vowels will retain one of its own sounds. The rule is: 'When two vowels go walking the first one does the talking' (mostly) 'and it usually says its own name' e.g. raid, bean, soak.
*   A **diphthong** – this is a blend of two vowels in one syllable in which neither quite retains its own sound (oy and ah-oo). There are four vowel diphthongs in English and these are: oi (oil); oy (boy); ou (out); ow (cow). Two of them contain y and w acting as semi-vowels and 'ow' can also be a digraph as in 'snow'.

Gradual linguistics

As the teaching of phonics progresses, linguistic strategies should be taught as soon as they can help a pupil unravel a spelling problem or develop a spelling skill. Just learning the CVC structure is not enough; we need to teach the significance of the long and short vowels within syllables which control suffixing (see Chapter 6).

Rules

Rules can be an aid to good spelling but the pupils need to be ready for them and this means they need to be able to understand the basis of the rule, not just learn to chant it such as: 'i before e except after c'. This one is better taught as a problem-solving activity first to generate 'c' words using the dictionary if necessary and examine their spellings to see if there is a principle which governs them e.g. as in *can cat cut cycle cede cop cook clean cram cream cup cuss cull cell cello* etc., then receive, conceive, deceive, thief, grief, piece.

   In summary, both developmental and remedial phonics need a much more careful teaching plan. Magic 'e' is not a rule, it is a confusion. Long vowel sounds in syllables are denoted by 'e'. They make the vowel say its own name. For example: late, hope, line, wire, -ate.

Mnemonics

Mnemonics are very popular as an aid to spelling. The process consists of using the initial sound of each letter in the word to make up a memorable sentence. As the word becomes longer so making the mnemonic becomes a bigger chore. The main problem is that a new mnemonic has to be made up for every misspelled word for there is no generalisation to other words. It is more cognitively efficient to find another strategy such as a morphemic one.

Personalised programmes

A number of teachers and researchers have designed their own remedial pro- grammes. Nicolson and Fawcett (1994) reported on a multimedia program for Apple Macintosh which they had devised and used with 10–12 year old dyslexics. The pupils had to learn 20 spellings, ten with a mnemonic approach they called 'Selfspell' and the other ten with a mastery learning whole word approach, 'Spellmaster'. In each there was an overlearning strategy which they said was 'gen- erally considered to be one of the most effective for dyslexic children' (p. 519). Both programmes were effective in remediating the 20 errors, with Spellmaster showing more improvement on the immediate post test. Performance on the elapsed test however gave equivalent results for both tests. On the whole the dyslexics found the mnemonics-making method in Selfspell more attractive. This is not surprising for it has some appeal to the intellect and the dyslexics selected for such pro- grammes are usually well above average in intelligence. Indeed they come to believe that rote learning by visual means is their only route to successful reading and spelling and use mnemonics for the really 'hard ones'.

What is of note is that both are mainly based upon rote learning and the strate- gies lack the power of generalisation to new and different words. The elapsed test results are what might be expected from such methods.

Learning and not learning

If the pupil appears to know the sound one day and forgets it the next day, conclude that the sound has not been securely learnt. It is far better to spend five sessions ensuring that one sound is learnt than that five sounds, particularly vowel sounds, should be presented in one session and none of them be learnt. In the latter case all that has happened is that the teaching programme has been completed without regard to the pupil's learning need and the real learning agenda.

Reappearance of errors

Sometimes an old error is repeated next day as though the new correct version has been forgotten. What has occurred is that the new version does not have a high enough profile in the memory and so both versions become available. How to over- come this is dealt with in Chapter 6.

Forms of phonics teaching

Basic phonics – one-to-one correspondence

Teachers unfamiliar with the range of phonics methods when introducing phonics use a very basic strategy. They teach the sounds of the alphabet and then move on to consonant – vowel – consonant or regular words and then move on to blends. When sounds are used to blend words this is sometimes regarded as synthetic phonics as words are being synthesised.

However, the strategy emphasises one-to-one correspondence between a single letter and its sound; the blending comes late. It appears to work with some regular words e.g. c-a-t, b-i-g, but then not so well with s-t-r-ee-t, s-a-n-d or s-c-h-oo-l. It is a less powerful form of phonic synthesis, and can seem to have little relationship for early years learners to most of the words they want to spell. It may be better than no phonics at all.

Thirty pupils of average age eight years ten months, all in Years 4 and 5, who had been assessed as children with learning difficulties were given a weekly session of one hour in class support for learning to help with their reading and writing. Each was also given half an hour of individual teaching each week using phonic and other worksheets. When they were tested after a six month period there was an average loss in reading age of 8.6 months. In reality one subject made no gain but no loss, keeping up with his increasing age; one subject made 20 months' progress above the six months' increase in age, five subjects made an average gain of three months over chronological age; and 23 subjects made a loss of 12.74 months.

In relation to spelling in the group of subjects overall there was a loss of 0.04 months or no observable gain over chronological age; they were now keeping pace with it. Twelve subjects made 7.6 months' progress over their increased age; five subjects made 14.6 months' progress – a ratio of more than two to one; 14 subjects lost 6.6 months in progress – in other words they stayed where they were when they entered the programme.

It can be seen that this phonics programme was helping just over half the pupils in spelling to keep up with their age but except for one pupil it was not transferring to reading. The help was not enough to remedy their problems. This is typical of the analytic and basic phonics presented in school worksheets.

Gittelman and Feingold (1983) claimed to have undertaken a carefully controlled experiment with subjects randomly assigned to treatment groups. Their remediation involved 'intensive' phonics training which they suggested directly transferred in a limited manner to the spelling but was not so good for reading. Their remediation training also included intersensory integration training in reading, whole word recognition training and all perceptual motor training techniques! A classic example of 'hedging bets', including anything under remediation which might conceivably work – the shotgun approach.

Although the phonics work did not show much transfer to reading, reading skills did improve in a limited way. This was not surprising since four types of treatment were given to it! It can only be presumed that they were not effective as remedial strategies.

Analytic phonics

Analytic phonics is more suitable for reading. It provides pupils with the strategies for decoding words during reading. For example, the first and most important strategy is the letter sounds needed to detect the onsets in words. Systems such as Letterland (see below) help to do this. If we apply it to the traditional example: 'The cat sat on the mat' the analytic phonics would work like this: th-e c-at s-at o-n th-e m-at. In other words we teach the onset and rime strategy. The pupil uses phonic knowledge to guess the word from the initial sound and its sentence or picture context. If in addition the semantic and syntactic structure of the sentence mirrors that of ordinary speech it makes the process easier. Blends and digraphs are specifically taught to assist this decoding activity e.g. st - still, bl - blend. As all the letters in the word for reading are already present it does not help to sound every single one in English. Instead the *onset and rime strategy* (Bryant and Bradley 1985) is more effective, especially at the beginning.

Sometimes blending is taught without regard to this and runs against the natural order e.g. 'sand' s-a-n-d, sa-n-d, san-d, sand. Dyslexics told us during the development of TRTS that they found onsets and rime strategies (s-and) the easiest for reading and blending.

Synthetic phonics

Synthetic phonics is a sound and blend method. It is most suitable for teaching spelling. The word to be spelt has to be pronounced clearly and then constructed or transformed from this abstract auditory form into concrete graphemes. Rather than teaching single sounds separately for each letter in order through the alphabet ('basic phonics') the initial sounds including blends, middles and end blends are taught as well as other useful phonograms and rules. The children learn to sound and write two or three letters such as a, p, t and then learn to blend them immediately to make word sounds and regular words such as ap, at, pap, tap, tat and pat. Thus children learn to build words at the very beginning. This is the essence of the TRTS and Hickey dyslexia programmes.

Three hundred children from disadvantaged backgrounds in Clackmannanshire with 93 per cent of the average child's word knowledge were taught by the synthetic phonics method starting with a, p, t and used a magnetic board to assemble their spellings (Watson and Johnston 1998). The children were found to be three-and-a-half years ahead at 11 compared with those from the same backgrounds taught by NLS methods (basic phonics), and one sound per week. More controlled studies are needed.

Phonetics (Smith and Bloor 1985)

Children who are having difficulties in learning to spell often have to engage in a self help approach when it comes to phonics and their errors can be misinterpreted. This can create problems in a teaching programme and time can be wasted on the wrong kind of input. A knowledge of some aspects of phonetics can be helpful to remedial teaching. Phonetics is a system of 46 symbols which represent the separate speech sounds which are made in the English language.

The speech sounds are described by how they are made: plosive, fricative, nasal and lateral in relation to the key articulators. For example, the movement of the tongue, alveolar ridge, nasal cavity, velum – the position of the soft palate and where it directs the air and vocal cords – whether they vibrate or not, and the shape of the lips.

The consonant 'm' is made with lips closed and voicing; 'n' is made with the tongue contacting the alveolar ridge; and 'ng' is velar. M and n are frequently confused and helping the pupil articulate and identify the *feel* of these consonants can help spelling. When 'n' is followed by d or t in the final blends (-nd and –nt) the result is that the preceding vowel is nasalised and the pupil can easily fail to detect this and so makes spelling errors, for example fed for fend, bed for bend, wet for went, set for sent, and so on.

Pupils may make reversals in spelling such as 'was' for 'saw' and 'on' for 'no'. If they were to prepare to mouth or articulate the initial sound (the onset) subvocally they could not then write 'was' for 'saw' and 'on' for 'no' because their formation is quite different. They may also omit final consonants such as 'd' and 't' even when trying to articulate clearly for spelling.

Another common error is in b and d confusions. As these are characteristic of many poor spellers' scripts their appearance or reappearance can be misinterpreted. If when they are noted multisensory retraining is given again to correct the error a lot of time can be fruitlessly spent when the pupil actually thinks that the football ticket 'abmits' one and has a similar notion about 'abvantage'. Teaching the prefixes 'ad' and 'ab' along with the meanings which they convey and their clear expression in speech will be a more appropriate method.

Some knowledge of *assimilation* can also be helpful for it is then possible to identify spelling error patterns which might seem like articulation immaturities or difficulties such as 'bab boys', 'fak cat', and 'temmen'. *Elisions* may also be directly transcribed such as 'tem pence', and 'dome be' for don't be.

Multisensory training and phonics

The universal cry seems to be that phonics *must* be multisensory and most early reading teachers and remediators have taken it up. It is a practice adopted from the remedial field from the 1970s as distinct from what was going on in early years teaching and was regarded as somehow being effective with dyslexics. Multisensory phonics works! But does it? We need to exercise caution, for multisensory training seeks to establish the link between the visual symbol, its auditory sound, and its motor graphemic shape, i.e. the VAK triangle (visual – auditory – kinaesthetic) linkage in those who have problems. It can become a terrible waste of time in overtraining for those who have no such problems. It can also waste dyslexics' time unmercifully if the ariculatory dimension is not included or goes on long after the breakthrough has been made. Applying the principle ad nauseam to learning all new spellings brings us back to the spelling grind of the nineteenth century modes of teaching.

Careful observation of pupils' needs should enable the teacher to stop multisensory training in good time and switch to new strategies, even with dyslexics!

Literacy Acceleration (LA) (Lingard 2005)

Pupils who were 'slow readers' received daily LA help which consisted of individualised phonic help given by trained teaching assistants (TAs). The pupils only moved forward as they mastered the phonics, not at a predetermined rate as in the NLS.

They followed a structured spelling programme at least twice a week, grouped by attainment. The method was multisensory with regular and systematic repetition drawing on different learning styles. They wrote weekly as a group and also studied text and genres. Non-readers and near non-readers were given LA tuition in pairs or alone with a TA. Lingard's cautious interpretation of the results found these methods successful in comparison with those following the National English Strategy in mixed ability groups in Years 7 and 8. He stated: 'it is a mistake to believe that the secondary school English programmes, designed for those who can already read, spell and write, are effective with pupils with literacy difficulties' (2005: 76).

Some issues for subskills approaches

The substantial problem of 'ecological validity' has already been raised with regard to identifying what are relevant subskills in the acquisition of reading and writing and their development. Acquisition skills may not be the same as developmental skills. For example, decoding a word in order to read it may not use the same processes as reading whole words as they begin to become familiar or when we are fluent readers. Similarly, spelling words automatically from the lexicon (word memory store) will involve different processes from encoding unknown spellings from spelling particles.

It has already been suggested that increasing phonological skills of awareness and segmentation may be the result of, not the precursor to, literacy progress. Now a further issue is relevant and that refers to effectiveness judgements when training on subskills or using a lack of them to identify the nature and extent of literacy problems. This is the issue of predictive validity – can their poor results on the test predict exactly who will be dyslexic and be seen to fail in two years' time? How many errors in prediction might be involved? Then there is the issue of significance, or what exactly does 'a very significant' improvement or high correlation mean? For example, the correlation between handwriting and keyboarding skills is highly significant in a large sample but the correlation of +0.34 actually overlaps or accounts for 11.56 per cent of the variance. The one cannot be used to predict performance on the other, as most of the time you would be wrong. A correlation of +0.8 between a word recognition reading test and a spelling test looks very strong but there is only 64 per cent predicitive validity between them and we need correlations of above +0.95 (90.25 per cent) to reliably say that the poor scores on the one will mostly predict which individuals will fail on the other. The predictive validity of most early screening tests is seldom higher than 50 per cent but when Torgesen (1995) finds something which is 96 per cent then it must be important.

Phonological Awareness Training (PAT) – onsets and rimes (Wilson 1994)

Wilson, an educational psychologist, described the background to a PAT project she had devised as based upon research on phonological skills and phonological awareness. She referred to the work of Rack et al. (1992), Bryant and Bradley (1985), Goswami and Bryant (1990) and Goswami (1994) in particular. She described traditional phonics programmes as the progressing from letter – sound relationships to consonant-vowel-consonant words (c-v-c words) and then moving on to blends and so on, and stated that 'This route now appears to work entirely against the course of the development of phonological skills' (Wilson 1994: 5).

But Wilson failed to examine synthetic phonic programmes and compare their effects. On the basis of work with case study 'A' who was ten years old and at the end of Year 5, she devised a system of phonological training. She reported that A had already received a great deal of 'specialist' remedial teaching and had worked on 'word families' without success. This time he was to spend not more than ten minutes each day during the summer holiday generating words which shared the same rime. She gave him the onsets and a selection of common rimes giving examples of how to word build using them. If necessary his mother was simply to remind him of what a specific rime said. Two months later he was tested with words using the rimes, some familiar and some new ones. He could read them all and spell those with the training rimes.

She then piloted the system with colleagues in schools and found that all the children benefited, although not all to the same extent as A. The teachers used it with their children and a test project was set up of 48 children aged 8–12 years old. They all had reading difficulties (spelling not mentioned) as identified by the schools. After a psychological assessment 24 children followed the PAT programme over a 20-week period and the other 24 followed a programme arranged by the schools. They were all then reassessed by the psychologists before the names of those in each programme were revealed.

Of the two matched groups the PAT group was found to have made significantly more progress in reading *and* spelling than the others. Wilson did not recommend this particular strategy for use for children below the age of seven years because the basis of the intervention is through making and finding analogies which younger children, unless reading advanced, would find difficult. It is essentially a spelling learning strategy different from using onset and rime in beginning reading and spelling. She suggested that younger children might find the strategy confusing and recommended other forms of phonological awareness training. The PAT programme has been implemented in primary and secondary schools in Buckinghamshire.

There are now three PAT programmes. They are not designed to replace reading schemes but are used to supplement and underpin them. There are five placement sheets and placement is based upon the pupil's ability to read the words on the reading lists in them. If longer than 60 seconds is taken to read a particular list then placement begins at the next level down. The programme only deals with regularly spelled words and there are 25 photocopiable worksheets and 25 related reading lists and dictation sheets.

The procedure is to spend 10–15 minutes a day, five days per week on the programme. The first three days are spent on worksheets. These are headed by the whole alphabet and underneath there are four columns, each beginning with a different rime. Pupils are given a new worksheet each day but only if their score on the previous sheet shows more than 14 out of 20 correct. On the fourth day the pupil does reading and ten spellings and on the fifth day five sentence dictations are given and there is a special format for these too. It is important that the procedures laid down are carefully followed and this includes supervision of the worksheets and 'slicing' or cutting the task to half a worksheet for those with the severest difficulties.

According to Thomas (1998), 'the children enjoy the worksheets and find them exciting and challenging although teachers looking at them at first think they look dull and uninteresting ... one cannot fail to notice the excitement as the children begin to improve' (p. 17). One of Thomas' referrals reported to her teacher, 'I am doing very well now because I have this special programme which really makes me spell better and has helped my reading. I find that I say words automatically without the struggle I used to have' (p. 18). This pupil had made progress in reading age from 7.9 to 10.1 years in 12 weeks on the programme.

Once again we can see the dominance of the reading approach and the visual memory training rote method applied to the rimes. It is more to do with analytic phonics for reading than spelling, except for the dictations. It is wise to use the programme sparingly to give a boost in confidence as it does provide one strategy a pupil can use – that of analogy with a known word. Dyslexics, however, even beyond the eight-year-old level may not have the necessary phonological subskills to cope with the onsets (spelling) or generating real word rimes and can find the whole process very trying.

A common ending, rime or unit is said to be useful for spelling and reading such as -ent in tent, bent, dent and sent, but what about meant? And how does the dyslexic learn to spell 'ent' in the first place? It may come out as 'et' or 'tne'.

In a review of 30 reading teaching methods, Brooks et al. (1998) found that the most effective were those which worked on both phonological skills and self-esteem. However, none of the methods were able to achieve more than keeping pace with increasing age. This is of course better than no progress at all but not sufficient for full remediation.

Phonological training effects (Bryant and Bradley 1985; Bradley 1990)

Sixty-five pre-readers identified as having difficulty on a rhyme judgement test were matched and assigned to three treatment groups. Children in group one were given phonological training and half the group were shown how the phonemes in the words they categorised could be represented by graphemes, using plastic alphabet letters. In the second group they were trained to categorise the same words semantically. The third group received no training.

The training consisted of 40 ten-minute sessions over two years. Two years later, aged eight–nine years, the phonologically trained group were four months ahead of the trained control group and ten months ahead of the untrained controls. On the spelling test, children who had received phonological training and letter mapping were 13 months ahead of the phonological training only group, 17 months ahead of the trained controls, and nearly 24 months ahead of the rest. The specially trained group were also now three months ahead of their 300 peers who had initially performed well on the rhyme test.

Five years later Bradley tested them again and found more than half the children from the control groups had received remedial help. Although all the children had made some progress those given the letter mapping were still as far ahead as they were earlier. 'The particular advantage gained by the children taught to understand the connection between sound categories and orthographic spelling patterns suggests the two together make a formidable contribution to children's early progress in spelling' (Bradley and Huxford 1994: 431).

What we can tease out from this is that the predictive capacity of the rhyme test to later literacy attainment appears to be around 50 per cent (a correlation of +0.71) and that the explicit teaching of spelling sound-symbol correspondences (using the plastic letters) at this early stage gives gains later of two years over the untrained groups whereas phonological awareness training on its own is much less effective.

A similar but larger scale study was carried out by Lindberg and Frost (1988). They trained 235 Danish children daily over eight months on a range of phoneme awareness tasks, games and stories. It was only those games which involved dividing spoken words into smaller segments which later were found to have enhanced spelling.

In the USA Ball and Blachman (1991) tested three groups of kindergartners, then Group A was trained to segment phonemes and on rhyming and letter knowledge, Group B was trained in language activities and letter knowledge, and Group C was given no training. After four 20-minute sessions for seven weeks Group A had made significantly more progress in spelling than the other two groups and there was no difference between the groups in letter name knowledge. Again we can conclude that segmenting phonemes with or without rhyming was the effective element. Is segmenting phonemes a euphemism for teaching a spelling skill?

In a comprehensive NFER-funded review of programmes offering help to slow readers Brooks *et al.* (1998) found the following results among others:

- no treatment, or normal schooling, does not enable them to catch up;
- most approaches which concentrated heavily on phonological approaches to reading showed little impact.

In addition, comprehension can be improved if directly targeted; work on self-esteem and reading together had potential; and IT approaches needed to be targeted and teacher-supported (Brooks 1999: 30). Again we see the emphasis on reading in the research and treatments but we can learn from them that the type of phonological training given – awareness-training may be misdirected and they needed to use segmentation training or 'spelling approaches'.

Some phonics schemes in use in the UK

Letterland

This scheme was first devised by Lynn Wendon (1984) and was originally known as the Pictogram System. 'Letterland' is a secret place lying invisibly inside the written word. Clever Cat, Eddy Elephant and Wicked Water Witch live there. Each letter shape is a pictogram in which picture clues have to be fused to give its shape. Stories have been developed which explain the behaviour of each letter and how it reacts with other letters. There are two teaching programmes – *First Steps in Letterland* and *Big Strides in Letterland*. Included in them is work on language, phonics, whole word recognition, reading development, writing and spelling. Story telling, drama role play and singing are integral to the scheme. Although correct letter formation is taught from the outset it is presented in print script form.

The scheme has a great appeal to children in nursery and reception classes but will not be appreciated by older learners; for them, remedial phonics approaches are needed. The stories about the letters are so powerful with small children that teachers are loath to adopt any scheme which does not accommodate them and their letter forms. They do not accept that they can teach a different script for spelling from that for reading. The Letterland approach fits with one-to-one correspondence and promotes the basic phonics format in which only the simplest and most regular words can be spelled. It is more helpful for reading than spelling.

Phonetic alphabet system: i.t.a.

The initial teaching alphabet (*i.t.a.*) (Pitman 1961) was introduced as a phonemic system of 44 symbols representing all the speech sounds of English. There was only one correct sound response to each symbol and there was a graded introduction based upon frequencies. It had direct phoneme–grapheme correspondence but a considerable number of new graphemes had to be invented and it was these which, in the end, adults trained in the 26 letters of the Roman alphabet found difficult to accept.

In the i.t.a. system, transfer to traditional orthography was achieved towards the end of second year where difficulties ensued only for the minority (Downing 1964). It was once quite a popular scheme but by 1996 was only used in one school because parents and governors found the script too different to accept and there was a lack of up-to-date reading material being published.

The average advantage reported was that they were about a year ahead of children taught by look and say at seven years, and an NUT film of the period showed them reading away very rapidly and fluently. This advantage corresponds to the findings of Chall (1967) in the USA with phonics methods. Few children failed to learn in this system but those who did would have been likely to have difficulties in other systems and began to show these difficulties at transfer.

Jolly Phonics: The Phonics Handbook (Lloyd 1993)

This scheme is thought to be used in about 68 per cent of English primary schools. It uses an action, picture, story and song to represent each letter sound. *The Phonics Handbook* was an adaptation of the i.t.a. approach. Sue Lloyd had had extensive experience in the teaching of reading using the look and say system with i.t.a., a system in which all the 44 sounds of the initial teaching alphabet were learned before starting the reading books. In her *sounds first* method, at the end of the second year the children were reading as well as they used to at the end of the third year. Before the change in method the average score on Young's Reading Test was 102 and afterwards it was between 110 and 116 and the reading itself was more fluent. Lloyd also reported that the pupils' independent writing was far better although it was not always in conventional spelling at first but the teachers could read what the children had written.

In this multisensory synthetic phonics teaching system, what Lloyd has done is instead of using i.t.a. symbols for the 18 sounds which do not correspond to single letters of the alphabet, she has used the 'digraphs' which most closely matched them. In making this simple but ingenious step traditional orthography can be made to carry all the benefits of i.t.a.

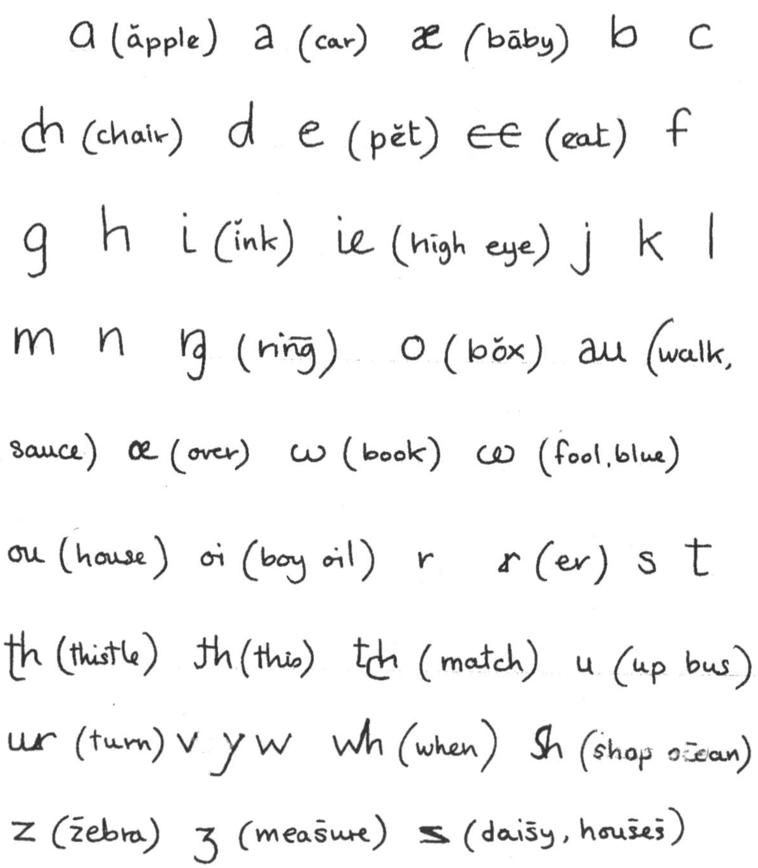

a (ăpple) a (car) æ (bāby) b c

ch (chair) d e (pĕt) ee (eat) f

g h i (ink) ie (high eye) j k l

m n ŋ (riñg) o (bŏx) au (walk,

sauce) œ (over) w (book) ധ (fool, blue)

ou (house) oi (boy oil) r ᴦ (er) s t

th (thistle) th (this) tch (match) u (up bus)

ur (turn) v y w wh (when) ᶴh (shop oᴄean)

z (żebra) ʒ (measure) s (daiᶴy, houᶴes)

Figure 5.3 The Pitman i.t.a. alphabet

All the sounds can be learned as part of the same system which is simpler for children than a two-tiered system consisting of monographs followed by digraphs. This means that children can write any words they wish by using this logical sound bank in a synthetic phonics approach. Multisensory training is used to help the sound and the grapheme connect. It includes saying and sounding, and the ears, eyes, larynx, body and finger muscles are all drawn into the action.

The manual describes auditory skills training, the order of introduction of the symbols, and tracing and copying exercises. Finally, more advanced spelling skills and rules are dealt with. Teachers who have used the scheme in general remedial settings have been very enthusiastic about it. It is very similar to the Spalding and Spalding (1967) phonogram system which has 70 phonograms, as is the following.

Phono-Graphix (McGuinness and McGuinness 1998)

This is another multisensory synthetic phonics programme. It starts from what the child knows, the language. It teaches that the sounds of the language correspond to 'sound pictures' (letters). There are 79 pictures to learn, including blends. At the first level, the Basic Code, children are introduced to all the sound pictures that represent one sound and so they learn to read and spell phonically regular three-letter words (van, cat, jug; bell, buzz; lamp, hand). Later, at Advanced Code, they learn consonant and vowel digraphs (sh-i-p, cha-t), that most of the sounds are represented by more than one picture (boat, train, play, paper) and then where some of the sound pictures are used for more than one sound (show, frown).

At Level 3 pupils learn multisyllable management in words of up to five syllables for encoding and decoding.

In a research study in Gloucester schools, Dias and Juniper (2002) compared the results of using Phono-Graphix or the NLS in which teachers incorporated their favoured approaches such as Jolly Phonics. The experimental groups used Phono-Graphix (N=17) or Phono-Graphix plus Onset and Rime (N=14) and the control group (N=34) used NLS/Jolly Phonics. At the outset all the groups were five years and three to four months old. The results after seven months showed that all the groups had similar phonemic code knowledge but the Phono-Graphix only group had a better level of segmenting and blending skills and could generalise these to reading non-words. The NLS 'eclectic mix' group 'all knew their alphabet work and letter sounds but did not know how to apply this to new words' (2002: 37). On the Middle Infant Screening Test in Year 1 only two children from the Phono-Graphix group were highlighted for concern compared to eight in the parallel class. It was the best result since the school had started using MIST. In the comparison schools 25–30 per cent of children needed additional literacy support. Greater success was achieved by not combining Onsets and Rime with Phono-Graphix. Solity *et al.* (1999) reported similar results and advised that mixing analytic and synthetic phonics did not produce consistent results. As with Jolly Phonics the Gloucester teachers reported the children's motivation at reading and writing real words from the beginning. They also enjoyed the table-top objects which are used for stimulating spoken language.

Wirth (2001) described another study with 30 schools in Gloucestershire. Ten followed the NLS and their own school phonics schemes, ten followed Jolly Phonics and ten followed Phono-Graphix in the 15 minutes per day devoted to NLS word level work in reception classes. Instead of one or two sounds per week, the pace of these special programmes enabled them to teach four to six and all 42 in nine weeks on Jolly Phonics. After the first week even the less able pupils could write simple words and read them.

Teaching Handwriting, Reading and Spelling Skills (THRASS) (Davies and Ritchie 1998)

It is claimed that over 8000 schools worldwide use THRASS although most are in the UK and Australia. It is similar in design to the Spalding method and Phono-Graphix and has a range of resources such as CD-ROMs, videos, Big Books, charts, picture boards, and tapes. The focus is on blending for reading and segmenting for spelling supported by Raps and Sequencing tapes.

The THRASSboard has 44 phoneme boxes, 24 for consonant phonemes and 20 for vowel phonemes. For vowels the authors distinguish seven short monophthongs, five long monophthongs and eight diphthongs as in the THRASSWORDS tray, hair, ear, fly, snow, toy, moor and cow. There is also a category called 'Grapheme Catch Alls' (GCAs); these are graphemes not included on the picture charts because they would make the chart difficult to use e.g. the quad eigh in 'eight' should be in the box with *a, a-e, ai* and *ay* and on the picture clue card with baby, tape, snail and tray. The writing style on the materials is simple print with some ligatures.

Hornsby (2000) recommended the spelling choice charts as useful mnemonics when children were unsure of which letters are needed e.g. *j, g, ge,* or *dge* for spelling, but said that they would need Alpha to Omega support to explain the reasons behind the choices.

Lindamood Phoneme Sequencing System (LiPS) (Lindamood and Bell 2005)

Although this is rarely used in the UK it is worthy of note. It was originally known as Auditory Discrimination in Depth. The multisensory articulation training (oral-motor) improves phoneme awareness, self checking, spelling and articulation and this is coupled with synthetic phonics.

Developmental Spelling Handbook (Montgomery 1997b)

This is a handbook for teachers which through 110 mini lessons shows how to teach synthetic phonics and morphemic linguistics. It is initially based on the TRTS and Hickey remedial systems and letter order. It teaches multisensory articulatory phonics and uses an ovoid cursive writing method. It was initially written for XLane school (p. 284). Further details on the morphemics methods may be found in Chapter 6.

Precision Teaching (PT)

Precision teaching was one of the techniques widely promoted by the Special Needs Action Programme (SNAP) leaders Ainscow and Muncey in 1979 and subsequent years through until about 1987 when its dominance waned, or it was promoted less. PT was originally designed by Lindsley in the 1960s. He was a student of Skinner and the method is based upon the behaviourist principles of operant conditioning. It is a method of assessment which can be applied to overcome small learning difficulties and is not a form of teaching. In a four-year study in Montana, students on the programme for 20–30 minutes per day showed gains of 19–40 points on the IOWA Test of Basic skills over other students in the district (Binder and Watkins 1990).

A typical pupil benefiting from PT is one who cannot concentrate for long. It can help overcome a learning block but should not be used continuously. In PT a few minutes' work each day for a period of a week can increase the pupil's motivation and attention. The opportunity for interaction with the teacher is productive as well as helping to identify needs. PT is particularly successful with a warm and supportive teacher.

PT concentrates upon skills-based activities and one of the major strategies is to test for fluency or the rate of performance. If for example sounds of some letters of the alphabet need to be learned they are first directly taught then tested with a 'probe'. Fluent readers read at the rate of 80 words per minute of text, 50 words per minute of words in isolation and 54 words per minute of sounds in isolation. Spelling rate needs to be assessed by checking the speed of peers.

A *probe* is a test given daily and usually lasts for one or two minutes. It usually takes the format: see-to-say, see-to-write, hear-to-write, or hear-to-say. It could be applied to initial sounds, blends, words, or numbers.

An example format of precision teaching for spelling:

Decision	Alex will learn to spell AND, THE, FOR and FROM.
Action	Alex has to spell the words correctly in cursive.
Conditions	The task will be presented multisensorily.
Criterion	Alex has mastered the skill when the words can be written 100 per cent correctly to dictation (by teacher or tape) at a rate of ten to the minute.
Probes	The dictation probe will be given daily for one to two minutes as appropriate; the order of the words will be randomised.
Implementing the programme	Alex will study the words for two minutes. The probe will be given at the same time each day if possible. The format will be HEAR TO WRITE.

The number of correct and incorrect responses will be counted and recorded on the ratio chart by Alex. PT will be discontinued after Alex has met the criterion on two successive days. If the task proves too difficult it will be sliced (made easier). If it still proves too difficult a different method will be introduced.

Alex was delighted with the timer, marking his results on the ratio chart and watching his scores improve each day as well as seeing his writing and spelling improve. His spelling was at a very limited level and learning to get these common words correct was very pleasing to him. His writing speed also improved and this transferred to other writing tasks and he was keen to continue with other words. The important factor was to ensure he had some success early on by choosing 'and' and 'the' and not having too many words for him to cope with. The two minutes' study time was well spent as he learned to focus on the 'tricky' parts. In the following weeks he retained the knowledge and it transferred to both his reading and writing.

Richards (2003) tried a modified PT version with AL, a 16-year-old A level student who had problems in summarising experiments in psychology prior to discussing them. She was given examples, set précis tasks and given feedback on them. In addition she was given a probe task – to summarise correctly in fewer and fewer words. The results were 195; 90; 69; 47; 39 words. AL became more confident as she progressed and in the mock exam she gained a D grade, just one mark below C instead of her predicted D/E. Her friend DG without the PT probe gained her predicted grade D/E.

Computer assisted learning and skill software packages for phonics

The majority of software programs are designed to produce phonic drills. Some of them only teach one aspect. Other programs address a range of skills and then care has to be taken that the speed of introduction is not too fast for remediating spelling. Similarly a lot of time can be taken using software when a particular set of skills has already been acquired, so careful monitoring is necessary. As corrective input they can be useful.

In addition to teaching software there are also a range of spell checkers and dictionaries which can find a word and its meaning from partial clues. The problem for dyslexics is that when they have a list of alternatives they find it difficult to choose the correct spelling and even the correct word from among them.

All of these should be regarded as aids to discovering spelling not a substitute for teaching it. The advantage of such software is that it can help separate out the secretarial skills from the composition and development of ideas, giving a chance for the latter to have free rein. Printing out and proofreading before using the spell checker can help identify areas of spelling difficulty which the pupil, with the teacher's help, can then address.

It is particularly noticeable that a number of software programs have inbuilt errors in what they regard as blends, digraphs, diphthongs and so on. For example, Starspell Plus does not distinguish vowel digraphs from diphthongs and groups double consonants, consonant digraphs and blends together.

In a review of using computers to teach spelling to dyslexics, Wise and Olson (1994) concluded that children can improve their spelling and thereby enhance their reading with computers. The programs should, they concluded, teach typing skills and involve handwriting if they are to be effective; they should not teach too many items at a time and 'should offer good support from a knowledgeable adult or from the program itself' (p. 498). In their studies in Colorado they found that students were more stimulated to work harder and study words longer when there was speech feedback on their own attempts. They found that computer programs can be motivating, easily individualised, provide as much checking and repetition as the student needs (and without impatience and criticism) and can with speech repeatedly dictate items to be spelled. With the synthetic speech they can hear their errors as well as the words to be spelled. Most importantly the studies showed only small gains if there were no teachers or tutors present offering support.

Alphabetics

The teaching of the alphabet has had a poor deal in literacy teaching over a number of decades. It was first associated with the endless chanting drills of the ABC method in the monitorial system of education and this continued in many schools into the twentieth century. Rote learning of the alphabet, sometimes singing it backwards and forwards, and associated with phonics drills followed in the early twentieth century. As look and say took hold, rote methods became unfashionable and by the 1970s some schools banned alphabet teaching until pupils were seven or eight years old. The rationale for this then was that the names of the letters did not contribute to learning to read or spell.

Of course this is patently untrue. When we use the long vowel sound it is in effect its name. Children do find this knowledge helpful. The alphabet names are also the only consistent form of identity that the letters actually have and they are absolutely essential for dictionary work. Alphabetical order is necessary for using a dictionary and though some children absorb this through contact with print a significant number need to be directly taught it. Dyslexics find it particularly difficult to learn and need a specific form of training as laid out in the APSL programmes. Alphabet names, the names of the days of the week, months of the year and naming left from right are difficult for dyslexics because they are arbitrary labels. Dyslexics do not fail to learn them because of a sequencing problem as is popularly thought but because they have verbal processing and naming problems.

Alphabet teaching can take a number of forms. A popular method is as in Letterland, outlined above. Alphabet tracking games where joining up alphabet letters in order produces line drawings of animals and other items. Direct methods include putting a set of wooden letters in a 'feelie' bag. Pupils feel one, describe it and guess which one it is, withdraw it and lay it down in its position/order in an arc (rainbow).

Each of the early APSL lessons begins with alphabet work and alphabet games. Each new lesson builds from where the alphabet learning was left last time and proceeds slowly so that each new letter or letter run is securely learnt. Success in this is followed by dictionary work to learn the quartiles and practise dictionary use.

In the SOS writing technique for correcting spelling, part of the procedure must include the naming of the letters for spelling. Some teachers switch this to saying the sounds and this leads to confusion again. Pupils find it tricky at first but it should not be omitted.

Parents and particularly grandparents are fond of helping pre-school children learn to write their own names and frequently do this in capital letters. They teach them the alphabet by rote and so on. The result of all this is that children learn to *draw* their letters, especially capitals, without them being associated with the language element in the left hemisphere and this does not prepare the brain well enough for literacy learning which involves the left hemisphere language areas (in most people). Dyslexics' writing is often all in capitals, and even if correctly spelled in adulthood, it indicates there has been a problem earlier. It is this drawing function that can be retained after a stroke when the person is unable to write or spell in the ordinary way. With training/remediation CAT scans show the relocation of the literacy activation in the left rather than the right hemispheres as seen in dyslexics (Kappers 1990).

In conclusion it perhaps needs to be stated that there is no harm in singing and chanting the alphabet as long as the pupils do actually *know and understand* the order and how it can be used.

Summary and conclusions

In this chapter a range of general and remedial phonic strategies and schemes are examined. Their value is discussed in relation to their use in the general classroom and the withdrawal setting. Selected research studies related to these methods are presented to gain some insight into their effectiveness.

It is argued that all primary school teachers should have a knowledge of the nature of different types of phonics teaching methods and strategies. Only then can they select the most appropriate methods and contents for particular learners' needs. The different phonics methods for reading and spelling are described including basic, analytic and synthetic phonics. The place of 'onset and rime' and phonological training strategies are analysed and schemes such as Letterland, Spelling Made Easy, Jolly Phonics and so on are discussed. The targets of the phonics schemes are quite clear whereas the phonological skills training needs to be probed in more depth. Phonological segmentation (vide spelling) training seems to be effective whereas awareness training only gives small effects.

The role of alphabet teaching is discussed with reasons for including it in many schemes. Evidence shows that alphabetic work and strategic systematic phonics are an essential component in literacy teaching for developmental, preventative and first stage remedial work for spelling. What is also of importance is that the further behind the pupils are, the more likely there will be impressive gains in the first stages. It is here that sound-based schemes have their limitations in that they deal in the main with the lower levels of spelling acquisition such as phoneme segmentation and phonics.

However, those schemes which include syllable knowledge and rules often do so in a rather limiting framework such as in the NLS. A sound-based scheme although essential is not sufficient for meeting the needs for good spelling development of all spellers and especially dyslexics. How programmes should develop from and within the phonics base will be discussed in the next chapter. The key construct is that English uses an orthographic system which is phonic but governed by morphemics.

Chapter 6

Overcoming barriers to learning
Strategic cognitive and linguistic approaches

Introduction

Prominent amongst researchers in the spelling field over time has been Cramer. It was one of his papers 'Diagnosing skills by analysing children's writing' in *The Reading Teacher* in 1976 which first introduced me to the strategic way of thinking about spelling. He described the spelling of a particular pupil as a creative writing route. David was aged seven and had written the poem without help as follows:

> *My Ded cate*
> Ones I hade a cate
> He was white and yellow
> One night my father came fame my grandfathers house
> Wenn father come home fame
> my grandfathers house
> he said
> Ruste is ded

Good spellers are often good readers, but good readers can be poor spellers. Cramer (1998: 143) states that expert spellers tend to have an 'implicit understanding of the rules that govern the English spelling system'. He emphasised the need to take a positive approach to misspellings and advocated that as soon as children have assembled any spelling knowledge they should be encouraged to use it. David had made a total of seven misspellings out of 32. Cramer argued that David's superior spelling skills were demonstrated in his correct spellings of father, grandfather, white, night, house, said and yellow. He analysed the misspellings as common but near-miss good equivalents. The misspelling, he said, would gradually disappear with further writing practice as David became more familiar with orthographic conventions through reading.

He counted 'ded' for dead as a good generalisation from basic knowledge for /e/ as in bed. It is the most common way of spelling that sound. Hade is counted as an overgeneralisation of the final 'e' rule, of which he has good knowledge as he spells come, home and white correctly. 'Wenn' for 'when' is a good phonetic equivalent when one takes into consideration that the use of double n is common, particularly in the middle of words (tunnel, funnel). His 'Ruste' for 'Rusty' indicates that he needs to learn that the /i/ sound at the end of English words is represented by /y/.

'Fame' for 'from' shows lack of knowledge and sensitivity to the two-letter blend /fr/ but he correctly uses /f/ and /m/ for the first and last sounds. He adds 'e' possibly because he is aware that there are four letter places in the word. *Place knowledge* is not an uncommon finding in memory span research (Wing and Baddeley 1986) and he chooses silent 'e' for the fourth place as that is a common ending.

Cramer's approach here is to permit spelling to be absorbed during reading but what we really want to do is speed up the spelling development by inserting some teaching points. We would want to teach David the /wh/ question words as a group e.g. Where? Why? What? When? Who? (later Whither? Whether? Whence?) and their formal pronunciation with aspiration to aid spelling, which for fun he could listen for in different speakers' accents.

David could also be taught the closed syllable structure with the short vowel sound which does not require the addition of silent 'e' as in had, bed, pig, lot and but. Later when this has been absorbed he can learn the use of silent 'e' to denote the long vowel sound in the closed syllable, e.g. fame, cede, ride, mole, rude. These can be followed by the suffixing rules which they govern.

The sound and use of 'y' in the final position in English words (except 'taxi', a shortened form of the word taximeter, a measuring instrument fitted to a cab) would be pointed out and reinforced in practice games. David was, according to Cramer, a satisfactory speller for his age. More recently Cramer stated that: 'strategies are tools for tackling spelling problems. Strategies must be applied at different levels, within different contexts, using different example words. When students have many ways of approaching spelling challenges, the chances are increased that they will succeed' (1998: 161).

This is most certainly true but not what is found in English schools. An infant life of 'look and say' can limit children's strategies to purely visual ones. Introducing phonics suggests there is another range of strategies which they can use.

The two routes – logographic and phonological – have been evident in the research literature for two decades; however, there is a third which tends to be ignored and that is the cognitive, strategic and metacognitive route where the strategies generate the spellings within the individual's brain and present them to the lexicon. The reason for emphasising three routes to reading and not just two is to lay stress on the need to teach and encourage pupils to use all three, instead of two or even just one.

Words in the lexicon do not appear to be stored alphabetically but by association, and are not stored as actual words but as rules of some kind relating to words. We do know that they appear to be stored as base word rules to which affixes may be attached (Kuczaj 1979) and this makes another good reason for teaching to this strength and as a strategy.

Fulk and Stormont-Spurgin carried out a review of published research on spelling interventions for students with learning disabilities and found that it showed three main features (1995: 489):

- The spelling skill of students with learning disabilities is similar in developmental terms to non-disabled students.
- Cognitive strategies, such as those employed for spelling, are generalised to other academic areas, particularly with training for transfer and teacher prompts.

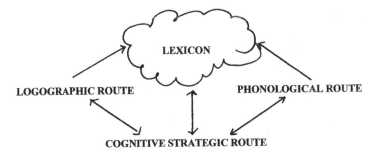

Figure 6.1 Three routes to spelling

- In 35 of the 38 spelling interventions presented in their review, explicit spelling instruction resulted in improved spelling performance.

Despite such evidence much research and teaching still considers dyslexia as a function of a disordered system and spelling a non-transferable skill, but is it?

Dyslexia: developmental delay or disorder?

In working with dyslexics it struck me forcibly that their writing at age ten and eleven was similar to the writing of David, their junior by several years. The 'Developmental Hypothesis' in dyslexia states that the difficulties we observe in dyslexics are due to a developmental delay of some kind. When the reasons for the delay are overcome or maturation takes place then development in spelling and reading will proceed and follow a normal pattern: a pattern similar to that of pupils who do not have dyslexia but who are several years younger. Bryant and Bradley (1985) supported the developmental hypothesis. The alternative position is held by Frith (1980), Snowling (2000), Nicolson and Fawcett (1994), and Miles and Miles (1992) among many others, that dyslexic problems stem from a deficit or a deficiency in verbal processing, in particular in phonological processing but it leads to spellings which are often 'bizarre' and the dyslexia is resistant to remediation especially in the area of spelling. It leaves the adult dyslexic with slow reading and problems with spelling which can never be successfully 'treated'. Evidence is adduced for this from adult dyslexics whose problems remain throughout life.

However, we can argue that those dyslexics whose problems have been cleared up do not present themselves for testing and some of them do not know they have been dyslexic. Their difficulties may only become observable in their slow reading and difficulties in spelling new and technical vocabularies. It is also true to say that we have not yet been able to give effective forms of remediation to a wide enough range of dyslexics. This was particularly true of the past and also there will be many adult dyslexics who have had no help at all. Some LEAs for example would not recognise dyslexia until the Code of Practice (DfEE 1994) referred to it. There will also be some dyslexics who have complex and multiple problems which are very resistant to remediation. These are most certainly likely to find their way to clinics and research centres for dyslexia.

There is a considerable amount of evidence to support the developmental hypothesis if we look at dyslexics' spellings in comparison with those of controls. It is necessary to compare the data from the same spelling test given to both groups or from a dictation.

Are dyslexics' spellings bizarre?

To test this, 23 dyslexics and 23 controls were given the Daniels and Diack spelling test (Montgomery 1997a) and the results are shown in Table 6.1.

As can be seen, the dyslexics were two-and-half-years older on average than the controls and the spelling age match was not perfect but showed that the controls were just over four months ahead. This amounts to doing about two words better on the test. It was the quality of the errors which was the target of interest. For this purpose the words that both groups had made errors on were collected. This resulted in 15 words' spellings for comparison, as shown in Table 6.2.

As can be seen, the number and nature of errors on the different words and on the test as a whole were very similar for both groups (xxx indicates the spelling was omitted on the test). In addition, the nature of the spelling errors is also similar. Each group has some examples of what someone not used to studying misspellings might consider bizarre such as 'dutwely' from a control for 'beautiful'. The d is a reversal for b and then we can see the control speller beginning to lay the word out phonetically with intrusive 'schwa' and getting lost. A dyslexic writes dualful, a lack of consonants and an attempt to reconctruct the word visually, which typically gets lost in the medial positions.

Only in the word friend did the dyslexics go more for a straight phonetic spelling as 'frend' whereas the controls introduced the letter 'i' more often. This reflects the phonics-based remedial programme the dyslexics were pursuing.

These lists of misspellings were presented to groups of 120 qualified teachers who had completed special needs and dyslexia training and 280 student teachers in their fourth years of training who had taken similar courses. They were asked to determine which group of misspellings had been written by the dyslexics. Only a handful managed to do this correctly. Most of the teachers said that it was impossible for them to say. The rest and the student group as a whole almost without exception but with lengthy time for study decided that the dyslexic group's spellings were in fact those of the controls. In evidence of this they pointed to the slightly larger number of 'bizarre' spellings amongst the matched controls, e.g. dutwely, fitghe, frenind, woner.

Table 6.1 Mean scores on spelling and writing tasks of a group of controls and dyslexics

	Mean chronological age	Spelling ratio score	Mean words written	Spelling age
Controls N = 23	8.04	X = 0.83	30.09	7.85
Dyslexics N = 23	10.65	X = 0.71	32.69	7.44

Table 6.2 The number and nature of errors made on the 15 target words

Target words	Controls	Dyslexics (errors in brackets)
1. so	sow sow sow (sow sow sowe soe sowh)	3 (5)
2. of	off off ov oft (off off ov ov ov)	4 (4)
3. form	fom from fom fom (fom forme)	4 (2)
4. seem	seam sean sem sean (seam seen sem seeme sem sheem sims)	3 (7)
5. who	hoo hoo ho hoow how ho ho (hoo hoe ho hoow how ho)	7 (6)
6. fight	fite fite fiter fit fite fite fite figth (fite fite firt fit fite fite fut fitghe)	8 (8)
7. great	grayt grayt grat grat grat grat grate grate grate (graet graet grate grat grat grate grate grate grate grade)	9 (10)
8. done	don doun dane dun dun dun dun dunit don (down don dune dun dun dun dun dun)	9 (8)
9. loud	loaed loaed loght lowd lowd loow lord lawd (lard loaed lawd lowd lad lod lawd)	9 (7)
10. friend	frend freind frend frend frend fred frend frend frend frend (freind freind frein freand freind frenid frend freind frenind frend frend frend)	10 (12)
11. women	whimm wimon wimin xxx xxx wimmen whimin wimen wim wiminn wimin (wimon wemen wimin wimen wimin wimen wimin winim wimming wimen woner wimin wiming)	11 (12)
12. any	neary eney eny eney eney enylen eny xxx eney eney ene ene (eany enry aney enay enay eney eney ener eney eney emey eny)	12 (12)
13. answer	answar answerwer aweser arser arser unser arser aser arnwa rser xxx answar arse (anweser answar answer ansire anrsoer answer awer asaw anrer unser ansir unser anser)	13 (13)
14. sure	shoer shoe shor shor shor sor shor sor shore shor shor shor shor shor (Shure chore shaw shore shoe shore shour shore shore shorshore shore sor shor shore)	14 (15)
15. beautiful	beautifo bueaful beutiful beatifal buitiful brotoful dualful buitfull xxx biterful birteeful botiful buoolefle biootf burooteforl butiful (bauetyful beatyful beutiful beutiful buatfull beatfull dutwely xxx xxx xxx beautifull buliefull beutiful beauitfull builfull builfull)	16 (16)

Total errors by dyslexics = 137
Total errors by controls = 134
Mean errors by dyslexics = 9.13
Mean errors by controls = 8.95

From these results it was inferred that dyslexics make no more bizarre spellings than younger controls of a matched spelling age. Their spellings appear to follow a normal pattern but characteristic of much younger spellers. Dyslexics also do not make any more reversals than we would expect of younger spellers; what they do is typical for their spelling age and extra experience.

Error analyses of spelling – miscues

Many of the miscues analyses of spelling bear little relationship to the needs of learners or teachers in correcting them. This criticism applies in particular to quantitative analyses – counting slips of the pen and errors at syllable boundaries; see Van Nes (1971) or Wing and Baddeley (1980) who found an error rate of 1.5 per cent in 40 undergraduate scripts with an estimated word count of 10,000 words in total. They categorised the errors as 'slips of the pen' – correctable errors attributable to lapses or inattention on the part of the writer, which should have been amended if they had been noticed. This form of error made up 79 per cent of the corpus, of which 73 per cent had been corrected. The other category was 'convention errors' – words which were consistently misspelled and were departures from conventional spelling, requiring some remedial input. These errors made up 21 per cent of the corpus. Their studies went on to investigate 'slips of the pen'; we are concerned here with convention errors. The differences however are not great. The following are misspellings taken from the first ten 'slips of the pen' items on their list: intele (intellect), censorsored (censored), likly (likely), an (any), immediatly (immediately), prodi (producing), wull (will), ho (how), unabiguous (unambiguous), chose (choose). These seem to me to be typical 'convention' errors except perhaps 'prodi'.

Even the categorical miscues classifications such as of Spache (1940) and Neale (1958) using 'additions, omissions, substitutions, reversals' and so on were not at all helpful in spelling error analysis. Even more recent classifications such as of Miles (1993) giving the 'thirteen milestones in spelling' relate to the way in which an observer might categorise a misspelling rather than devise a category which has some explanatory power and which may help in the error's correction.

Miles' (1993) 13 'dyslexic milestones'

In brackets are my comments and as can be seen the errors are not confined to dyslexics alone.

1 The impossible trigram. A collection of letters sequenced in a way that is impossible in the English language: lqu for liquid. (But incomplete phonic knowledge and incomplete articulation can lead to this error in spelling development in controls and dyslexics.)
2 The misrepresentation of a sound such as the incorrect use of a vowel or consonant: benane for banana. (Again a common phonetic transcription error, a simple schwa error.)
3 Wrong boundaries. Words may be run together or be incorrectly separated: halfanhour, a nother. (This is how we say them.)

4 Incorrect syllabification: too many or too few syllables; rember for remember, choclate. (Common transcription errors overcome by articulation and syllabification when spelling, plus work on base words and prefixes.)

5 Inconsistent spelling: scool, skule, scole. (Common phonetic variations are stored and used.)

6 A doubling of the wrong letter: eeg for egg. (Place numbers for letters remembered and doubling of something recalled, lack of knowledge of short vowel syllable rule.)

7 Poor recall of the order of letters within a word: pakr for park. (Visual recall used and invariably order errors made in medial positions.)

8 The letters in a word are correct, but in the wrong order: sitser for sister. (See 7 above.)

9 Omission of sounding letters: amt for amount. (Articulation/pronunciation error typical of beginning spellers, phonic transcription just beginning to develop.)

10 Duplication of one or more sounding letters: piyole for pile. (Overarticulation leading to incorrect transcription.)

11 Incorrect phonetic attempt to spell a word: yuwer for your. (Phonetic transcription, conventions only partly known.)

12 Intrusive vowels: tewenty for twenty. (Phonetic transcription resulting from pronunciation.)

13 B/D substitution: bab for dad. (Common error found in all spellers up until the age of eight years and later in dyslexics as they learn to spell, results from arbitrary nature of the letter sounds and names; a cursive writing strategy overcomes this.)

Each one of these milestones can be found in the misspellings of younger normal spellers. They reflect immature syllabic and phonic knowledge and mispronunciations for spelling. They are typically found in dyslexics' scripts as they too pass through the same stages towards correct spelling.

Hornsby's (1994) error analysis

1 Writes letters in a word in an incorrect order: tiem for time. (Phonetic transcription or the use of a visual recall strategy.)

2 Mirrors words: nomiS for Simon. (Writing problem, visual strategy used.)

3 Reverses b for d and p for d.

4 Inverts n for u and m for w.

5 Mirror writes. (Writing problem.)

6 Spells phonetically: bizzy for busy.

7 Spells bizarrely with spellings unrelated to the word: lenaka for last. (Writes initial sound then guesses the rest, usually closer to correct length/number of letters.)

8 Omits letters: lip for limp, wet for went. (N and m nasalify the preceding vowel and are difficult to sense.)

9 Adds letters: whent for went, whant for what. (Overuse of 'wh' knowledge.)

In an interpretation of errors by Hornsby (1989: 130–1) of one of her pupils (e.g. famel (family); punshment (punishment); pont (point); perhas (perhaps); continu (continue); poshon (portion); constucted (constructed), she writes,

> His spellings of family and punishment indicate his tendency to omit syllables when writing words. It is interesting that the final syllable -tion has been partly mastered but without good sequencing skills words with this ending cannot be spelled accurately. … [His] pronunciation needs sharpening in 'dis drif' (disc drive) and 'Chrismas' (Christmas).

As one example it is arguable that an ending such as -tion can best be learnt by a dyslexic through training in sequencing its sounds t-i-o-n, or 'she-un', for it is variously spelled -tion, -cian and -sion and sounded 'shun' in attention, mansion and magician. What might prove more effective as a means of learning would be some knowledge of morphemics.

The same type of criticism applies to the categories of misspelling produced by Hornsby to represent dyslexic scripts. They are developmental errors and mainly relate to the dyslexics' incomplete grasp of phonics and the use of visual strategies to supplement this. The only error which is different is the mirror writing. It does appear in the scripts of both ordinary and dyslexic spellers, but is perhaps more frequently seen in young dyslexics and is associated with it rather than a part of the problem. In word processing this whole book the mouse was reversed, but I am not dyslexic.

Selkowitz's (1998) six categories of dyslexic error

One final error classification to illustrate the point.

1   Phonetic errors: these are spellings that look similar to the attempted word, but when pronounced sound out differently: lap for lip, goase for goose. (But not when the dyslexic sounds them out or scribes them?)
2   Visual errors: these are spellings that are phonetically correct, but visually incorrect: lite for light, sed for said (This does not make them visual errors, you cannot proofread what you do not know.)
3   Letter substitution errors: these are errors usually made as a result of auditory or visual perception difficulties: pig for big, bab for dad. (These are the usual B/D labelling confusions in younger spelling.)
4   Insertion or omission errors: where extra letters are added e.g. blore for bore, or omitted e.g. bicyle for bicycle. (Blore may result from the 'bl' being the more frequently used than 'b'. Bicycle – usually because a visual strategy is relied upon for spelling.)
5   Sequential errors: confusion in the sequence of letter position within a word: birdge for bridge. (Visual strategy used, needs to be taught the 'br' blend and articulatory phonics.)
6   Irrational errors: errors that look irrational to the reader but have some logic for the speller: lift for laugh or ritt for right. (Substitutes word for laugh with similar elements l and f, ritt is nearly 'correct'.)

This error analysis we can infer comes from a number of implicit theories about dyslexia which are widely held, i.e. that dyslexia stems from visual perceptual and/or auditory perceptual difficulties as well as sequencing problems. None of these theories when put to the test by Vellutino (1979) were shown to have any validity. The categories are essentially not error types.

The most frequent and basic types of spelling error found by Nelson (1980) were letter order errors e.g. 'asy' for 'say'; the production of phonetically implausible spelling as in 'for' for 'from', 'seam' for 'seem'; and that of orthographically illegal spelling such as 'ckak' for 'cake' which contains a letter group that does not occur in that position of order in English. After studying the errors of 11-year-old dyslexics compared with seven-year-old controls she concluded that their level and types of spelling errors showed no significant differences. Moats (1983) followed the same procedure and came to the same conclusions about beginner groups' spelling at grade two level and dyslexics, but the dyslexics were better informed about spelling conventions, which is to be expected as their experience of print was that much longer.

Bruck and Treiman (1990) investigated phonological awareness and spelling skills among controls and dyslexics who were defined as being at the same spelling level. They found that both had difficulties with consonants in initial blends during word recognition and phoneme deletion tasks, and both had problems with producing correct blends, most of the time failing to represent the second consonant of the blend. They concluded that both showed similar patterns of performance whilst dyslexics' actual phonological awareness and spelling skills were poorer than those of the matched controls. In 1994 Treiman concluded that spelling errors and errors in phonological knowledge reflect inadequate knowledge rather than sound-to-spelling translation problems. From this we can conclude that if we actually teach dyslexics the knowledge they need then their spelling can be brought up to grade level. It is a teaching issue that we need to resolve.

When Bourassa and Treiman (2003) tested dyslexics' and younger controls' oral and written spelling performance using T-BEST (Treiman-Bourassa Early Spelling Test) they found that the groups showed a similarity in their advantage for words over non-words. This was on both the phonological and orthographic basis as well as an equivalent advantage for written over oral spelling, on the phonological measure. Their linguistically based errors were more or less the same. The assumption made was that their spelling performances appeared to be quite similar and that children with dyslexia performing at second grade commit spelling errors that are similar in quality and quantity to those of younger normally progressing children.

Finally, Cassar and Treiman (2004) compared the phonological and orthographic accuracy of real word spellings at the second grade level. They found dyslexics produced 'spellings statistically indistinguishable on all measures' (p. 17) from controls. After testing the knowledge of long and short vowels and initial and final consonant clusters (blends), they reported that even reversals, considered to be the most common characteristic of dyslexia, showed similar results.

Even the research on dyslexics remaining poor at non-word reading and spelling despite having achieved the necessary phoneme-grapheme information is not as straightforward as it seems. When computer models are established to look at this process (Brown and Loosemore 1994; Rumelhart and McClelland 1986) it is found that a similar restricted input leads to a difficulty and slowness in spelling non-words. In other words it is not a result of a disordered system but of an early low level of input to the system.

Given all this evidence it is surprising that some people still believe that dyslexic spelling is 'bizarre' and use this together with reversals as key indicators of dyslexia. This can mean that if no reversals and no orthographic illegalities are seen in test scripts then that individual will not be referred for dyslexia support. It may even be seen as a way of saving money but it is at great cost to the individual.

These results suggests that on entry into school and in the pre-school period the dyslexic has a difficulty which for some reason delays the onset of the develop-ment of reading and spelling skills. When this barrier is overcome, or it may clear up of its own accord, then reading and spelling development can proceed nor-mally. It was suggested in Chapter 3 that this early barrier was an articulation awareness problem. A training technique for helping to assert early awareness called 'multisensory mouth training' was described. Most dyslexics finally do appear to break through this barrier even without training but at a stage too late so that their literacy progress is severely affected, thus it is that remedial techniques are still required at present.

Coffield *et al.* (2000: 86) found that: 'There is mounting evidence to support the belief that not all students learn to spell by immersion in reading and writing alone'.

In a DfEE funded project (Brooks and Weeks 1999), individual case work with six children showed that building on the strengths of individual learning styles was effective and a group experiment was organised. There were 12 children in each group of spelling-age-matched dyslexics, children with moderate learning difficul-ties and controls. The average ages were eight, eleven and six years respectively. The results were not significant; however, the authors went on to conclude that the children with 'dyslexic features' learned the greatest number of word spellings when using Neurolinguistic Programming, a visual learning method 'which appeared to tap into their visual strengths and reduce their reliance on their phono-logical weaknesses' (p. 3). The dyslexic children were encouraged to continue to use their best learning method and over 15 months six of them made gains 50 per cent greater than would be expected. Better results were obtained using best learning method from a much broader band of children in three schools.

Using one preferred method and compensatory strategies seems to serve to nar-row the options available to spellers rather than to grow their opportunities. In addition there have been warnings about the notion and validity of 'learning styles' (Riding and Rayner 1998; Coffield *et al.* 2004; Mortimore 2005).

Some strategic approaches to correcting misspelling

Getting words into the long-term memory bank is the purpose of a spelling strategy. Research indicates that good spellers have a broader repertoire of spelling strategies than poor spellers and good spellers are more likely to use the more efficient and effective strategies. Good spellers, for example, are more likely to cite visualisation or meaning as a spelling strategy than poor spellers.

(Cramer 1998: 162)

The second finding of Fulk and Stormont-Spurgin (1995) was that cognitive strategies, such as those employed for spelling, are generalised to other academic areas. Encouraging reflection and a problem solving approach to spelling can demystify the process and support the same approach to other problems. It perhaps builds confidence in the students' own abilities to sort out an issue. It certainly seems to overcome the 'learned helplessness' that is observed so often in poor spellers.

In an analysis of researches on spelling, Coffield *et al.* concluded that:

> the research was effective in paving the way for the majority of the students to become metacognitive in their use of spelling strategies. Researchers ... believe that students must have knowledge of the process involved and their own characteristics as learners before they can strategically control the process.
>
> (2000: 95)

As well as research into metacognition and spelling there have been a number of practical contributions to strategic spelling made from experience, case work and research. Some details of these contributions appear below.

Multisensory spelling programme for priority words (MUSP) (Lee 2000)

Jenny Lee writes and lectures on adult dyslexia and is a basic skills coordinator in County Durham LEA. She draws on the research of Paulesu *et al.* (1996) and Nicolson and Fawcett (1996) to underpin her method to link visual and auditory and motor memory, and develop automaticity. Informal research at her adult dyslexia unit finds that if the students use MUSP exactly as prescribed for learning priority words then a success rate of between 85 and 97 per cent can be obtained.

The advised procedure is to select only a small number from 5–15 priority words at a time, that the person really needs to spell. On the left of a page all the words in the first list (A) must be written in joined up or cursive writing. On the right hand side of the page the words are written showing the strategy chosen, for example:

permanent   perma frost at Nent Head

solicitor   sol ICI tor

opportunity   op port unity

The advice accompanying these examples is to notice the symmetrical patterns or find the hidden words, split up the double consonants auditorily and visually, and

LOOK	at the word and study the strategy
SAY	the word and then say the strategy
COVER	the word and the strategy
PICTURE	each bit of the strategy in your mind's eye as you SAY it
WRITE	the word as a whole unit in joined up writing but SAY the strategy as you write it, telling your hand what to write
CHECK	letter by letter to see if it is right

Over a period of four weeks the list is rehearsed and the teacher helps the student with it at intervals. In week four the teacher puts the words into sentences and then dictates them to the student and they start on list B. At intervals of a few months the list should be retested.

As can be imagined this is a labour-intensive procedure but it does have some good elements about it. An important element is at the beginning where the student chooses a strategy to deal with the area of error. No information is given about this, except to notice patterns and look for words in words. No doubt the teacher helps here but it could be developed into so much more.

Moseley's intervention strategies (1994)

There are a whole host of older pupils who, although not classified as dyslexic, have poor spelling. They conceal this whenever they can by using a range of compensatory strategies. Moseley (1989) for example found that the 13–15 year olds whose free writing he was studying:

- used fewer words outside a core of 500;
- used more short words;
- used more regularly spelled words;
- avoided common hard-to-spell words;
- repeated words and phrases to play safe.

He suggested that the constant criticism which poor spelling engendered caused a lack of self-esteem and a tendency to avoid putting pen to paper if at all possible. These findings are similar to those of Myklebust (1973), who found that disabled spellers would write at least one-third less than age-matched peers. They would also substitute known words for those whose spelling they knew they were unsure of. My adult students reported that they took longer in examinations as they tried to avoid known difficult words and select/replace them with a known one. In a similar effort ten-year-old Gavin substituted 'box' when the teacher had read out 'parcel' (see Figure 3.2). This is just an indication of his commitment and motivation to try to do what was required and to show the teacher he was not careless.

Moseley reported successful interventions with his 13–15-year-old poor spellers, in which spelling ages increased by 19 months in five, an average of 3.7 per month. This was in comparison with controls who received a 'look – cover – write – check' strategy and whose scores remained the same. The best results were obtained by the teacher who also gave daily tests to monitor learning. The successful intervention strategies were (Moseley 1994: 469):

- say the word to suit the spelling
- trace and say
- sky write
- visualise the word and count the letters
- use mnemonics
- use spelling patterns and some rules
- focus on the tricky parts

- say the alphabet names
- make a rhyming word

Again the emphasis is upon rote learning in four of the strategies: trace and say, sky write, mnemonics and visualisation. It may be that the activities of focusing on the tricky part, counting the letters, saying for spelling, alphabet names, and making a rhyme all supported by regular testing contributed as much as the rote elements. We are not clear either how many of the strategies were to be used for each word; presumably subjects chose the ones they preferred after noting the tricky part.

Enhanced visualisation strategies

Radaker (1963) manipulated one variable in his study, that of visualisation. He found that visualisation training strategies did help improve the spelling of his experimental groups over controls. His subjects had to imagine the word they were learning set in glossy black letters on a white background or cinema screen. If the image was unstable they had to imagine pasting the letters in place, or fixing them as large metallic letters with holes in the bottom and top to 'nail' them in place. His subjects were pupils of 8.5 to 10.5 years.

Visualisation techniques such as this can prove helpful as they encourage pupils to inspect the word very carefully and this is something they cannot do when reading text. Some young pupils have a facility for visualising which will support this and all of us can improve with practice. It can be imagined that being introduced to such a technique will produce an enhanced effect over controls who have been given no extra support. If used as the only strategy, visualisation is too limited even when used in NLP (neurolinguistic programming) where visualisation is used plus looking into the upper left quadrant.

We also have to consider in all this 'sky writing', tracing and visualisation the distinct possibility that the unwilling learner in secondary school will not want to be seen doing these things. It is not 'cool'.

Rote strategies are particularly unappealing to the more able students who have spelling problems, and they are not particularly helpful to the rest, as Moseley found. The look – cover – write – check effect is temporary, for within a day or two the original error returns.

Unscrambling Spelling (Klein and Millar 1990)

In their book *Unscrambling Spelling* Klein and Millar described work with dyslexics in further education. They identified the following types of errors in students' writing and had developed a series of strategies for dealing with them.

- Spelt like it sounded
- Rule not known
- Letters out of order
- Mixed up sounds
- Missed out or added bits

These are reminiscent in part of the Spache (1940) categories of substitutions, additions, reversals and omissions as they are found throughout reading test literature. The strategies that Klein and Millar suggest to address the errors and improve the spelling are as follows:

- 'look – cover – write – check'
- chunk words for reinforcing the visual aspects
- teach word building i.e. roots, prefixes and suffixes
- find rule from spelling patterns and lists
- proofreading
- dictation
- teach cursive writing

They provided 17 example resource sheets to illustrate their various proposals which they had successfully used with their FE students.

We can see the influence of dyslexia training courses in the use of LCWC and cursive writing as well as the teaching of word building and rules, proofreading and dictation. There are definitely more cognitive elements involved in their strategies.

Prompt spelling (Watkins and Hunter-Carsch 1995)

This technique was based upon the paired reading concept and trialled in three secondary schools with more than 30 pupils over three terms. There is a prompter (a more skilled speller – teacher, pupil etc.) and a promptee who work as a pair. There are five steps in the process.

1   The pair identify five misspellings in the promptee's work.
2   They consider the word and the prompter says it clearly, stressing beginnings, syllables and endings and the promptee says it in a similar way.
3   The promptee underlines the area thought to be wrong and they discuss it and promptee attempts to correct the error.
4   The promptee uses the spellchecker to correct the spelling and it is entered in the second column of the worksheet. More discussion and suggestions about blends and rules.
5   The pair discuss similar words and they are entered in column three. There is then a recapitulation.

Every fifth session the promptee was tested against the 20 words dealt with thus far.

In the ten closely monitored students, spelling improvements ranged from 0.3 to 1.7 years. Gains of over one year were made in six cases out of ten in less than a third of a year of actual time in school (p. 135).

Cognitive Process Strategies for Spelling (CPSS) (Montgomery 1989, 1997a, 1997b, 2003)

In a series of experiments and case studies the cognitive process strategies for spelling approach was first devised to help teachers and undergraduate student teachers improve their own spelling and correct their errors. The possibilities of using the techniques in schools were then investigated and were positive and then the strategies were also found to be particularly useful and motivating for more able school learners with spelling problems (Montgomery 2000a, 2000b).

In the development period over 1700 teachers and undergraduates were given a misspelled spelling test. Twelve different strategies were collected as they tried to spell the words. Since that period more than double those numbers have been exposed to the same test and the results remain stable. Strategies that required rote memorising, visualisation and mnemonics as the key elements were excluded. Another popular rote strategy was the singing rhyme (MI – SSI – SSI – PPI – Mississippi!) but we could not think of another.

The undergraduates were too advanced in literacy skills to need a dyslexia APSL programme but they did need help. They came individually with an essay script showing their typical problems and were set to identify the errors. A list was made and strategies discussed for dealing with two of them. The students then wrote the two words out three times using the SOS procedure and left. A few days later in the coffee queue the students would come and spell the word orally as a check they still had the spelling correctly stored. After the first half hour spent on the tutorial the next one or two took only a few minutes as the two new misspellings were dealt with. Quite soon armed with a list of CPSS they felt able to handle the rest on their own and became independent in developing their spelling.

The target dyslexics' misspellings in the undergraduate cohort dropped significantly from 20 or more per script in Year 3, to four or five in the Year 4 examinations and the nature of the errors changed towards higher order errors and homophones.

Twelve cognitive process strategies for spelling (CPSS) were elicited from the research.

Articulation – The misspelt word is clearly and precisely articulated for spelling. Teachers need to encourage clear, correct speech, during classwork and in reading aloud explaining why. Mispronunciations should be corrected such as 'chimney' not 'chimley'; and 'skellington' to 'skeleton'. The point where stress comes in a word can also be noted for this will help in correcting the spellings such as harass and embarrass.

Over articulation – The word is enunciated with emphasis on each of the syllables but particularly the one normally not sounded or in which there is the schwa sound e.g. parli(a)ment, gover(n)ment, w(h)ere, sep(a)rate.

Table 6.3 Spelling error types of 55 undergraduate final year scripts analysed for types of error in order of frequency of occurrence

Error type	Total	Error type	Total
Suffixing error	43	Homophones	5
Baseword error	36	Long vowel rule error	4
Prefixing error	26	Phonic/phonetic error	3
Root errors	19	Short vowel rule error	2
Syllabification error	9	Articulation/pronunciation	0
Slips of the pen	7	Noun/verb confusion	0

Cue articulation – The word is pronounced incorrectly, e.g. Wed-nes-day, Feb-ru-ary. This points up the area of difficulty to cue the correct spelling.

Syllabification – It is easier to spell a word when we break it down into syllables, e.g. misdeanor – mis / de / mean / our, criticed – crit / i / cise / d. Poor spellers and young spellers need to be taught to do this and learn to clap the beats in names and words to help them. Although the syllable division will vary, as they learn more about the structure of language they will learn to build this in to the syllabification.

Phonics – The pupil needs to learn to try to get a comprehensible skeleton of the word's sound translated into graphemic units. At first the skeletons or scaffolds will be incomplete e.g. bd for bed, and wet for went in regular words. If the words are irregular such as cum / come at least the phonic scaffold is readable and other strategies can be taught to build the correct word.

Origin – Often the word's root in another language may give clues e.g. -op / *port* / unity. The medial vowel in this word is a schwa sound and is often spelt incorrectly with 'e' or 'u'. Finding that the original meaning comes from an opening, a port or a haven means the pupil has a strong clue to the spelling.

Rule – A few well-chosen rules can help unravel a range of spelling problems e.g. the l – f– s rule, that is l, f, and s are doubled in a one-syllabled word after a short vowel sound – ball, puff, dress; and i before e except after c, or the two vowel rule – when two vowels go walking the first one does the talking (usually). Exceptions to these rules are saved and learned as a group e.g. pal, nil, if, gas, yes, bus, us, plus, thus, by writing them into a sentence – 'My pal gets nil if …'.

Linguistics – The syllable types open, closed, accented and unaccented need to be taught as well as the four suffixing rules which govern most words, and also the difference between and uses of base words and roots.

Family/base word – This notion is often helpful in revealing silent letters and the correct representation for the schwa sound e.g. Canada, Canadian; bomb, bombing, bombardier, bombardment; favour-ite, sign, signature, signal. These are real families of words not common letter strings.

Meaning – Separate is commonly misspelled as sep / e / rate. Looking up the meaning in a dictionary can clear this up because it will be found to mean to divide or part or even to pare. The pupil then just needs to remember 'cut or part' and 'pare' to separate.

Analogy – this is the comparison of the word or a key part of it with a word the pupil does know how to spell, e.g. 'it is like boot, hoot, root' or 'hazard' is one 'z' like in 'haze' and 'maze'. This is the closest to the letter string approach that we want to come.

Funnies – Sometimes it is not possible to find another strategy and so a 'funny' can help out e.g. 'cess pit' helped me to remember how to spell necessary.

The seven-step protocol for using CPSS

Younger pupils and those with poorer spelling will need more of the first five CPS strategies and little or no dictionary work to begin with.

1   The pupil selects *two* misspellings to learn in any one session.
2   The pupil identifies the *area of error*, usually only one letter, with the help of the teacher or a dictionary.

3   The pupil puts a *ring round* the area of error and notices how much of the rest is correct.
4   The pupil is taught (later selects) a *cognitive process spelling strategy* (CPSS) to correct the misspelling. A reserve strategy is also noted where possible.
5   The strategy is *talked over* with the teacher and is used to write the corrected spelling.
6   The spelling is *checked* to see if it is correct – the dictionary can be used again here.
7   If correct the pupil covers up the spellings and writes the word three times from memory in *joined up/full cursive* writing using *SOS*.

Examples: Acco(m)modate: Ac (prefix) – com/mod (Linguistic rule – double m after the short vowel in the closed syllable) – ate (common syllable ending); Potato(e) – tomato – vibrato, 'toes are plural, o is one'; long vowel /o/.

Adults whose spelling is advanced may well profit from having the whole list with some examples; younger spellers benefit from having the list taught two at a time.

An adult 40-year-old poor speller (dyslexia undiagnosed) giving a report on car repairs

REAR FLor L/R (rear floor left)
PEDDER RUBDER (pedal rubber)
BUSHER Top STAIRG COM (bushes, top of steering column)
WASH NOT WORKING P L (washer not working)
DIS pad (disc pad)
STNIMG BOX ARM (steering box arm)
L/H STOP LAMP

As can be noted this poor speller needs help with the five more basic levels of CPSS, especially clear articulation and pronunciation for spelling, syllabification, syllable structure and synthetic phonics.

Johnson and Myklebust (1967: 24; 1995) illustrated the effect of different forms of dictation on the spelling of a 15-year-old dyslexic as follows:

When spelling from his own head and no auditory and articulatory stimulation:

cabinet	was spelled	kntrs
window	as	wror
recorder	as	rkrrd

When spelling from words dictated one syllable at a time:

hundred	indent
represent	represent

When spelling words dictated normally:

pencil	pnsl
manufacture	mufnctur
candidate	cndati

Teaching clear articulation and syllabification for spelling will help all poor spellers improve their spelling.

Developmental spelling handbook (Montgomery 1997b)

This scheme is partly based upon the TRTS programme for dyslexics but was written for an infant school which was having severe problems with improving the pupils' spelling SATs. It is a handbook of 110 mini lessons which could be included as part of the general class or individual literacy teaching strategies, from reception through to secondary and further education.

The programme teaches synthetic phonics AND morphemic linguistics including CPSS and multisensory training and cursive writing. It includes examples of authentic assessment techniques. Overall 53 different teaching strategies are presented throughout the booklet. The programme does not use the intensive dyslexia training methods or spelling and reading packs of TRTS and Hickey. These are reserved for the dyslexics.

The developmental spelling teaching can begin at any time in pre-school or reception and it begins or is based on early language work. When it accompanies early work on the letter sounds it is undertaken by a method called *multisensory mouth training for spelling*. This can be run in parallel with the motor coordination games and training for beginning writers. It emphasises clear speaking and articulation for spelling.

The effect of the spelling programme also enhanced the reading results in a significant way (see Table 6.4). Interestingly the school was already teaching cursive from the outset but had not linked this to direct teaching of spelling; it was still taught by the copywriting method.

It needs to be stressed that some basic phonics teaching techniques may be so narrow they only transfer to similar regular word items found in the early levels of spelling tests. Drilling in basic phonics without syllabic linguistics may result in the pupil being 'over phonicked'. In Figure 6.2 it can be seen how much Thomas needed some syllabic-linguistic strategies to be built into his remedial phonics programme. What teachers or researchers might think on seeing this example is that he has had too much phonics and that it is not good for the early years pupil. He needs his phonics knowledge extended with blends and digraphs and to be praised for what he knows, then be taught to synthesise regular words.

I w I t fg w my cat d b iw vy

I s b in m gdn

Translated as: 'I would like to forget when my cat died because I was very sad it is buried in my garden'.

Figure 6.2 Phonics and spelling by Thomas aged 7.5 years

Table 6.4 XLane infant school SATs before and after use of developmental spelling

	1997	1998
Reading	46%	56%
Spelling	16%	44%
Writing	57%	58%
Maths	83%	85%

Now he has finally cracked the alphabetic code a helpful approach would be to go over the text with him to get him to articulate it slowly and clearly to see if he can feel and identify some more of the consonants and syllables. A series of redrafts with him and one on his own could reveal quite a bit more knowledge. At another session he could write it again from memory to see what had been retained and then the single *closed syllable structure* could be introduced – cvc with the short vowel sound. He can be taught the rule that all syllables must have a vowel in them. He can practise beating syllables in words. One word could then be addressed e.g. 'sad' and he could learn to generalise this knowledge to other words with the same sound – dad, pad, mad. He should be the one to try and generate them. At first he will find this difficult and need a lot of support.

Now Thomas has cracked the alphabetic code and has some whole word knowledge such as 'cat' and 'in' he could be taught 'my' as a whole word writing unit and the scaffold 'gdn' shows the potential for progress if more linguistics teaching is built in.

Why CPSS and cursive writing are both needed for correcting misspellings

In earlier chapters the underpinnings of the skills of spelling and handwriting have been discussed. When we come to correcting misspellings what has to be understood is that the incorrect spelling has already been stored in the lexicon in the cerebral hemispheres, and the memory for motor programme and pathways by which it is activated and written is also stored but this time in the cerebellum. No amount of visualisation of the correct spelling on the one hand and the look – cover – write – check strategy on the other is going to succeed in stopping the incorrect version from emerging, especially under pressure. Automaticity has already been established and it is this which has to be replaced by a higher profile version in both the lexicon and the cerebellum.

The CP strategic approach serves the purpose of opening up the misspelling in the lexicon to intellectual scrutiny by the cerebral cortex so that when we want to spell the word correctly we have given it a higher profile. As we write we can then feel it coming and can pause long enough to select the correct spelling by using the cognitive strategy. At the same time we use the cursive strategy to write over the area of error.

The SOS strategy used with the CPSS in the correction stage helps establish a new motor programme and pathway so that the correct word elicits the new motor programme from the cerebellum, not the old one. The more the new form of the word is elicited and used in writing the stronger the links become so that after a while the pause and use of the CPSS is no longer needed as the correct version comes out each time.

Teacher research and case work using CPSS

In-classroom research (Adrusysgyn 2002) demonstrated the effectiveness of CPSS techniques. Within a dozen short intervention sessions spelling errors were reduced from 55 per cent to 5 per cent and the pupils overcame their 'learned helplessness'. They could also generalise what they had learned to new learning situations. The techniques were based upon their own creative writing work and it was found that there was a transfer from the remedial/corrective setting to general classroom work which is usually more problematic.

Another teacher, Heather Parrant (1989) ran a six-week research project in her classroom to test the effect of CPSS. The experimental subjects were a mixed class group of 11-year-olds in an ordinary middle school. There were 21 pupils in the class and eight of them were identified as having specific special needs in relation to reading and spelling problems. A parallel class of 23 pupils in the same school was used as the control group. At the outset of the investigation all the subjects were given a dictation of 100 words drawn from their current favourite book *Charlie and the Chocolate Factory* by Roald Dahl.

Parrant reported that although pupils might begin to misspell the words in free writing as they approached them, warning bells would ring in their heads that this was one of their 'specials'. They would then either misspell it and then correct it using their key strategy or they would slow down and use the strategy to get the correct spelling first time.

As they used the word more often, they could begin to correct it before writing it down for they were cued to attend carefully and avoid the old error. Eventually, they found that words frequently used were spelled easily and without pause as the old motor programme was substituted for the new higher profile one. The cursive writing assisted in this. The control group received the usual look – cover – write – check strategy for correcting their misspellings, also written three times.

The same dictation was given after the experimental period. Not surprisingly, and as we would hope, the total numbers of errors made by both groups fell. However, the control group's level of improvement was not statistically significant whereas that of the experimental group was ($p < 0.01$). The experimental group's errors fell from 273 to 162 over the six weeks. All the subjects' error scores in this group diminished markedly except for two good spellers, one who made one error on each test and another who made no errors on the pre-test and one on the post-test. A change in attitude was also reported for the experimental group. They had moved from learned helplessness or neutrality to a positive interest and self-esteem through finding a way through to improving their own spelling. Within the class the special needs group's spelling also improved but less significantly ($p < 0.05$).

Case work using CPSS with an able student named Maia in a school in Nairobi was described by Morey (2001). Maia's abilities were in the high average range (nine years eight months); however her spelling age was seven years five months and her reading age was eight years four months. She was a highly articulate pupil aged nine years and two months. She was given remedial withdrawal tuition twice a week for 35 minutes each for a term using TRTS. The opportunity was taken to consolidate sound-to-symbol correspondence especially using the multisensory mouth training techniques as she seemed unaware of the feel of the consonants in her mouth. During this period she made progress then regressed. Morey concluded that Maia's problem was due to her inability to see why the segmenting of a sound was worthwhile for spelling, so she would use a mixture of phonetic and visual cues to aid her spelling. Onset and rime strategies were tried but nothing worked if she was not interested. The general structured approach of TRTS had helped but she needed something more to gain her interest. She would spell words correctly in one place and then incorrectly in another. She lacked the ability to self-monitor and proofread and so CPSS was tried.

Morey reported, 'Immediately cognitive strategies were implemented there was an overwhelming change in the relationship between teacher and student' and 'Whilst there are still weaknesses in her spelling her ability to focus on words is having a dramatic effect on her reading (p. 29). The TRTS was started in September and by the end of November the reading was four months behind chronological age (12 months advance in three months); by March with CPSS it had moved a further five months ahead of chronological age (nine months' advance). Spelling progress was slower but by March it had progressed to eight years two months (an advance of nine months in six months). Morey concludes that more importantly the strategic approach was helping Maia not only in the literacy area but also to become reflective about her work as a whole and it was transferring to other contexts.

Another case example is by Folland (2004). Natalie was a student in Year 10, aged 15. She was somewhat impulsive and had dyslexic type difficulties (spelling age 12.4 years). She had been in the learning support class for three years. 'There are numerous difficulties in school as Natalie does not like to listen to criticism and does not accept help to improve her work' (p. 10).

Her writing was sometimes difficult to read, especially when writing words she was unsure of. Her written work did not reflect her level of understanding, she wrote the minimum required, did not proofread, made many grammatical errors and was very slow at writing.

In the first CPSS session the teacher and Natalie spoke at length about the strategies and then Natalie was given a dictation. She selected the words 'edge' and 'comfortable' to tackle, put a ring round her area of error, looked them up in the dictionary, and cue articulation was suggested for ED-ge and then a 'funny' which arose when Natalie said she was reminded of a dog called 'Edger/ Edgar', then they used the phrase 'edger has the edge'.

Natalie then chose cue articulation for the word com-FORT-able as well as the phrase which amused her 'The fort is comfortable'. She became very keen on using CPSS and over the next few weeks kept asking if she could have her spellings checked and if she could have new ones. 'It was a struggle to keep her to two per session as she thought she could cope with more' (p. 12). She enjoyed identifying the word, looking it up in the dictionary and thinking of strategies to overcome it. However, what she did not enjoy was the SOS and cursive writing. She was reluctant to use them despite being told why and felt they were too much like other spelling programmes she had been given before but which had failed.

> A few days after the first session Natalie came to find me very excited because she had 'heard alarm bells ringing' when writing the word 'edge' in Food Technology and as a result of 'the bell' she had taken more time over the word and been able to correct her own writing.
>
> (p. 12)

Over the next three weeks they spent ten minutes every learning support lesson reviewing spelling. Only in these sessions could Natalie be persuaded to use SOS. After a few more weeks all the words she had been learning were put into a dictation. Although Natalie complained she had not had time to review them in fact all were spelled correctly except 'thought' which was given as 'though'. She said that now whenever she used the target words the alarm bells would ring although sometimes it took her a while to remember the strategy. For example, she still wanted to spell the word leisure as 'leasure' but now her brain told her not to.

Other important things emerged during the mini lessons such as that Natalie became willing to share some of the stresses her problems with spelling had caused and opened a floodgate on homonyms that had troubled her for years. She was surprised that no one had thought to teach her the suffixing rules before. As the sessions progressed she gained in confidence and was enjoying studying spelling and getting very obvious benefit which she herself could see and experience. She even determined to look again at developing cursive.

Folland in reflecting on the experience of using CPSS writes:

> Many of the students I work with have been following dyslexia spelling programmes with private tutors for years with little or no improvement in their ability to spell accurately when under pressure especially in a test or exam. When I first read about CPSS I was a little dubious as it seemed a time consuming way of teaching students correct spelling however I was desperate to find something which would work after years of repeatedly correcting the same errors. [...] It did not take long for Natalie to feel confident about what she was doing ... it has been an extremely positive experience as it really helped raise her self esteem as well as improving the accuracy of her spelling ... I have now introduced the CPSS to all the classes I teach.
>
> (p. 13)

Carl was nine years eleven months old with a spelling age of eight years four months and diagnosed by an educational psychologist as 'moderately dyslexic'. Wraith (2001) gave him a 100-word dictation from his Harry Potter reading book. He misspelled 12 words and identified five of them: monning (morning); itsalf (itself); bewiching (bewitching); foled (followed); turbern (turban) and: cristmas, midde, coverd, sevulal, soled, punshed, thay.

In the period of a fortnight they dealt with his errors. Lesson One follows.

Christmas

Carl missed the 'h' in this word and said he sometimes missed the 'r' as well.

Cue articulation: 'We pronounced the word 'Christ mas'. We talked about the fact that Christmas is all about Jesus i.e. Christ. We looked up 'mass' in the dictionary and discovered that it can mean a meal or a body and that at Christmas we have a big meal to celebrate that Jesus came to earth in human body. Carl had never realised the word 'Christ' was in Christmas.

'Funny': As soon as I spelt this word correctly Carl said 'Oh look, my brother's name.' Carl has a brother called 'Chris' whose name he can spell quite happily so it really helped him to remember that the name 'Chris' is in 'Christmas'.

SOS: He found it quite hard to make himself use the cursive writing at first but said it got a lot easier as he repeated the word. He also found it easier to remember the spelling if he shut his eyes.

Followed

Carl spelt this as 'foled'.

Syllabification: Carl needed help to see how the base word 'follow' can be broken down into syllables, then he spotted the word 'low'.

Analogy: He was able to think of a rhyming word for 'foll' i.e. 'doll'. As soon as I mentioned the past tense he remembered he needed an 'ed' ending.

SOS: (After analogy with doll it might have been useful to introduce the l-f-s rule and/or doubling after the short vowel sound).

At the outset of lesson two he spelt the two words correctly and they proceeded with the next two words. After the six sessions he was given the dictation again and Carl correctly spelled all the target words. Initially he resorted to the former spelling of 'covered' and 'punishment' but in both cases he immediately realised his error and self-corrected. He was quite hesitant over 'several' but got it correct after some thought. He initially put 'terban' for 'turban' but corrected it immediately. His writing in the post test was more joined.

This case example is typical and one of many such cases. A quote from another teacher working with CPSS will serve to reinforce these points. She is writing about a Year 8 pupil 'J' (chronological age = 13.6; reading age = 9.1; spelling age = 8.7). J had had small-group withdrawal teaching in junior school for reading and spelling. Now in secondary school she was in the bottom set for English in a group of 15 with some teaching assistant support. She had a half hour group withdrawal session per week but no special programme was in place. J said she felt stupid, other children laughed at her reading and spelling, and often teachers were cross with her for spelling words incorrectly. She really wanted to be a successful reader and speller. Over a period of four weeks in a one-on-one withdrawal session they used CPSS with the following result.

The student and I gained a lot from this experience. The student said she thought that she'd never learn to spell words that she got wrong and she felt that now at secondary school they had given up on her. She felt by working together that she had used a lot of her own ideas when investigating words and she had enjoyed having the responsibility. She said that when we talked about things together she understood more than if she was just listening ... . She said she'd always thought she wasn't as clever as other children and had labelled herself as 'thick'... . I had seen a marked improvement in J's confidence, enthusiasm and spelling abilities.

(p. 47)

This writing was better laid out and more fluent, joined and legible. Obviously more work on spelling is needed but some useful progress has been made.

Before:
> he eat him. now I'm no exspert but <u>anemals</u> do behve <u>lick</u> that. and he did the same to the others but the had a <u>difrent</u> larws and the <u>PLeos</u> <u>cort</u> him eath is the most <u>stangest</u> <u>plac</u> J <u>onow</u> <u>Yors</u> <u>fafhly</u>
> hoblar

The underlined words were those chosen by Alex to tackle in the sessions.

After:
> Dear Hoblar I fanck you for your letter, I've looked up your animal consirns and animals on earth have a good reputasn like Robin Hood, the Fox and Bugs Buny. I have beny watching a lat of films and cartoons and I disagree with you. For example police dog's save live's and guide dog's help blind people. I'll meet you at the space cafe on Wednesday 4th July
> See you soon
> Blar

Figure 6.3 An example of 13 year old Alex's work before and after 5 mini-sessions of CPSS

Error analyses based upon CPSS – some new directions

The scripts of two large cohorts of ordinary pupils in Year 7 were analysed for types of spelling error rather than just numbers of errors. The reason was to determine if the analysis applied to the undergraduate scripts would prove useful. If so it could be linked to CPSS and help guide teachers in intervention.

Even students classified in School B as having SEN, mostly specific learning difficulties, showed the same types of errors as the rest of the cohort. The main difference was that in developmental terms they made slightly more errors of a basic kind such as with articulation and phonics and in their grammatical knowledge. They also showed a profile of spelling development typical of younger children when compared with results from Year 5 cohorts. This is also significant in relation to studies of dyslexia.

Table 6.5 Spelling type data analysis in Year 7

Error type	% Errors SEN group (N=27) Cohort B	Cohort B (N=160)	Cohort C (N=251)	Cohort C Error % (all words)
Synthetic phonics				
Artic/Pronunciation/Syll	12.4 %	11.9 %	12.9 %	0.58 %
Phonetic/Phonic	32.8 %	28.7 %	29.1 %	1.23 %
Morphemics				
Baseword/ Origin	28.2 %	30.0 %	19.6 %	0.82 %
Suffix/Pref/vowel rules	11.8 %	18.4 %	17.2 %	0.73 %
Homophone	1.4 %	3.5 %	9.5 %	0.40 %
Grammatical	13.2 %	9.7 %	11.7 %	0.49 %
Total numbers of errors	773	1953	2651	4.25 %

Multiple errors of the same word's misspelling by an individual pupil were counted only once.

It was found that the children's errors were often more difficult to assign than those of the adults mainly because of the nature of the errors. For example, it was easy to detect articulatory, pronunciation and syllabic errors but not always to distinguish between them e.g. is 'mies' (minutes) to be counted as a pronunciation error for transcription or a syllabification error? Hence they were grouped together in the overall analysis and both strategies could be applied in the remediation. The spelling of 'interest' was often 'intrest'. This was difficult to assign for it could be regarded as a phonetic transcription of the way the child said it or it could be classed as a base word error for teaching. When two error types were present in a word, which was not frequent, it was assigned to the lower of the two categories. The category 'Family' for intervention in CPSS was gathered into baseword errors e.g. bombing, where the family – bomb, bombardment, bombing, bombardier – gives the clue to correct spelling of the baseword – bomb.

In Table 6.5 the categories of diagnosis bear a close relationship to the CPSS strategies. However, there is not and cannot be complete correspondence, just as the categories themselves cannot be seen as absolutes but rather inferences from the data which might prove useful.

The categorising of spelling errors based upon their strategic value can be a useful guide to the intervention on a general scale that English departments could provide, and for the SEN group to what the SENCo interventions could be offering.

A topic-based approach to strategic spelling with CPSS – 'the 15 spells'

Although many English spellers have learnt to spell accurately without ever having any knowledge of morphemics or linguistic rules, when they are introduced to them it can give them a special interest and pleasure. Spelling teaching instead of being laborious, a 'spelling grind', can be enjoyable and flexible more like a problem solving piece of detective work.

According to Hanna *et al.* (1966) it is possible to spell 85 per cent of the English language with a knowledge of phonics and some basic rules although spellers complain that it is a very irregular language to learn. These researchers found that it was possible to program a computer to spell 17,000 basic words with some 300 rules and knowledge of how sounds are transcribed and represented by alphabetic symbols – phonics. However, they were dealing with rules governing letter order and frequencies, often called surface rules, rather than with deep structure rules about word and syllable structure, morphemics and linguistics. Henry (1995) in the USA suggested that with a knowledge of roots the rules governing only 14 words could teach all the spellings that an elementary school child might be expected to know.

With this principle in mind I set out to see if this was feasible and discovered that 15 words are needed to do this in English using linguistics and morphemics. The idea is that every school should develop a policy towards spelling which includes CPSS and every subject area should convert the principles and practices to their subject area vocabulary so that all the teachers should be reinforcing the same approaches rather than rely on sightword training alone. The following is a list of the 15 key words built round a sailing trip on a Thames sailing barge which pupils from around the country go on in Essex. They can be changed to fit topics on the Victorians, the Elizabethans and the Second World War in history or topics in science, PE, art and geography, or devised for year groups and so on.

1 CUT (cvc). Short vowel, closed syllable. DOUBLING rule for adding suffixes – cut-t-ing, putting, running, bedding, hopping, sitting, in polysyllables – rudder, potter, kipper, cutter.

2 HULL (cvcc). Short vowel and l-f-s rule. Must double l-f-s after short vowel in single syllable till, hill, pill; off, boff, sniff; hiss, miss (some exception words – if, gas, bus, yes).

3 ROPE (cvce). After long vowel sound in closed syllable, silent /e/ denotes long vowel sound. DROP silent /e/ when adding suffixes: roping, hoping, riding.

4 SAIL (cvvc). 'When two vowels go walking the first one does the talking, usually': rain, paint, cleats, load, tear. Just ADD suffix – raining, painted, cleated, loads.

5 COOK (cvvc). book, look, took, hook, good; double /oo/ short vowel sound, ADD rule cooking.

6 MOON (cvvc). Long vowel /oo/ in noon, cool, saloon, tool and school, ADD rule, schooling, schooled.

7 LIST (cvcc). Short vowel followed by double consonants simply ADD rule applies – listing, rushed, missed, rusting, posted. Master, lasting, faster, bath – dialect change in south of England from short to longer /ar/ sound.

8 BARGE (vowel r, ge). R changes a in words large, are, art, mart; e softens g –ge.

9 WHEEL (wh digraph) teach /wh/ question words as a group. Teach the six consonant digraphs ch, ph, ch, sh, wh and th voiced and unvoiced.

10 CABIN (cvc/ic/id/in) 'cabin' words robin, rapid, titanic probably pronounced with the long vowels once cf Titanium. The rest follow the long vowel rule – open, bacon, spoken, laden, token.

11 WATER (wa /or/ and wo /ir/ rules). W changes the vowel sounds of a and o – war, ward, walk, warm. Work, world, whorl, word, worm, worst.

12 PAY (cvy). CHANGE rule. Change y to i when suffixing. Paid, said, laid.

13 ROUND (diphthong /ou/ow sound is ah -oo or two sounds). Ground, bound, found, sound, hound, rouse, louse; row, cow; oi diphthong in oil, boil, toil. Ow is also a digraph low, row, know.
14 SIGN (cv – gn, silent letters). Family words will help with detecting some silent letters – sign, signal; bomb, bombardment. Some letters were once pronounced knife, knight, knave, knitting.
15 PAIR (air/are words). Air, fair, lair, stair; care, stare, pare, dare (often verbs) mare, fare.

Several schools may volunteer to try the 'Spells Approach' following the 2007 cohort analyses of their writing results and through this collaboration we hope to improve the structure and develop the idea as a new LDRP project.

A misspelling dictionary

In order to help teachers with the CPSS intervention, a dictionary of misspelled words from the cohorts is in development and each entry has suggestions for different types of cognitive intervention related to the type and level of the error. For example, the word 'minute' has entries for the following misspellings: mies, minits, minuet, minut.

Summary and conclusions

This chapter suggests that spelling development of dyslexics follows a normal pattern similar to that of non-dyslexic younger spellers. It looks in some detail at the nature of the spelling errors and a review is made of the research and confirms the developmental hypothesis.

A discussion of various strategic approaches to spelling correction in the literature is undertaken and illustrations are given. A particular form of strategic intervention called CPSS is discussed in more detail and case work and teacher research with controls and dyslexics at the second level stage, after they have cracked the alphabetic code, are shown and confirm that the strategic approach to assessment and intervention can help in directing the ways in which we can correct spelling. The essential components are discussed in terms of higher cerebral functions and the role of the cerebellum in writing showing both must be alerted and retrained in remediation or correcting misspellings.

Some dyslexia programmes follow on from basic phonics and syllable work to give structured teaching on morphemics and linguistics but this again is highly structured and teacher directed, which many older students reject. Case work with these dyslexics shows that they are just as able as 'normal' subjects to use the CPSS methods effectively and carry them into their other areas of work. It shows that spelling teaching and learning need not be laborious, a 'spelling grind', but can be flexible, more like detective work, with the transfer to the compositional abilities in evidence as well as to reading. Formalised research studies are now needed to check this.

The link is then made between strategic assessment and strategic interventions which all teachers could learn if the school policy directed. New developments using CPSS are outlined for cross curricular and project work and for a special misspelling dictionary.

It would appear from a number of researches (Goswami 1993; Lennox and Siegal 1994) that children will use any method to spell and that the strategies operate in parallel rather than sequentially unless the teaching programme has been heavily biased to one type. As Ellis (1995: 7) wrote, 'different sources of knowledge constantly interact and are brought to bear on the spelling process'. His longitudinal studies confirmed the importance of spelling to the development of reading.

Appendix

An informal hearing reading inventory (photocopiable material)

Name:			At test	After test
Class:		Chronological age:		
Date of birth:		Reading age:		
Reading scheme:		Reading test:		
Spelling age:		Spelling test:		
Dates	*Examples (use ticks if possible)*	*Month*	*Month*	
Text	Reading scheme book and page number. Criticism if any.			
Word attack skills	Guesses from initial sound. Tries blend. Self corrects. Syllabifies. Sounds out word.			
Comprehension skills	Can answer factual recall questions. Can predict using picture, syntax or general meaning. Answers inferential question. Pauses at full stops.			
Audience effects	All one tone, word by word reading. Drops voice at full stop. Reads in units of meaning. Speed. Takes account of speech marks. Fluent. Reads with good audience effect.			
Behavioural signs	Reading position close to page or distant. Body posture. Finger or book mark used. Hand left out. Smooth eye scan.			
Emotional signs	Tenseness cues: jiggling, breathlessness, nervous smiling, avoidance of task if possible. Lack of fluency and monotone.			
Other comments	Select one thing to help the next month's/week's reading, e.g. using initial sound to help guess word. Teach appropriate sounds.			

D. Montgomery 2007

Epilogue

The intention behind this book was to try to help teachers establish a better balance between reading and writing in literacy teaching by focusing on spelling and handwriting issues and problems. There are several reasons for this, one being that learning to spell has a more fundamental contribution to make in becoming literate than it is given credit for in the UK. Handwriting associated with spelling has an equally significant role. It has been established that until both spelling and handwriting have been automatised, compositional skills cannot fully develop. Failure to acquire automaticity at an early stage hampers progress in the wider curriculum not only in schools but also later at university level. Writing difficulties are thus widely seen as some of the main reasons for underachievement in schools across the ability range.

In relation to dyslexia it has been suggested that a greater priority must be given in the early stages to spelling and handwriting teaching in order to establish the multisensory connections between sounds, symbols, articulation awareness and motor skills components. A synthetic phonics approach must be built from the moment two sounds have been learnt. In the later stages dyslexics need to be given a wider range of skills, especially strategic approaches to deal with the dominant morphemic aspects of the language.

Dyslexics were also identified who had learnt to read to grade level or beyond but who had many problems with spelling and writing. Their underachievement tended to go unnoticed and unsupported and they had to make tremendous efforts to gain their goals and conceal their difficulties. They had spent their school years labelled as 'stupid' or 'lazy' and felt failures, whatever they achieved later. It has been argued that a whole school approach to developing handwriting and spelling skills is needed in the form of a *Developmental Writing Curriculum* for both primary and secondary schools to help conteract these problems. It should include teaching scaffolds to support weak organisational skills; an agreed format for teaching fluent joined handwriting in both primary and secondary schools starting in reception; and a programme of developmental spelling teaching and correction which goes well beyond rote training and engages the pupils' problem solving abilities so that they do not develop a learned helplessness.

Writing is still widely used as the main response mode in schools and so developing a school policy towards writing can help teachers develop kinder attitudes to writing difficulties and help them intervene to support and develop writing skills. To this end we may never need to read of adult dyslexics looking back on their school experiences (Hughes and Dawson 1995) and perceiving themselves as stupid and failures, bullied and degraded by teachers and peers alike just because they had reading and writing difficulties.

References

Adams, M. J. 1990 *Beginning to Read*. Cambridge, MA: MIT Press.

Adonis, A. (Lord) 2005 'Dyslexia does exist'. Ministerial statement. At: http://news.bbc.co.uk/2/hi/uk.

AFASIC 2006 *Suggestions for Teachers' Leaflets*. Association for All Speech Impaired Children, Smithfields, London: AFASIC.

Allcock, P. 2001 'Update September 2001: Testing handwriting speed'. *PATOSS Bulletin* November: 17.

Alston, J. 1993 *Assessing and Promoting Writing Skills*. Stafford: NASEN.

Alston, J. and Taylor, J. 1993 *The Handwriting File*. Wisbech: Learning Development Aids.

Amano, I. 1992 'The light and dark sides of Japanese education'. *Royal Society of Arts Journal* 145: 5424.

Andrusysgyn, K. 2002 'An investigation of CPSS with a group of poor spellers'. Module 2 MA SpLD. London: Middlesex University.

APA (American Psychiatric Association) 1994 *The Diagnostic and Statistical Manual of Mental Disorders (DSM-IV)*. Washington, DC: APA.

APU (Assessment of Performance Unit) 1991 *Assessment of Writing Skills*. London: Further Education Unit.

Ashman, A. 1995 'How effective is remediation in school?' *Journal of Cognitive Education* 4 (2): 1–3.

Augur, J. and Briggs, S. (eds) 1991 *The Hickey Multisensory Language Course* (2nd edition). London: Whurr.

Baddeley, A. D. 1986 *Working Memory*. Oxford: Clarendon.

Bailey, C. A. 1988 'Handwriting: ergonomics, assessment and instruction'. *British Journal of Special Education* 15 (2): Research Supplement, 65–71.

Bakker, D. J. 1972 *Temporal Order and Disturbed Reading*. Rotterdam: Rotterdam University Press.

Bakker, D. J. 1992 'Neuropsychological classification and treatment of dyslexia'. *Journal of Learning Disabilities* 25 (2): 102–9.

Ball, E. and Blachman, B. A. 1991 'Does phoneme awareness training in kindergarten make a difference in early word recognition and developmental spelling?' *Reading Research Quarterly* 26 (1): 46–66.

Barker-Lunn, J. C. 1984 *NFER Survey on Teaching Basic Skills in Primary Schools*. Windsor: NFER-Nelson.

Barnard, H. C. 1961 *A History of English Education*. London: London University Press

BDA (British Dyslexia Association) 1981 British Dyslexia Asociation Expert Group Minutes, personal communication from J. Alston BDA.

BDA 1999 *Dyslexia Handbook*. Reading: BDA.

BDA 2004 'Dyslexia Information' at www.bda-dyslexia.org.uk/

Beaton, A. A. 2002 'Dyslexia and the cerebellar deficit hypothesis'. *Cortex* 38 (4): 479–90.

Becker, W. C. and Engelmann, S. 1977 *The Oregon Direct Instruction Model.* University of Oregon: SRA.

Berninger, V. W. 2004 'Review of handwriting research and intervention'. Keynote paper at Annual DCD Conference, Oxford: April.

Berninger, V. W., Mizokawa, D. and Bragg, R. 1991 'Theory based diagnosis and remediation of writing'. *Journal of School Psychology* 29: 57–79

Berninger, V. W., Vaughan, K., Abbott, R., Abbott, S., Rogers, L., Brooks, A., Reed, E. and Graham, S. 1997 'Treatment of handwriting problems in beginning writers: transfer from handwriting to composition'. *Journal of Educational Psychology* 89: 652–66.

Binder, C. and Watkins, C. L. 1990 'Precision teaching and direct instruction: Measurably superior instructional technology in schools.' *Performance Improvement Quarterly* 3 (4): 74–96.

Birch, H. G. 1962 'Dyslexia and the maturation of visual function'. In J. Money (ed.) *Reading Disability.* Baltimore: Johns Hopkins Press.

Birch, H. G. and Belmont, L. 1964 'Auditory-visual integration in normal and retarded readers'. *American Journal of Orthopsychiatry* 34: 352–61.

Bishop, D. V. M. 2002 'Cerebellar abnormalities in developmental dyslexia: cause, correlate or consequence?' *Cortex* 38: 491–8.

Bladon, H. 2004 'An investigation into the relationship between unusual penhold and school performance'. Unpublished MA SpLD dissertation. London: Middlesex University.

Bloom, B. S. 1956 *Taxonomy of Educational Objectives Volume 1* London: Longman.

Blythe, P. and McGlown, D. J. 1979 *An Organic Basis for Neurosis and Educational Difficulties: A New Look at the Old MBD Syndrome.* Chester: Insight.

Boder, E. 1973 'Developmental dyslexia: a diagnostic approach based on three atypical reading patterns'. *Developmental Medicine and Child Neurology* 23: 663–87.

Bourassa, D. and Treiman, R. 2003 'Spelling in children with dyslexia.' *Scientific Study of Reading* 7 (4): 301–3.

BPS (British Psychological Society) 1989 *Deliberations of the Expert Group on Dyslexia.* Leicester: BPS.

Bradley, L. L. 1980 *Assessing Reading Difficulties: A Diagnostic and Remedial Approach.* Basingstoke: Macmillan.

Bradley, L. L. 1981 'The organisation of motor patterns for spelling: an effective remedial strategy for backward readers'. *Developmental Medicine and Child Neurology* 23: 83–97.

Bradley, L. L. 1990 'Rhyming connections in learning to read and spell'. In P. D. Pumfrey and C. D. Elliott (eds) 1990 *Children's Difficulties in Reading, Spelling and Writing: Challenges and Responses.* Basingstoke: Falmer Press.

Bradley, L. L. and Huxford, L. 1994 'Organising sound and letter patters for spelling'. In G. D. A. Brown and N. C. Ellis (eds) *Handbook of Spelling: Theory, Process and Intervention*, pp. 425–38. Chichester: Wiley.

Brand, V. 1998 *Spelling Made Easy.* Baldock, Herts: Egon.

Bravar, L. (2005) 'Studying handwriting: an Italian experience'. *6th International DCD Conference*, Trieste: May.

Briggs, D. 1980 'A study of the influence of handwriting upon grades in examination scripts'. *Educational Review* 32: 185–93.

Brooks, G. 1999 'What works for slow readers'. *Support for Learning* 14 (1): 27–31.

Brooks, G., Flanagan, N., Henhusens, Z. and Hutchinson, D. 1998 *What Works for Slow Readers? The Effectiveness of Early Intervention Schemes.* Slough: NFER.

Brooks, P. and Weeks, S. 1999 *Individual Styles in Learning to Spell: Improving Spelling in Children with Literacy Difficulties and All Children in Mainstream Schools.* Nottingham: DfEE Publications (also Research Brief No. 108, DfEE).

Broomfield, H. and Combley, M. 1997 *Overcoming Dyslexia: A Practical Handbook for the Classroom.* London: Whurr.

Brown, N. E. 1990 'Children with spelling and writing difficulties: an alternative approach'. In P. Pumfrey and C. D. Elliott (eds) *Children's Difficulties in Reading, Spelling and Writing,* pp. 289–304. London: Falmer.

Brown, G. D. A. and Ellis, N. C. (eds) 1994 *Handbook of Spelling: Theory, Process and Intervention.* Chichester: Wiley

Brown, G. D. A. and Loosemore, R. P. W. 1994 'Computational approaches to normal and impaired spelling'. In G. D. A. Brown and N. C. Ellis (eds) *Handbook of Spelling: Theory, Process and Intervention,* pp.319–36. Chichester: Wiley.

Bruck, M. and Treiman, R. 1990 'Phonological awareness and spelling in normal children and dyslexics: the case of initial consonant clusters'. *Journal of Experimental Child Psychology* 50: 156–78.

Brunswick, N., McCrory, E., Price, C. J., Frith, C. D. and Frith, U. 1999 'Explicit and implicit processing of words and pseudowords by adult developmental dyslexics'. *Brain* 122: 1901–17.

Bryant, P. and Bradley, L. 1985 *Children's Reading Problems.* Oxford: Blackwell.

Bueckhardt, G. 1986 Unpublished thesis on Learning Difficulties. Kingston-upon-Thames: Kingston Polytechnic.

Burnhill L, P. Hartley, J., Fraser, L. and Young, D. 1975 'Writing lines: an exploratory study'. *Programmed Learning and Educational Technology* 12 (2): 84–7.

Butler-Por, N. 1987 *Underachievers in Schools: Issues and Interventions.* Chichester: John Wiley.

Butt, H. 2003 'An investigation into the cognitive process strategies for spelling in the development of spelling skills of a group of Year 2 Pupils'. Unpublished MA SpLD dissertation. London: Middlesex University.

Butterworth, B. 2006 BBC Radio 4 Interview, *Today* Programme 2 April.

Calder, N. 1970 *The Mind of Man,* pp. 150–4. London: BBC Publications.

Calfee, R. C., Lindamood, P. and Lindamood, C. 1973 'Acoustic-phonetic skills and reading in kindergarten through twelfth grade'. *Journal of Educational Psychology* 64: 293–8.

Cassar, M. and Treiman, R. 2004 'Developmental variations in spelling: comparing typical and poor spellers'. In C. A. Stone, E. R. Silliman, B. Ehren and K. Apel (eds) *Handbook of Language and Literacy: Development and Disorders.* New York: Guilford.

Chall, J. 1967 *Learning to Read: The Great Debate.* New York: McGraw-Hill.

Chall, J. 1985 *Stages in Reading Development.* New York: McGraw-Hill.

Chalmers, G.S. 1976 *Reading Easy 1800–1850.* London: Broadsheet King.

Chesson, R., McKay, C. and Stephenson, E. 1991 'The consequences of motor/learning difficulties in school age children and their teachers: some parental views.' *Support for Learning* 6 (4): 172–7.

Childs, S. 1968 *Education and Specific Language Disability.* Connecticut: The Orton Society.

Chomsky, C. 1971 'Write first, read later'. *Childhood Education* 47 (6): 296–9.

Christensen, C. A and Jones, D. 2000 'Handwriting: an underestimated skill in the development of written language'. *Handwriting Today* 2: 56–69.

Clark, M. M. 1970 *Reading Difficulties in Schools.* Harmondsworth: Penguin.

Clay, M. M. 1975 *What Did I Write? Beginnings of Writing Behaviour.* London: Heinemann.

Clay, M. M. 1979 *The Early Detection of Reading Difficulties.* London: Heinemann.

Clay, M. M. 1989 'Observing young children reading texts'. *Support for Learning* 4 (1): 7–11.

Clay, M. M. 1993 *Reading Recovery: A Guidebook for Teachers in Training*. Auckland: Heinemann.

Clements, S. D. 1966 *National Project on Minimal Brain Dysfunction in Children – Terminology and Identification Monograph No. 3 Public Health Service Publication No. 1415*. Washington, DC: Government Printing Office.

Coffield, F., Moseley, D. and Ecclestone, K. 2004 'Should we be using learning styles? What research has to say to practitioners'. At: http://www.LSDA.org.uk.

Combley, M. (ed.) 2000 *The Hickey Multisensory Language Course* (3rd edition). London: Whurr.

Connelly, D., Campbell, S., MacLean, M. and Barnes, J. 2005b 'Handwriting fluency and essay writing in university students with dyslexia'. *Handwriting Today* 4 (Autumn): 39–41.

Connelly, V. and Hurst, G. 2001 'The influence of handwriting fluency on writing quality in later primary and early secondary education'. *Handwriting Today* 2: 50–7.

Connelly, V., Dockrell, J. and Barnett, A. 2005a 'The slow handwriting of undergraduate students constrains the overall performance in exam essays'. *Educational Psychology* 25 (1): 99–109.

Connor, M. 1994 'Specific learning difficulty (dyslexia) and interventions'. *Support for Learning* 9 (3): 114–19.

Cooke, A. 1992 *Tackling Dyslexia the Bangor Way*. London: Whurr.

Cowdery, L. L. 1987 *Teaching Reading Through Spelling (TRTS): The Spelling Notebook*. Kingston: Learning Difficulties Research Project.

Cowdery, L. L., Morse, P. and Prince-Bruce, M. 1985 *Teaching Reading Through Spelling (TRTS) The Early Stages of the Programme Book 2C*. Kingston: Learning Difficulties Research Project.

Cowdery, L. L., Montgomery, D. (ed.), Morse, P. and Prince-Bruce, M. 1984 *Teaching Reading Through Spelling (TRTS): The Foundations of the Programme Book 2B*. Kingston: Learning Difficulties Research Project.

Cowdery, L. L., Montgomery, D., Morse, P. and Prince-Bruce, M. 1994 *Teaching Reading Through Spelling Series*. Wrexham: TRTS.

Cowdery, L. L., McMahon, J., Montgomery, D. (ed.), Morse, P. and Prince-Bruce, M. 1983 *Teaching Reading Through Spelling (TRTS): Diagnosis Book 2A*. Kingston: Learning Difficulties Research Project.

Cox, A. R. 1992 *Foundations of Literacy*. Cambridge, MA: Educators Publishing Service.

Cramer, R. L. 1976 'Diagnosing skills by analysing childen's writing'. *The Reading Teacher* 30 (3): 276–9.

Cramer, R. L. 1998 *The Spelling Connection: Integrating Reading, Writing and Spelling Instruction*. New York: Guildford Press.

Cripps, C. 1988 *A Hand for Spelling*. Wisbech: Learning Development Aids.

Cripps, C. and Cox, R. 1987 Data reported in C. Cripps (1989) *Joining the ABC*. Wisbech: Learning Development Aids.

Cunningham, A. E. and Stanovich, K. E. 1990 'Early spelling acquisition: writing beats the computer'. *Journal of Educational Psychology* 82: 154–62.

Daniels, J. C. and Diack, H. 1958 *The Standard Spelling Test*. London: Chatto and Windus. Reprinted by Hart Davis Educational, 1979.

Davies, A. and Ritchie, D. 1998 *THRASS Teachers' Manual*. Chester: THRASS (UK).

DDAT 2004 *DDAT Centre Report*. Kenilworth: DDAT.

de Hirsch, K. and Jansky, J. 1972 *Predicting Reading Failure*. New York: Harper and Row.

Delpire, R. and Monory, J. 1962 *The Written Word*. London: Prentice-Hall.

DES 1989 *English from Ages 5–16 (The Cox Report)*. London: HMSO.

DfE 1994 *Code of Practice on the Identification and Assessment of Special Educational Needs.* London: HMSO.

DfE 1995 At: www.standards.dfe.org.uk.

DfEE 1997 *Excellence for All Children: Meeting Special Educational Needs.* London: The Stationery Office.

DfEE 1998 *The National Literacy Strategy: Framework for Teaching.* London: DfEE.

DfEE 2001a *Developing Early Writing, Section Three.* London DfEE.

DfEE 2001b *Code of Practice for SEN (Revised).* London: DfEE.

DfES 2004 *Removing Barriers to Achievement: The Government's Strategy for SEN (Executive Summary).* Nottingham: DfES Publications.

DfES 2006 'The sounds of English'. At: www.Standards.dfes.gov.uk

Diack, H. 1965 *In Spite of the Alphabet.* London: Chatto and Windus.

Dias, K. and Juniper, L. 2002 'Phono-Graphix – Who needs additional literacy support?' *Support for Learning* 17 (1): 34–8.

DILP 1993 *Dyslexia Institute Language Programme.* Staines: Dyslexia Institute.

Downing, J. 1964 *The Initial Teaching Alphabet* (2nd edition). London: Cassell.

Duane, D. 2002 *The Neurology of NLD Keynote Lecture, Policy into Practice Conference on Dyslexia.* Uppsala, Sweden: 14–16 August.

Durham LEA 2005 At: www.durhamtrial.org.

Early, G. H. 1976 'Cursive handwriting, reading and spelling achievement'. *Academic Therapy* 12 (1): 67–74.

Eccles, J. C. 1973 *The Understanding of the Brain.* New York: McGraw Hill.

Eckert, M. A., Leonard, C. M., Richards, T. L., Aylward, E. H., Thomson, J. and Berninger, V. W. 2003 'Anatomical correlates of dyslexia: frontal and cerebellar findings'. *Brain* 126: 482–94.

Edwards, J. 1994 *The Scars of Dyslexia.* London: Cassell.

Ehri, L. C. 1979 'Linguistic insight threshold of reading acquisition'. In T.G. Waller and G. E. MacKinnon (eds) *Reading Research: Advances in Theory and Practice.* New York: Academic Press.

Ehri, L. C. 1984 'How orthography alters spoken language competencies in children learning to read and spell'. In J. Downing and R. Valtin (eds) *Language Awareness and Learning to Read.* New York: Springer Verlag.

Ehri, L. C. and Robbins, C. 1992 'Beginners need some decoding skills to read words by analogy'. *Reading Research Quarterly* 27: 13–26.

Eisenberg, L. 1962 'Introduction'. In J. Money (ed.) *Reading Disability: Progress and Research Needs in Dyslexia,* pp. 4–5. Baltimore: Johns Hopkins Press.

Elliott, D. 1996 *British Ability Scales II.* Windsor: NFER Nelson.

Elliott, J. 2005 'Row erupts over dyslexia denial'. At: http://news.bbc.co.uk/1/hi/uk-news/education/4205932.stm (accessed September 2005).

Ellis, A. W. 1995 *Reading, Writing and Dyslexia* (2nd edition). Hove: Erlbaum.

Fassett, J. H. 1929 *The New Beacon Readers: Teachers' Manual* (Revised edition). London: Ginn.

Fawcett, A. J. and Nicolson, R. I., 1996 *Dyslexia Early Screening Test (DEST).* London psychological Corporation.

Fawcett, A. J. and Nicolson, R. I. 1999 'Dyslexia: the role of the cerebellum'. *Dyslexia and International Research and Practice* 5: 155–77.

Fawcett, A. J. and Nicolson, R. I. 2000 'Systematic screening and intervention of reading difficulty' In N. A. Badian (ed.) *Prediction and Prevention of Reading Failure.* Baltimore: New York Press.

Fawcett, A. J., Nicolson, R. I. and Dean, P. 1996 'Impaired performance of children with dyslexia on a range of cerebellar tasks'. In *Annals of Dyslexia, Volume 46.* Baltimore: The International Dyslexia Association.

Fawcett, A. J., Singleton, C. H. and Peer, L. 1998 'Advances in early years screening for dyslexia in the United Kingdom' In *Annals of Dyslexia, Volume 48.* Baltimore: The International Dyslexia Association.

Fawcett, A. J., Nicolson, R. I., Moss, H. Nicolson, M. K., and Reason, R. 2001 'Effectiveness of reading intervention in junior school'. *Educational Psychology* 21 (3): 299–312.

Feiler, A. and Webster, A. 1998 'Success and failure in early literacy: teachers' predictions and subsequent intervention'. *British Journal of Special Education* 25 (4): 189–95.

Fernald, G. M. 1943 *Remedial Techniques in Basic School Subjects.* New York: McGraw-Hill.

Ferreiro, E. 1978 'What is written in a written sentence? A developmental answer'. *Journal of Education* 160 (4): 25–39.

Fiderer, A. 1998 *Rubrics and Checklists to Assess Reading and Writing,* Leamington Spa: Scholastic Books

Folland, C. 2004 Case work using CPSS with Natalie. Unpublished Module 2 Portfolio, London: Middlesex University

Forsyth, D. 1988 'An evaluation of an infant school screening instrument'. Unpublished dissertation. Kingston-upon-Thames: Kingston Polytechnic.

Francis, H. 1982 *Learning to Read: Literate Behaviour and Orthographic Knowledge.* London: Allen and Unwin.

Francis, M., Taylor, S. and Sawyer, C. 1992 'Coloured lenses and the Dex frame: new issues'. *Support for Learning* 7 (1): 25–7.

Frank, J. and Levinson, D. 1973 'Dysmetric dyslexia and dyspraxia: hypothesis and study'. *Journal of American Academy of Child Psychiatry* Reprint 12 (4): 690–701.

Frederickson, N. and Reason, R. (eds) 1993 'Phonological assessment of special learning difficulties'. *Education and Child Psychology* 12 (1).

Frederickson, N., Frith, U. and Reason, R. 1997 *Phonological Assessment Battery (PhAB).*

Frith, U. 1974 'Internal schemata for letters in good and bad readers'. *British Journal of Psychology* 65 (2): 113–23.

Frith, U. 1978 'Spelling difficulties'. *Journal of Child Psychology and Psychiatry* 19: 279–85.

Frith, U. (ed.) 1980 *Cognitive Processes in Spelling.* Chichester: Wiley.

Frith, U. 1985 'Beneath the surface of developmental dyslexia'. In K. Patterson and M. Coltheart (eds) *Surface Dyslexia.* London: Routledge and Kegan Paul.

Frith, U. 1993 'Dyslexia. Can we have a shared theoretical framework?' *Education and Child Psychology* 12 (6): 18–24.

Frith, U. 2000 'Dyslexia: a theoretical framework' 27th International Conference on Psychology, Stockholm.

Frostig, M. and Horn, D. 1964 *The Frostig Programme for the Development of Visual Perception.* Chicago: Follett.

Fry, E. 1964 'A frequency approach to phonics'. *Elementary English* 41: 759–65.

Fulk, B. M. and Stormont-Spurgin, M. 1995 'Spelling interventions for students with disabilities. A review'. *Journal of Special Education* 28 (4): 488–513.

Gagne, F. 1995 'Learning about gifts and talents through peer and teacher nomination'. In M. W. Katzko and F. J. Monks (eds) *Nurturing Talent: Individual Needs and Social Ability Proceedings of the 4th ECHA Conference* pp. 20–30. Assen, The Netherlands: Van Gorcum.

Gagne, R. 1973 *The Essentials of Learning.* London: Holt, Rinehart and Winston.

Gaines, K. 1989 'The use of reading diaries as a short term intervention strategy'. In P. Pumfrey and R. Reason (eds) 1991 *Specific Learning Difficulties (Dyslexia): Challenges and Responses.* London: NFER-Nelson.

Galaburda, A. M. 1993 *Dyslexia and Development.* Cambridge, MA: Harvard University Press.

Gelb, I. J. 1963 *A Study of Writing* (2nd edition). London: University of Chicago Press.

Gentry, J. R. 1981 'Learning to spell developmentally'. *The Reading Teacher* 34 (4): 378–81.

Geschwind, N. 1979 'Specialisations of the human brain'. *Scientific American* 241 (3): 156–67.

Gibson, R. J. and Levin, H. 1975 *The Psychology of Reading.* Cambridge, MA: MIT Press.

Gilger, J. W., Pennington, B. F. and Defries, J. C. 1991 'Risk for reading disabilities as a function of parental history in three family studies'. *Reading and Writing* 3: 205–18.

Gillingham, A. M., Stillman, B. U. and Orton, S. T. 1940 *Remedial Training for Children with Specific Disability in Reading, Spelling and Penmanship.* New York: Sackett and Williams.

Gillingham, A., and Stillman, B. 1956 *Remedial Training for Children with Specific Disability in Reading, Spelling and Penmanship.* New York: Sackett and Williams.

Gittelman, R. and Feingold, I. 1983 'Children with reading disorders.' *Journal of Child Psychology and Psychiatry* 24 (2): 169–93.

Goddard Blythe, S. 2004 *The Well Balanced Child.* Stroud: Hawthorne Press.

Godinho, S. and Clements, D. 2002 'Literature discussion with gifted and talented students'. *Educating Able Children* 6 (2): 11–9.

Goldberg, H. K. and Schiffman, G. B. 1972 *Dyslexia: Problems of Reading.* London: Grune and Stratton.

Golinkoff, R. M. 1978 'Phonemics awareness and reading achievement'. In F. R. Murray and J. J. Pikulski (eds) *The Acquisition of Reading.* Baltimore: University Park Press.

Goodacre, E. J. 1971 *Reading in Infant Classes* (2nd edition). Windsor: NFER.

Gorman, T. and Fernandes, C. 1993 *Reading in Recession.* Windsor: NFER-Nelson.

Goswami, U. 1993 'Orthographic analogies and reading development'. *The Psychologist* (July) 313–15.

Goswami, U. 1994 'The role of analogies in reading development'. *Support for Learning* 9 (1): 22–5.

Goswami, U. 2003 'How to beat dyslexia'. *The Psychologist* 16 (9): 463–5.

Goswami, U. and Bryant, P. 1990 *Phonological Skills and Learning to Read.* Hove: Lawrence Erlbaum.

Goulandris, N. K. 1986 'Speech perception in relation to reading skill. A developmental analysis'. *Journal of Experimental Child Psychology* 41: 489–507.

Graham, S., Harris, K. R. and Fink, J. 2000 'Is handwriting causally related to learning to write? Treatment of handwriting problems in beginning readers'. *Journal of Educational Psychology* 92 (4): 620–33.

Graham, S., Berninger, V. W., Abbott R. D., Abbott, S. P. and Whitaker, D. 1996 'The role of mechanics in composing of elementary students: a new methodological approach'. *Journal of Educational Psychology* 89 (1): 70–182.

Gubbay, S. S. 1976 *The Clumsy Child.* London: W. B. Saunders.

Hanna, P. R., Hanna, J. S., Hodges, R. E. and Rudorf, E. H. 1966 *Phoneme-Grapheme Correspondence as Cues to Spelling Improvement.* Washington DC, US Office of Education.

Harris, D. (ed) 1963 *Harris-Goodenough draw a person test: The revised version of the goodenough draw a man test.* New York: Grune & Stratton.

Helene, M. 2004 'A critical evaluation of an APSL programme'. Unpublished Module 4 portfolio investigation, MA SpLD. London: Middlesex University.

Henderson, S. E. and Green, D. 2001 'Handwriting problems in children with Asperger Syndrome'. *Handwriting Today* 2: 65–71.

Henderson, S. E. 2003 'Getting it right'. *Special* 30–3.

Henderson, S. E. and Hall, D. 1982 'Concomitants of clumsiness in young school children'. *Developmental Medicine and Child Neurology* 24: 448–60.

Henry, M. K. 1995 'The importance of roots in the English spelling system'. *Annual Conference of the Orton Society* Houston, Texas: 2 November.

Hickey, K. 1977 *Dyslexia: A Language Training Course for Teachers and Learners.* Available from the Staines Dyslexia Institute.

Hines, C. 1998 Personal Communication of school's SATs.

Hinson, M. and Smith, B. 1986 'The productive process: an approach to literacy for children with difficulties'. In B. Root (ed.) *Resources for Reading: Does Quality Count?*, pp. 161–71. London: UKRA/Macmillan.

Hinson, M. and Smith, B. 1993 *Phonics and Phonic Resources.* Stafford: NASEN.

HMCI (1998) *Annual Report of the Chief Inspector for English Schools 1996–1997.* London: Stationery Office.

HMI 1990 *The Teaching and Learning of Reading in Primary Schools.* London: HMSO.

HMI 2001 *The Teaching of Writing in Primary Schools: Could Do Better.* London: DfES.

Holmes, B. 1994 'Fast words speed past dyslexia'. *New Scientist* 10: 27 August.

House of Commons 1995 Education Sub Committee Enquiry. Westminster: House of Commons.

House of Commons Enquiry 2005 Oral Evidence presented on the Effectiveness of the National Literacy Strategy to the Education and Skills Committee, Session 2005.

Hornsby, B. 1989 *Before Alpha.* London: Souvenir Press.

Hornsby, B. 1994 *Overcoming Dyslexia.* London: MacDonald.

Hornsby, B. 2000 Written communication to THRASS, Chester: 27 March.

Hornsby, B. and Farrar, M. 1990 'Some effects of a dyslexia-centred teaching programme'. In P. D. Pumfrey and C. D. Elliott (eds) *Children's Difficulties in Reading, Spelling and Writing*, pp. 173–96. London: Falmer Press.

Hornsby, B, and Shear, F. 1976–1995 *Alpha to Omega* (Revised Edition). London: Heinemann.

Hughes, W. and Dawson, R. 1995 'Memories of school: adult dyslexics recall their schooldays'. *Support for Learning* 10 (4): 181–84.

Hulme, C. 1981 *Reading Retardation and Multisensory Teaching.* London: Routledge and Kegan Paul.

Humphries, T. W., Snider, L., and McDougall, B. 1993 'Clinical evaluation of the effectiveness of sensory integration and perceptual motor therapy in improving sensory integrative function in children with learning disabilities'. *The Occupational Therapy Journal of Research* 13: 163–82

Hurry, J., Silva, K., and Riley, S 1996 'Evaluation of a focused literacy teaching programme in Reception and Year 1'. *British Educational Research Journal* 22 (5): 617–30.

Irlen, H. I. and Lass, M. J. 1989 'Improving reading problems due to scotopic sensitivity using Irlen lenses and overlays'. *Education* 109: 413–17.

Jansky, J. and de Hirsch, K. 1972 *Preventing Reading Failure.* New York: Harper and Row.

Jarman, C. 1979 *The Development of Handwriting Skills.* Oxford: Blackwell.

Johnson, D. R. and Myklebust, H. R. 1967 *Learning Disabilities: Educational Principles and Practices* London: Grune and Stratton.

Johnson, M., Phillips, S. and Peer, L. (eds) 1999 *MTSR: A Multisensory Teaching System for Reading: UK Edition.* Manchester Metropolitan University: Manchester.

Johnson, R. and Watson, J. 1999 'Synthetically successful'. *Literacy Today* (June):19.

Jones, D. and Christensen, C. A. 1999 'Relationship between automaticity in handwriting and students' abilty to generate written text'. *Journal of Educational Psychology* 91 (1): 44–9.

Kappers, E. J. 1990 'Neuropsychological treatment of dyslexic children'. *Euronews Dyslexia* 3: 9–15.

Kellmer-Pringle, M. 1970 *Able Misfits.* London: Longman.

Kent County Council 2003 *Writing in the Air: Nurturing Young Children's Dispositions for Writing.* Maidstone: Schools Advisory Service.

Klein, C. and Millar, R.R. 1990 *Unscrambling Spelling*. Sevenoaks: Hodder and Stoughton.

Knight, B. and Smith, J. 2000 'The effect of word study and cognitive strategy training on student's spelling abilities.' *Australian Journal of Special Education* 24 (2/3): 84–97.

Kokot, S. 2003 'A neurodevelopmental approach to learning disabilities, diagnosis and treatment'. In D. Montgomery (ed.) *Gifted and Talented Children with Special Educational Needs: Double Exceptionality*, pp. 11–24. London: David Fulton.

Koppitz, E. M. 1977 *The Visual Aural Digit Span Test*. New York: Grune and Stratton.

Kuczaj, S. A. 1979 'Evidence for a language learning strategy: on the relative ease of acquisition of prefixes and suffixes'. *Child Development* 50: 1–13.

Kussmaul, A. 1877 'Disturbance of speech'. *Cyclopaedia of the Practice of Medicine* 14: 581–75.

Laszlo, M., Bairstow, P., and Bartrip, P. 1988 'A new approach to perceptuomotor dysfunction. Previously called clumsiness'. *Support for Learning* 3: 33–40.

LDA 1993 *The Handwriting File*. Wisbech: Learning Development Aids.

Leach, D. 1983 'Early screening'. *School Psychology International* 4 (1): 47–56.

Lee, J. 2000 'How to teach the spelling of priority words to dyslexic learners'. In J. Townend and M. Turner, (eds) *Dyslexia in Practice: A Guide for Teachers*. Kluwer Academic/ Plenum Publishers.

Lehmkule, S., Garzia, R. P., Turner, L. Hash, T. and Baro, J. A. 1993 'A defective visual pathway in children with reading disability'. *New England Journal of Medicine* 328: 989–96.

Lennox, C and Siegal, L. S. 1994 'The role of phonological and orthographic processing in learning how to spell' in G. D. Brown and N. C. Ellis (eds) *Handbook of Spelling*. Chichester: Wiley.

Liberman, I. J. 1973 'Segmentation of the spoken word and reading acquisition'. *Bulletin of the Orton Society* 23: 365–77.

Liberman, A. M., Shankweiler, D. P., Cooper, F. S. and Studdert-Kennedy, M. 1967 'Perception of the speech code'. *Psychological Review* 74 (6): 431–61.

Lie, K. G. and O'Hare, A. 2000 'Multidisciplinary support and the management of children with specific writing difficulties'. *British Journal of Special Education* 27 (2): 95–9.

Lindamood, P. and Bell, N. 2005 *Lindamood-Bell Program(s) 3rd Edition*. www.lblp.com/programs/phonemiclips

Lingard, T. 2005 'Literacy Acceleration and the Key Stage 3 English Strategy – comparing two approaches for secondary-age pupils with literacy difficulties'. *British Journal of Special Education* 32 (2): 67–77.

Lloyd. S. 1993 *The Phonics Handbook*. Chigwell: Jolly Learning.

Lloyd, S. 2005a, 'How to ... use synthetic phonics'. *Special Children* (Sept/Oct issue): 198.

Lloyd, S. 2005b *Evidence presented to the House of Commons Select Committee*. Westminster: House of Commons.

Lockhead, J. 2001 *THINKBACK: A User's Guide to Minding the Mind*. London: Lawrence Erlbaum.

Lovegrove, W. 1996 'Dyslexia and a transient/magnocellular pathway deficit: the current situation and future directions'. *Australian Journal of Psychology* 48: 167–71.

Low, G. 1990 'Cursive makes a comeback'. *Education* 6 April: 341.

Lundberg, I., Frost, J. and Petersen, O-P. 1988 'Effects of an extensive program for stimulating phonological awareness in pre-school children'. *Reading Research Quarterly* 23 (3): 472–5.

Lupart, J. L. 1992 'The hidden gifted. Current state of knowledge and future research directions'. In F. Monks and W. Peters (ed.) *Talent for the Future*, pp.177–90. Assen, The Netherlands: Van Gorcum.

Lyth, A. 2004 'Handwriting speed: an aid to examination success?' *Handwriting Today* 3: 30–5.

McGuinness, D. 1997 *Why Our Children Can't Read: And What We Can Do About It.* New York: Free Press.

McGuinness, C. and McGuinness, G. 1998 *Reading Reflex.* Harmondsworth: Penguin.

McGuinness, C and McGuinness, G. 1999 *Reading Reflex – The Foolproof Phono-Graphix Method for Teaching Your Child to Read.* Hemel Hempstead: Simon and Schuster.

MacIntyre, C. 2001 *Dyspraxia 5–11: A Practical Guide.* London: David Fulton.

McPhillips, M. 2001 'On reading reflex and research'. *The Psychologist* 14 (2): 82–3.

McPhillips, M., Hepper, P. G. and Mulhern, D. 2000 'Effects of replicating primary-reflex movements on specific reading difficulties in children: a randomised double blind trial' *The Lancet* 355 (9203): 537–41.

Makita, K. 1968 'The rarity of reading disability in Japanese children'. *American Journal of Orthopsychiatry* 38: 599–613.

Manson, J. and Wendon, L. 1997 *Letterland: Early Years Handbook.* London: Collins Educational.

Marsh, G., Friedman, M. P., Welch, V. and Desberg, P. 1980 'The development of strategies in spelling'. In U. Frith (ed.) *Cognitive Processes in Spelling,* pp. 339–54. London: Academic Press.

Mastropieri, M. and Scruggs, T. (eds) 1995 *Advances in Learning and Behavioural Disorders 9.* Greenwich, CT: JAI Press.

Miles, T. R. 1978 *Understanding Dyslexia.* Sevenoaks: Hodder and Stoughton.

Miles, T. R. 1993 *Dyslexia: The Pattern Of Difficulties* 2nd edition. London: Whurr.

Miles, T. R. and Miles, E. 1992 *The Bangor Teaching System* (2nd edition). London: Whurr.

Miles, T. R. and Miles, E. 1999 *Dyslexia 100 Years on* (2nd edition). London: Routledge.

Miskin, R. 2005 *Ruth Miskin Literacy Programme – Just Phonics Handbook (Read Write Inc.).* Oxford: Oxford University Press.

Moats, L. C. 1983 'A comparison of the spelling errors of older dyslexics and second grade normal children.' *Annals of Dyslexia* 33: 121–40.

Monroe, M. 1932 *Children Who Cannot Read.* Chicago: Chicago University Press.

Montgomery, D. 1977 'Teaching pre-reading through training in visual pattern recognition'. *The Reading Teacher* 30 (6): 216–25.

Montgomery, D. 1981 'Do dyslexics have difficulty accessing articulatory information?' *Psychological Research* 43: 235–43.

Montgomery, D. 1989 *Managing Behaviour Problems.* Sevenoaks: Hodder and Stoughton

Montgomery, D. 1990 *Children with Learning Difficulties.* London: Cassell.

Montgomery, D. 1993 'Spelling difficulties in able dyslexics and their remediation'. In K. A. Heller and E. A. Hany (eds) *Competence and Responsibility,* pp. 224–36. Gottlingen: Hogrese and Huber.

Montgomery, D. 1995 'Social abilities in highly able disabled learners and the consequences for remediation'. In M. W. Katzko and F. J. Monks *Nurturing Talent: Individual Needs and Social Abilities,* pp. 226–38. Assen, The Netherlands: Van Gorcum.

Montgomery, D. 1996 *Educating the Able.* London: Cassell.

Montgomery, D. 1997a *Spelling: Remedial Strategies.* London: Cassell.

Montgomery, D. 1997b *Developmental Spelling: A Handbook.* Maldon: LDRP.

Montgomery, D. 1998 *Reversing Lower Attainment.* London: Fulton.

Montgomery, D. (ed.) 2000a *Able Underachievers.* London: Whurr.

Montgomery, D. 2000b 'Supporting the bright dyslexic in the ordinary classroom'. *Educating Able Children* (Spring) 4 (1): 23–32.

Montgomery. D. 2002 *Helping Teachers Develop Through Classroom Observation.* London: David Fulton.

Montgomery. D. (ed.) 2003 *Gifted and Talented Children with Special Educational Needs: Double Exceptionality.* London: David Fulton.

Montgomery, D. 2004 'Barriers to learning in gifted children'. *NAGC Newsletter* 22–30.

Montgomery, D. 2005 'Boys' underachievement: what the research tells us about uplifting achievement'. NACE London Conference, April.

Montgomery, D. 2006 'Cohort analysis of writing after 2, 4 and 7 years of the National Literacy Strategy', paper presented at the 2005 BERA Conference, at: www.leedsedu.ac.uk

Morey, K. 2001 'Casework with an able dyslexic in Nairobi'. *Educating Able Children* 5 (1): 27–30.

Morse, P. 1984 'Handwriting and handwriting difficulties'. In L. L. Cowdery, D. Montgomery, P. Morse and M. Prince-Bruce *Teaching Reading Through Spelling (TRTS): Foundations of the Programme*, pp. 32–68. Kingston: Learning Difficulties Research Project.

Morse, P. 1986 *Teaching Reading Through Spelling: The Handwriting Copy Book*. Kingston: Learning Difficulties Research Project.

Morse, P. 1988 *Teaching Reading Through Spelling: The Handwriting Copy Book for Infants*. Clwyd: Frondeg Hall Publishers.

Morse, P 1991 'Cursive in Kingston-upon Thames'. *Handwriting Review* 5: 16–21.

Mortimore, T. 2005 'Dyslexia and learning style – a note of caution'. *British Journal of Special Education* 32 (3): 145–8.

Moseley, D. 1994 'From theory to practice: errors and trials' in G. D. Brown and N. C. Ellis (eds) *Handbook of Spelling*. Chichester: Wiley.

Moseley, D. 1989 'How lack of confidence in spelling affects children's written expression.' *Educational Psychology in Practice* 5 (1): 42–6.

MSL 1998 *The Complete Structured Literacy Course: Literacy for All*. Peterborough: Multisensory Learning.

MTSR 1999 *Multisensory Training System for Reading*. Manchester: Manchester University/DfEE.

Muter, V. 1994 'Influence of phonological awareness and letter knowledge on beginning reading and spelling development'. In C. Hulme and M. Snowling (eds) *Reading Development and Dyslexia*, pp. 45–62. London: Whurr.

Myklebust, H. 1973 *Development and Disorders of Written Language Volume 2: Studies of Normal and Exceptional Children*. London: Grune and Stratton.

NCC 1989 *Non Statutory Guidelines in English*. York: National Curriculum Council.

NCE (National Commission on Education) 1995 *Standards in Literacy and Numeracy*. London: NCE.

Neale, M. D. 1958 *The Neale Analysis of Reading Ability*. British Adaptation London: Macmillan London

Nelson, H. E. 1980 'Analysis of spelling errors in normal and dyslexic children' in U. Frith (ed.) *Cognitive Processes in Spelling*. London: Academic Press.

Newton. M. and Thomson, M. 1976 *The Aston Index*. Cambridge: LDA.

NFER 1992 *Standards in Literacy and Numeracy: Briefing Paper No. 10*. London: National Commission on Education.

NFER 1996 *Standards in Literacy and Numeracy 1948–1995*. Windsor: NFER.

Nicolson, R. I. and Fawcett, A. 1994 'Spelling remediation for dyslexic children: errors and trials' in G. D. Brown and N. C. Ellis (eds) *Handbook of Spelling*. Chichester: Wiley.

Nicolson, R. I. and Fawcett, A. 1996 *Manual of The Dyslexia Early Screening Test*. London: The Psychological Corporation.

Norrie, E. 1917 *The Edith Norrie Letter Case*. London: Word Blind Institute (1946), Reprinted Helen Arkell Centre.

Norrie, E. 1973 *Edith Norrie Letter Case Manual*. London: Helen Arkell Centre (1993).

O'Brien, K. 2004 'An investigation into the use of Cognitive Process Strategies as a proposed effective means of teaching spelling and remediating or correcting errors'. Unpublished MA dissertation. London: Middlesex University.

OfSTED 1998 *The National Literacy Strategy:An HMI Evaluation.* London: OfSTED.

OfSTED 2001 *The Teaching of Phonics: A Paper by HMI.* London: OfSTED.

OfSTED 2002 *The National Literacy Strategy: The First Four Years.* London: OfSTED.

OfSTED 2004 *The Annual Report of the Chief Inspector for Schools in England 2002–2003.* London: OfSTED.

Ott, P. 1997 *How to Detect and Manage Dyslexia: A Reference and Resource Manual.* Oxford: Heinemann.

Parrant, H. 1989 'An investigation of remedial approaches to children's spelling difficulties'. Unpublished SEN dissertation. Kingston Polytechnic.

Paulesu, E., Frith, U., Snowling, M., Gallagher, A., Morton, J., Frackowisk, R. and Frith, C. 1996 'Is developmental dyslexia a disconnection syndrome? Evidence from PET scanning'. *Brain* 199: 143–57.

Pavlidis, G. Th. 1981 'Sequencing eye movements and the early objective diagnosis of dyslexia'. In G. Th. Pavlidis and T. R. Miles (eds) *Dyslexia Research and Its Application to Education,* pp. 99–164. Chichester: Wiley.

Peters, M. L. 1967 *Spelling: Taught or Caught?* London: Routledge and Kegan Paul.

Peters, M. L. 1985 *Spelling: Caught or Taught?* (revised edition). London: Routledge and Kegan Paul.

Peters, M. L. and Smith, B. 1986 'The productive process: an approach to literacy for children with difficulties'. In B. Root *Resources for Reading: Does Quality Count?,* pp. 161–71. London: UKRA/MacMillan.

Peters, M. L. and Smith, B. 1993 *Spelling in Context.* Windsor: NFER-Nelson.

Piggott, R. 1958 *Handwriting: A National Survey.* London: Allen and Unwin.

Pitman, Sir I. 1961 *The Initial Teaching Alphabet.* London: Pitman.

Polatajko, H., Fox, M. and Missiuna, C. 1995 'An international consensus in children with DCD'. *Canadian Journal of Occupational Therapy* 62: 3–6.

Pollack, J. and Waller, E. 1994/2001 *Day to Day Dyslexia in the Classroom.* London: Routledge.

Portsmouth LEA 2001 Headteachers' Conference, personal communication.

Portwood, M. 1999 *Developmental Dyspraxia: Identification and Intervention.* (2nd edition). London: Cassell.

Priest, N. and May, E. 2002 'Laptop computers and children with disabilities'. *Australian Journal of Occupational Therapy* 48: 11–23.

Prince-Bruce, M. 1978 *Spelling Difficulties.* Kingston: London Borough of Kingston L.E.A.

Prince-Bruce, M. 1986 *Teaching Reading Through Spelling (TRTS): The Later Stages of the Programme, Vols 1 and 2.* Kingston: Learning Difficulties Research Project.

Pumfrey, P. D. and Elliott, C. D. (eds) 1990 *Children's Difficulties in Reading, Spelling and Writing: Challenges and Responses.* Basingstoke: Falmer Press.

Pumfrey P. D. and Reason, R. (eds) 1991 *Specific Learning Difficulties (Dyslexia) Challenges and Responses: A National Inquiry.* Windsor: NFER-Nelson.

QCA (Qualifications and Curriculum Authority) 2002 *Standards at Key Stage 2 English: A Report on the 2002 National Curriculum Assessments for 11 Year Olds.* London: QCA.

QCA 2005 *Project 21.* London: QCA.

Rack, J. P. and Rudduck, S. 2002 'Dyslexia, severity and teaching outcomes'. *Dyslexia Institute Review* 13 (2): 21.

Rack, J. P., Snowling, M. and Olson, R. K. 1992 'The non-word reading deficit in developmental dyslexia; a review.' *Reading Research Quarterly* 27: 28–33.

Rack, J. P. and Walker, J. 1994 'Does Dyslexia Institute teaching work?' *Dyslexia Institute Review* 11 (3): 26 .

Radaker, L. D. 1963 'The effect of visual imagery in spelling performance.' *Journal of Educational Research* 54: 370–2.

Rae, C., Harasty, J. A., Dzendrowskyj, T. E., Talcott, J. B., Simpson, J. M., Blamine, A. M., Dixon, R. M., Lee, M. A., Thompson, C. H., Styles, P., Richardson, A. J. and Stein, J. F. 2002 'Cerebellar morphology in developmental dyslexia'. *Neuropsychologia* 40: 1285–92.

Raven, J. C. 1985 *Raven's Progressive Matrices*. Windsor: NFER/Nelson.

Rayner, K. 1986 'Eye movements and the perceptual span'. In G. Th. Pavilidis and D. F. Fisher (eds) *Dyslexia its Neurology and Treatment*, pp. 111–32. Chichester: Wiley.

Read, C. 1986 *Children's Creative Spellings*. London: Routledge and Kegan Paul.

Richards, S. 2003 'A report on the implemetation of a Precision Teaching programme'. Unpublished coursework, Module One MA SpLD. London: Middlesex University.

Richardson, A. J. (2002) 'Fatty acids in dyslexia, dyspraxia, ADHD and the autistic spectrum'. *Nutrition Practitioner* 2001 3 (3): 18–24.

Richardson, A. J., Allen, S. J., Hajnal, J. V., Cox, I. J., Easton, T. and Puri, B. K. 2001 'Association between central and peripheral measures of phospholipid breakdown revealed by cerebral 31-phosphorus magnetic resonance spectroscopy and fatty acid'. *Progress in Neuropsychopharmacology and Biological Psychiatry* 25: 1513–21.

Richardson, A J., McDaid, A M., Easton, T., Hall, J A., Montgomery, P., Corrie, A C., Clisby, C., Stein, J F., Puri, B K. and Stordy, B. J. 1998 'Is there a deficiency of long-chain polyunsaturated fatty acids in dyslexia?' National Institutes of Health presentation, Bethesda USA: 2–3 September.

Ridehalgh, N. 1999 'A comparison of remediation programmes and analysis of their effectiveness on a sample of pupils diagnosed as dyslexic'. Unpublished MA SpLD dissertation. London: Middlesex University.

Riding, R. and Rayner, S. 1998 *Cognitive Styles and Learning Strategies*. London: David Fulton.

Roaf, C. 1998 'Slow hand. A secondary school survey of handwriting speed and legibility'. *Support for Learning* 13 (1): 39–42.

Robertson, J. 2000 *Dyslexia and Reading: A Neuropsychological Approach*. London: Wiley.

Rose, J. 2005 *Independent Review of the Teaching of Early Reading Interim Report*. At: www.standards.dfes.gov.uk/rosereview/interimreport.doc (accessed 12 February 2006).

Rose Review 2005 (interim report) at: www.Standards.gov.uk/rosereview.

Rosenblum, S., Weiss, P. L., and Parush, S. 2003 'Product and process evaluation of handwriting difficulties'. *Educational Psychology Review* 15 (1): 41–81.

Roycroft, S. 2002 'A study to determine whether DILP would help Year 3 children in mainstream school showing difficulties with reading and spelling'. Unpublished MA SpLD dissertation. London: Middlesex University.

Rozin, P. and Gleitman, L. R. 1977 'The structure and acquisition of reading 11. The reading process and the acquisition of the alphabetic principle'. In A. S. Reber and D. L. Scarborough (eds) *Towards a Psychology of Reading*. Hillsdale, NJ: Erlbaum and Wiley.

Rubin, N. and Henderson, S. 1982 'Two sides of the same coin: variations in teaching methods and failure to learn to write'. *Special Education* 9 (4): 14–18.

Rumelhart, D. E. and McClelland, R. R. (eds) 1986 *Parallel Distributed Processing Volume 1: Foundations*. Cambridge MA: MIT Press.

Rutter, M. L., Tizard, J. and Whitmore, K. (eds) 1970 *Education, Health and Behaviour*. London: Longman.

Rutter, M. L., Maugham, B., Mortimore, P. and Ouston, J. 1979 *Fifteen Thousand Hours: Secondary Schools and their Effect on Children*. London: Open Books.

Rutter, M. L., Caspi, A., Fergusson, D., Horwood, L. J., Goodman, R., Maughan, B., Moffit, T. E., Meltzer, H. and Carroll, J. 2004 'Sex differences in developmental reading disability'. *Journal of the American Medical Association* 291 9 (16): 2007–12.

Sassoon, R. 1989 *Handwriting: A New Perspective.* Cheltenham: Stanley Thornes.

Scannel, D. and Marshall, J. C. 1966 'The effect of selected composition errors on grades assigned essay examinations'. *American Educational Research Journal* 2 (2): 125.

Scarborough, H. 1999 'Identifying and helping preschoolers who are at risk for dyslexia'. *Journal of Perspectives* 1 (1): 1. Baltimore: The International Dyslexia Association.

Schiffman, G. B. 1972 'Table to show percentage gains after two years remediation at different ages of identification'. In H. K. Goldberg and G. B. Schiffman *Dyslexia: Problems of Reading Disability*, p. 66. London: Grune and Stratton.

Schonell, F. J. 1942 *Backwardness in Basic Subjects.* Edinburgh: Oliver and Boyd.

Schonell, F. J. and Schonell, E. E. 1946 (reprinted 1985) *Diagnostic and Attainment Testing* 4th edition. Edinburgh: Oliver and Boyd.

SED (Scottish Education Department) 1978 *The Education of Pupils with Learning Difficulties in Primary and Secondary Schools: A Progress Report by HMSI.* Edinburgh: HMSO.

Selkowitz, M. 1998 *Dyslexia and Other Learning Difficulties.* Oxford: Oxford University Press.

Sharman, D. 2004 'Raising the underachievement of boys. Kent LEA's Approach'. NACE London Conference: April.

Sherman, G. F. 1995 'The anatomical basis of dyslexia'. Paper presented at the Annual Conference of the Orton Society, Houston, Texas: 3 November.

Silverman, L. K. 1989 'Invisible gifts, invisible handicaps'. *Roeper Review* 12 (1): 37–42.

Silverman, L. K. 2004 'Poor handwriting: a major cause of underachievement'. At: http://www.visualspatial.org/Publications/Article%20List/Poor_Handwriting.htm (accessed 12 March 2004).

Simon, D. P. and Simon, H. A. 1973 'Alternative uses of phonemic information in spelling'. *Review of Educational Research* 43: 115–37.

Singleton, C. 1996 'Computerised cognitive profiling and the early detection of dyslexia'. Proceedings of the British Psychological Society 4 (1): 63.

Smith, F. 1973 *Psycholinguistics and Reading.* New York: Holt Rinehart and Winston.

Smith, F. 1978 *Understanding Reading* (Reprint). New York: Holt Rinehart and Winston.

Smith, F. 1988 *Understanding Reading: A Psycholinguistic Analysis of Reading and Learning.* Hillsdale, NJ: Erlbaum.

Smith, J. and Bloor, M. 1985 *Simple Phonetics for Teachers.* London: Methuen.

Smith, P. A. P. and Marx, R. W. 1972 'Some cautions on the use of the Frostig test'. *Journal of Learning Disabilities* 5 (6): 357–62.

Smith, S. D., Kelley, P. M. and Brower, A. M. 1998 'Molecular approaches to the genetic analysis of specific reading disability: a review'. *Human Biology* 70: 239–56.

Smythe, L. 1997 'Incidence of dyslexia'. In R. Salter and L. Smythe (eds) *The International Book of Dyslexia*, p. 238. London: World Dyslexia Network Foundation and European Dyslexia Association.

Snowling, M. J. 2000 *Dyslexia* (2nd edition). Oxford: Blackwell.

Snowling, M. J. 2005 'Dyslexia is not a myth'. At: http://www.bda-dyslexia.org.uk/ (accessed 21 October.)

Snowling, M. J. and Hulme, C. 2003 'A critique of claims by Reynolds, Nicholson and Hambly 2003 that DDAT is an effective treatment for reading problems'. *Dyslexia: An International Journal of Research and Practice* 9: 1–7.

Snowling, M. J., Stackhouse, J. and Rack, J. 1986 'Phonological dyslexia and dysgraphia – a developmental analysis'. *Cognitive Neuropsychology* 13: 303–39.

Solity, J. E. and Bull, S. L. 1987 *Bridging the Curriculum Gap for Children with Special Needs*. Milton Keynes: Open University Press.

Solity, J. E., Deavers, R. P., Kerfoot, S. R., Crane, G. and Cannon, K. 1999 'Raising literacy attainment in the early years. The impact of instructional psychology'. *Educational Psychology* 19 (4): 1345–7.

Soloff, S. 1973 'The effect of non-content factors on the grading of essays'. *Research in Education and Related Disciplines* 6 (2): 44–54.

Southgate-Booth, V. 1986 'Teachers of reading: planning the most effective use of their time'. In B. Root (ed.) *Resources for Reading: Does Quality Count?* pp. 80–98. London: UKRA/Macmillan.

Southwell, N. 2006 'Truants on truancy – a badness or a valuable indicator of SEN?' *British Journal of Special Education* 23 (2): 91–7.

Spache, G. D. 1940 'Characteristic errors of good and poor spellers.' *Journal of Educational Research* 34 (3): 182–9.

Spalding, R. B. and Spalding W. T. 1967 *The Writing Road to Reading* (2nd edition). New York: Whiteside and Morrow.

Staghuis,W. L. and Pinkus, S. Z. 1993 'Visual backward masking in central and peripheral vision in late adolescent dyslexics'. *Clinical Vision Sciences* 8: 187–99.

Stainthorp, R. 1990 'The handwriting of a group of teacher education students'. Paper presented at the UKRA Conference: July.

Stainthorp, R., Henderson, S., Barnett, A. and Scheib, B. 2001 'Handwriting policy and practice in primary schools'. Paper presented at the British Psychological Society Education and Developmental Sections Joint Annual Conference, Worcester: September.

Stamm, M. 2003 'Looking at long term effects of early reading and numeracy ability: a glance at the phenomenon of giftedness'. *Gifted and Talented International* 18 (1): 7–16.

Ste-Marie, D., Clark, S. E., Findley, L. C. and Latimer, A. E. 2004 'High levels of contextual interferences enhance handwriting skill acquisition'. *Journal of Motor Behaviour* 36 (1): 115–26.

Stein, J. 2000 'The magnocellular hypothesis in dyslexia'. Paper presented at the 27th Biennial Conference in Psychology, Stockholm.

Stein, J. 2001 'The magnocellular theory of developmental dyslexia'. *Dyslexia* 7: 12–36.

Stein, J. F. and Fowler, S. 1981 'Diagnosis of dyslexia by means of a new indication of eye dominance'. *British Journal of Ophthalmology* 66 (5): 322–6.

Stein, J. and Taylor, K. (2002) 'Dyslexia and familial high blood pressure: an observational pilot study'. *Archives of Disease In Childhood* 86: 30–33.

Stern, C. and Gould, T. S. 1965 *Children Discover Reading: Introduction to Structured Reading*. New York: Random House.

Stone, C., Franks, E. and Nicholson, M. 1993 *Beat Dyslexia*. Wisbech: Learning Development Aids.

Summers, J. and Catarro, E. 2003 'Assessment of handwriting speed and factors influencing written output of university students in examinations'. *American Occupational Therapy Journal* 30: 148–57.

Syvla, K. 1998 'An international comparison of early years education'. World Service Television, 24 Hours, Strasbourg, 3 June.

Tallal, P. 1994 'New clue to cause of dyslexia seen in mishearing of fast sounds. An interview with Dr Tallal' by S. Blakeslee. *New York Times* 24 August.

Tallal, P. 1980 'Auditory temporal perception, phonics, and reading disabilities in children'. *Brain and Language* 9: 182–98.

Tallal, P. and Piercy, M. 1973 'Developmental aphasia: impaired rate of non-verbal processing as a function of sensory modality'. *Neuropsychologica* 11 (4): 369–98.

Tansley, A. E. 1967 *Reading and Remedial Reading.* London: Routledge and Kegan Paul.

Tansley, A. E. and Pankhurst, J. 1981 *Children with Specific Learning Difficulties: Critical Review.* Windsor: NFER.

Taylor- Smith, M. 1993 *MTS A Multisensory Teaching System.* Forney, Texas: EDMAR.

Thomas, D. 1998 'Catering for the needs of children with Specific Learning Difficulties on transfer to a secondary school,' unpublished MA dissertation in Specific Learning Difficulties. London: Middlesex University.

Thomas, S. 1997 'Near point gripping in pencil hold as a possible disabling factor in children with SEN'. *British Journal of Special Education* 24 (3): 129–32.

Thomson, M. E. 1989 *Developmental Dyslexia.* London: Whurr.

Thomson, M. E. 1990 'Evaluating teaching programmes for children with specific learning difficulties'. In P .D. Pumfrey and C. D. Elliott (eds) *Children's Difficulties in Reading, Spelling and Writing,* pp. 155–71. London: Falmer Press.

Thomson, M. E. and Watkins, E. J. 1993 *Teaching the Dyslexic Child.* London: Whurr.

Thorndike, R. L., Hagen, E. and France, N. 1986 *The Cognitive Abilities Tests* (revised edition). Windsor: NFER.

THRASS 1995 *Teaching Handwriting Reading and Spelling Skills.* Sheffield LEA Reading Recovery Team Project, London: Collins.

THRASS 2006 www.thrass.co.uk.

Tibertius, S. 2001 'Handwriting in the secondary school'. *Handwriting Today* 2: 71–5.

Tidmas, H. 2005 'An investigation into the writing of a Year 7 cohort after receiving five years of teaching according to the National Literacy Strategy'. Unpublished MA SpLD dissertation. London: Middlesex University.

TIMSS 1997 *Third International Mathematics and Science Study.* Washington. DC: National Center for Education Statistics, US Government Printing Office.

Torgeson, J. K. 1995 'Instructional alternatives for children with severe reading difficulties'. Paper presented at the Annual Conference of the Orton Society, Houston, Texas: 1 November.

Torgeson, J. K., Wagner, R. K., Rashotte, C. A., Rose, E., Lindamood, P., Conway, T. and Garvan, C. 1999 'Preventing reading failure in young children with phonological processing disabilities. Group and individual responses to instruction'. *Journal of Educational Psychology* 9 (4): 579–93.

Treiman, R. 1993 *Beginning to Spell.* Oxford: Oxford University Press.

Treiman, R. 1994 'Sources of information used by beginning spellers'. In G. D. A. Brown and N. C. Ellis (eds) *Handbook of Spelling,* pp. 75–92. Chichester: Wiley.

Treiman, R., Mullennix, J., Bijejac-Babic, R. and Richmond-Welty, E. D. 1995 'The special role of rimes in the description, use, and acquisition of English orthography'. *Journal of Experimental Psychology: General* 124: 107–36.

Turner, M. 1991 'Finding out'. *Support for Learning* 6 (3): 99–102.

Tymms, P. 2004 'Why this man scares Ruth Kelly'. Article by Warwick Mansell, *Times Educational Supplement* 9: 28 August.

Vallence, C. 2002 'A case study of the use of an APSL programme'. Unpublished Coursework, Module 4, MA SpLD. London: Middlesex University.

Van Nes, F. L. 1971 'Errors in the motor program for handwriting.' *IPO Annual Progress Report* 6: 61–3.

Vellutino, F. R. 1979 *Dyslexia: Theory and Research.* London: M.I.T.

Vellutino, F. R. 1987 'Dyslexia'. *Scientific American* 256 (3): 20–7.

Vincent, C. 1983 'A study of the introduction of cursive writing'. Unpublished inservice dissertation. Kingston-upon-Thames: Kingston Polytechnic.

Wallace, B. 2000 *Teaching the Very Able Child.* London: David Fulton.

Warnock, M. 1978 *Special Educational Needs: The Warnock Report.* London: HMSO.

Waterland, L 1986 'The apprenticeship approach to reading'. In P. Chambers (ed.) *Bright Ideas: Teachers' Handbooks – Reading.* Leamington Spa: Scholastic.

Watkins, G. and Hunter-Carsch, M. 1995 'Prompt spelling: a practical approach to paired spelling'. *Support for Learning* 10 (3): 133–7.

Watson, J and Johnson, R 1998 *Accelerating Reading Attainment: The Effectiveness of Synthetic Phonics.* Edinburgh: The Scottish Office.

Webb, M. 2000 'An evaluation of the SEN provision to improve literacy skills of Year 9 students at N.fields'. Unpublished MA SpLD dissertation. London: Middlesex University.

Wechsler, D. 1991 *Wechsler Intelligence Scale for Children (WISC III).* San Antonio, TX: The Psychological Corporation.

Wedell, K. 1973 *Learning and Perceptuomotor Difficulties in Children.* New York: Wiley.

Wendon, L. 1984 *The Pictogram System.* Barton, Cambridgeshire: Pictogram Supplies.

West, T. G. 1999 'The abilities of those with reading disabilities. Focusing on the talent of people with dyslexia'. In D. D. Duane *Reading and Attention Disorders - Neurobiological Correlates,* Ch.11. Baltimore: York Press.

Westwood, P. 2004 *Reading and Learning Difficulties – Approaches to Teaching and Assessment.* London: David Fulton.

Whitmore, J. R. 1980 *Giftedness, Conflict and Underachievement.* Boston: Allyn and Bacon.

Wilson, J. 1993 *P.A.T. Phonological Awareness Training: A New Approach to Phonics.* London: Educational Psychology Publishing.

Wilson, J. 1994 'Phonological awareness training: A new approach to phonics'. *PATOSS Bulletin* November: 5–8.

Wilson, J. and Frederickson, N. 1995 'Phonological awareness training: an evaluation'. *Education and Child Psychology* 12: 68–79.

Wing, A. M. and Baddeley, A. D. 1980 'Spelling errors in handwriting' in U. Frith (ed.) *Cognitive Processes in Spelling.* London: Academic Press.

WISC-IV 2006 *Wechsler Intelligence Scale for Children – IV.* Oxford: Harcourt Assessment, Psychological Corporation.

Wirth, C. 2001 'Phonics fun.' *Literacy Today* 29. At: www.literacytrust.org.uk/Pubs.

Wise, B. W. and Olson, R. K. 1994 'Using computers to teach spelling to children with learning disabilities' in G. D. Brown and N. C. Ellis (eds) *Handbook of Spelling.* Chichester: Wiley.

Witelson, S. F. 1977 'Developmental dyslexia: two right hemispheres and one left'. *Science* 195: 309–11.

Witty, P. and Kopel, D. 1936 'Preventing reading disability: the reading readiness factor'. *Educational Administration and Supervision* 28: 401–18.

WORD 2006 *Wechsler Objective Reading Dimensions.* Oxford: Harcourt Assessment Psychological Corporation.

Wraith, J. 2001 'CPSS case work with an able dyslexic'. Unpublished portfolio work, MA SpLD. London: Middlesex University.

Wray, D. 2004 'Raising the underachievement of boys in writing'. NACE London Conference: April.

Wright, D. L., Black, C. B., Immink, M. A., Brueckner, S., and Magnuson, C. 2004 'Long term motor programming improvements occur via concatenation of movement sequences during random but not during blocked trials'. *Journal of Movement Behaviour* 36 (1): 39–50.

Ysseldyke, J. E. 1987 'Annotation'. *Journal of Child Psychology and Psychiatry* 28 (1): 21–4.

Ziviani, J. and Watson-Will, A. 1998 'Writing speed and legibility of 7–14 year old school students using modern cursive script'. *Australian Occupational Therapy Journal* 45: 59–64.

Index